George Orwell

PHILOSOPHICAL OUTSIDERS

Philip Kitcher and Anjan Chakravartty, Series Editors

*

Philosophical Outsiders explores philosophical contributions made by influential thinkers well known for their work beyond the orthodox philosophical canon, including those who have advanced the sciences, political or social thought, or the arts and humanities. Through engagement with philosophical reflection in works usually viewed in a different light, this series aims to expand and diversify the canon itself, and to initiate wide-ranging conversations between philosophy and other traditions of inquiry.

*

Toni Morrison: Imagining Freedom
Lawrie Balfour

George Orwell: The Ethics of Equality
Peter Brian Barry

George Orwell

The Ethics of Equality

PETER BRIAN BARRY

OXFORD
UNIVERSITY PRESS

OXFORD
UNIVERSITY PRESS

Oxford University Press is a department of the University of Oxford. It furthers
the University's objective of excellence in research, scholarship, and education
by publishing worldwide. Oxford is a registered trade mark of Oxford University
Press in the UK and certain other countries.

Published in the United States of America by Oxford University Press
198 Madison Avenue, New York, NY 10016, United States of America.

CIP data is on file at the Library of Congress

ISBN 978-0-19-762740-2

DOI: 10.1093/oso/9780197627402.001.0001

Printed by Integrated Books International, United States of America

For SebAshtyn. May he read more.

Contents

Contents

Introduction

George Orwell: The Ethics of Equality is not a biography: several
biographies have already been written and more are forthcoming,
in spite of Orwell's wish that no biography of his life be produced.
Readers with some familiarity of the major events of Orwell's life
are at an advantage, since his ethics were shaped profoundly by crucial experiences: he was born abroad in India, named 'Eric Blair,'
the son of a middling civil servant tasked with fostering the opium
trade between England and its most lucrative colony; his youthful
experiences with working-class children shaped his view of class
and class dynamics; his time at St. Cyprian's School, a preparatory
school for boys, taught him hard lessons about class, wealth, punishment, and responsibility; his time at Eton was instrumental in
fostering his intellectual development, his contrarian nature, his
future literary contacts, and his strained relationship with literary
elites; his service to the British Raj provided source material for
early work and convinced him of the injustice of British coloni-
alism, generating in him a feeling of guilt he had to expiate; his guilt
led him to spend time with the down-and-outs of Paris and London
and shaped his ethical sympathies; his early work led him to Wigan
and to Spain, where he observed the ill treatment of the working
class and temporary ascendency of the Spanish resistance that led
him to embrace socialism; his betrayal by the Spanish Communists
and subsequent travels led him to loathe the orthodox Marxist
wing of the left and to work out his own version of socialism; living
through World War II confirmed his patriotism and led him to

George Orwell. Peter Brian Barry, Oxford University Press. © Oxford University Press 2023.
DOI: 10.1093/oso/9780197627402.001.0001

try to synthesize his love of England with his socialist convictions; the literature he read, his lifelong illness, the death of his first wife, Eileen, his work as a propagandist for the BBC, his time on the Scottish island of Jura and in British sanitoriums all affected him and made him the thinker he was; he passed in 1950 of tuberculosis at the age of forty-six and was buried in an Anglican graveyard with a tombstone that bears his birth name and not his more famous pseudonym. Biography can help us understand the events that shaped Orwell and his work, but, and this is central to *The Ethics of Equality*, philosophy has an important role to play as well. I argue that philosophy can help us to better understand Orwell and his works, a thesis that is perfectly consistent with the supposition that Orwell was at best indifferent to academic and abstract philosophy if not outright hostile to it. I also argue that there are important ethical principles that are detectable just about throughout Orwell's corpus that help to explain much of his writing and politics. If all goes well, both theses will be undeniable by the end of this book.

The cardinal sin of Orwell scholarship, a sin committed by some fellow philosophers among other readers, is to focus more or less exclusively on one of Orwell's works, usually *Nineteen Eighty-Four*, at the expense of his other work. There is much that should be of interest to philosophers in his late novels, but his other books, essays, reportage, newspaper columns, diaries, and letters are also laden with much that should be of interest and often contain more direct statements of his views about normative matters. I have tried to be as comprehensive as possible, drawing on his major works when necessary but pulling frequently from works that even an avid reader of Orwell has probably not reviewed: *The Complete Works of George Orwell* edited by the late Peter Davison spans twenty volumes. I do not refrain from criticizing him at times, and when I think he was in error or that his arguments are not sound I say so. I sometimes provide charitable interpretations of what he says when needed and friendly reconstructions to explicate when I think he could have been clearer. My approach to Orwell is hinted at in the cover image of this book. There are many iconic images of Orwell that have, quite reasonably, repeatedly adorned Orwell texts for the last several decades and have done much to ensure that some of his features—his equally iconic moustache, his wry and assured smile—are well known to even his casual readers. I had hoped for something less well known. The George Orwell Archive at University College–London includes "Orwell and the catapult" among the images of Orwell housed online, and that image struck me as appropriate, not only because it is, I think, a less well-known image of him. The blurred image appears to me as Orwell taking aim at his target none too confidently but seriously and soberly. It suggests a metaphor, one with its origins in Aristotle's dictum from *The Nicomachean Ethics* that "error is easy and correctness is difficult, since it is easy to miss the target and difficult to hit it."[1] Philosophy generally and ethics in particular are difficult subjects chock full of targets that are easy to miss. I do not say that Orwell always hit the target, but that he aimed at them at all merits comment and is worth discussing.

Reading the entirety of Orwell's *Complete Works* has yielded some surprises. An early work titled "A Summer Idyll," one that Davison suggests was possibly but not definitely written by Orwell during his time at Eton but published in a literary magazine that he facilitated, includes the following attempt at hard-boiled American-style fiction that would interest Orwell in the 1940s:

> [T]he next thing I knew was that a bum-guy in a Panama cranium lid with white knickerbocker pants and about eight foot of hairy shin caught me a clip over the head-piece. I went down like a felled prairie ox. When I came to I'd been clapped into a cell, a prison cell, mister, in a British prison, and me a free Yank from Milwaukee, Wisconsin! (X: 65)

---

[1] Aristotle, The Nicomachean Ethics, 2nd edition, translated by Terence Irwin (Indianapolis, IN: Hackett, 1999), p. 25.

I am Orwell's free Yank from Milwaukee, Wisconsin, who, like many of his readers, initially believed myself to be an avid fan having read only a small range of his corpus. Before attending university, I was assigned *Animal Farm* and *Nineteen Eighty-Four*, although I cannot recall reading either. Some of his essays, including "A Hanging" and "Shooting an Elephant," were familiar, but I do not recall reading them for the first time. I recalled that Orwell declined to shoot a pantsless enemy solider but wrongly thought the event was documented in *Homage to Catalonia*. When I first began to write in earnest, I hung a poster outside of my office with Orwell's somber and unsmiling mustached visage seated in front of a BBC microphone framed with the words "In a time of universal deceit, telling the truth is a revolutionary act." I did not then know that Orwell had spent two years working for the BBC creating wartime propaganda and writing things that he did not believe, nor that the quote is apocryphal and wrongly attributed to him. I have since taken the poster down.

I am not a literary scholar or theorist, merely a philosopher who has some experience teaching a course titled "Philosophy and Literature," which led to my second book, *The Fiction of Evil*, which utilized both philosophical and literary texts to better understand the concept of evil and what it is to be an evil person. I had no idea that I would become immersed in Orwell scholarship prior to being invited by Nathan Waddell to contribute a chapter to *The Cambridge Companion to Nineteen Eighty-Four*, a volume he edited, on the subject of evil and in the infamous Room 101, where Winston Smith, the protagonist of *Nineteen Eighty-Four*, was tortured and broken. I accepted with much enthusiasm and no idea just how much that I would find in Orwell that interested me as a philosopher. This book would not exist without Nath's kind invitation and I am grateful to him for drawing me into Orwell scholarship.

I am also grateful to The American Philosophical Society and the British Academy for awarding me the 2020 British Academy/

American Philosophical Society Fellowship, which I was unable to utilize until June of 2022, once a global pandemic receded enough to make international travel possible. The Fellowship allowed me to research at the aforementioned George Orwell Archive at UCL, where I was ably assisted by multiple archivists, although special thanks goes to Daniel Mitchell of UCL's Special Collections, who supplied access to source materials previously unknown to me. I also wish to thank Philip Kitcher for his invitation to submit for inclusion in the Philosophical Outsiders series and, I suspect, for supporting my proposal that led to the Fellowship in the first place. Mark Satta, Bobby Bingle, and David Dwan read parts and provided helpful feedback. But my greatest debt is to my wife, Felicia, who had to endure what must have seemed like an unending stream of Orwell commentary during a lockdown, when she could not easily avoid me and my newfound obsession. In his well-known essay, "Why I Write," Orwell wrote that "All writers are vain, selfish, and lazy" and that "Writing a book is a horrible, exhausting struggle, like a long bout of some painful illness" (XVIII: 320). She more than anyone has endured my vanity and selfishness during the horrible, exhausting struggle of writing this book, and I am, as always, endlessly grateful for her unceasing love and support.

1

George Orwell

Philosophical Outsider

There are endless towering descriptions of George Orwell. A tribute poem named him "A moral genius," adding that "Like Darwin playing his bassoon to plants / He too had lapses, but he claimed no wings."[1] He is, we are told, "the most widely read and influential serious writer of the twentieth century,"[2] "one of the most virtuous men of his day,"[3] "the wintry conscience of his generation,"[4] the "sea-green incorruptible of the Left,"[5] "half, but only the half of what the world needs,"[6] the "most devastating pamphleteer alive,"[7] "the most influential political writer of the twentieth century,"[8] "more quoted and referenced than any other modern writer,"[9] and

[1] Robert Conquest, "George Orwell," in *Collected Poems*, edited by Elizabeth Conquest (Baltimore: Waywiser, 2020), p. 125.

[2] Jeffrey Meyers, *Orwell: Life and Art* (Urbana: University of Illinois Press, 2010), p. 157.

[3] Stephen Spender, in *George Orwell: The Critical Heritage*, edited by Jeffrey Meyers (London: Routledge and Kegan Paul Ltd., 1975), p. 134.

[4] V. S. Pritchett, in *George Orwell: The Critical Heritage*, edited by Jeffrey Meyers (London: Routledge and Kegan Paul Ltd., 1975), p. 294.

[5] John Mandler, *The Writer and Commitment* (London: Secker and Warburg, 1961), p. 16.

[6] Bertrand Russell, in *George Orwell: The Critical Heritage*, edited by Jeffrey Meyers (London: Routledge and Kegan Paul Ltd., 1975), p. 301.

[7] V. S. Pritchett, "1984," in *Nineteen Eighty-Four to 1984: A Companion to Orwell's Classic Novel*, edited by C. J. Kupping (New York: Carroll and Graf Publishers, 1984), p. 151.

[8] Timothy Garton Ash, "Orwell for Our Times," *The Guardian*, 5 May 2001, https://www.theguardian.com/books/2001/may/05/artsandhumanities.highereducation.

[9] John Rodden, "Introduction," in *The Cambridge Companion to George Orwell*, edited by John Rodden (Cambridge: Cambridge University Press, 2017), pp. x–xi.

George Orwell. Peter Brian Barry, Oxford University Press. © Oxford University Press 2023.
DOI: 10.1093/oso/9780197627402.003.0001

"one of the greatest writers of the twentieth century."[10] He was also a philosophical outsider: perhaps no Anglophone writer is more worthy of the title.

In this and later chapters, I leave a more comprehensive discussion of his epistemology and philosophy of language to others[11] and focus primarily on Orwell's ethics, broadly construed, identifying and elaborating those ethical concepts and principles implicit in his work if not always explicitly identified or endorsed. In this opening chapter, I consider a popular interpretation of Orwell according to which he was indifferent to philosophy at best and positively hostile to it at worse. I close with some reflections on Orwell and offensive speech, partly to reveal just how surprisingly nuanced his ethical thinking was.

Philosophers, Meet Orwell; Orwell, Meet Philosophers

The literary intelligentsia of his day thought that he was "not one of us,"[12] and while Orwell is sometimes counted among the Auden generation[13] it was "a generation he was in but never a part of."[14] A fellow philosopher explains that "Orwell never felt as if he

---

[10] Gordon Bowker, *Inside George Orwell: A Biography* (New York: Palgrave Macmillan, 2003), p. 48.

[11] For a helpful introduction to Orwell's philosophical sympathies generally, see Mark Satta, "George Orwell," *Internet Encyclopedia of Philosophy*, https://iep.utm.edu/george-orwell/.

[12] Alfred Kazin, "Not One of Us," *New York Review of Books*, 23 January 1984. See John Rodden, "Not One of Us? Orwell and the London Left of the 1930s and '40s," in his *Every Intellectual's Big Brother: George Orwell's Literary Siblings* (Austin: University of Texas Press, 2006), pp. 9–31.

[13] Orwell shows up repeatedly in Samuel Hynes, *The Auden Generation: Literature and Politics in England in the 1930s* (New York: Viking Press, 1977).

[14] Stuart Samuels, "English Intellectuals and Politics in the 1930s," in *On Intellectuals*, edited by Philip Rieff (New York: Doubleday, 1969), p. 247.

belonged anywhere,"[15] and he is often enough characterized as "the loner; the outsider,"[16] as someone who "knew what it meant to be an outsider,"[17] as "the ultimate outsider in politics."[18] To be a philosophical outsider, one must be an outsider and, well, philosophical. Was Orwell?

There are reasons to answer in the affirmative. Some of his best writing is inarguably an attempt to work out political consequences of answers to essentially philosophical questions.[19] But it might also matter that philosophers have seen something in his work. For our part, philosophers are at least as interested in him as other scholars: a study of Orwell citations from 1976–2003 reveals that 4 percent are attributable to philosophers, about as many as those attributable to political scientists and sociologists and slightly more than those attributable to anthropologists, economists, and social scientists.[20] Philosophers are more interested than most in *The Road to Wigan Pier* and especially interested in *Nineteen Eighty-Four*,[21] and the better-known philosophical discussions of Orwell are mostly concerned with that book. Here is Peter van Inwagen:

> Before we leave the topic of Realism and anti-Realism, however, I should like to direct the reader's attention to the greatest of all attacks on anti-Realism, George Orwell's novel *1984*. Anyone who is interested in Realism and anti-Realism should be steeped

[15] Robert Solomon, "Ant Farm: An Orwellian Allegory," in *Reflections on America, 1984: An Orwell Symposium*, edited by Robert Mulvihill (Athens: University of Georgia Press, 1986), p. 114.

[16] Robert Colls, *George Orwell: English Rebel* (Oxford: Oxford University Press, 2013), p. 68.

[17] William Steinhoff, *George Orwell and the Origins of 1984* (Ann Arbor: University of Michigan Press, 1975), p. 127.

[18] Philip Bounds, *Orwell & Marxism: The Political and Cultural Thinking of George Orwell* (London: I. B Tauris, 2009), p. 2.

[19] Martin Tyrell, "Orwell and Philosophy," *Philosophy Now* (1996), https://philosophynow.org/issues/16/Orwell_and_Philosophy.

[20] Neil McLaughlin, "Orwell, the Academy, and the Intellectuals," in *The Cambridge Companion to George Orwell*, edited by John Rodden (Cambridge: Cambridge University Press, 2007), pp. 163–164.

[21] Ibid., pp. 167–168.

in the message of this book. The reader is particularly directed to
the climax of the novel, the debate between the Realist Winston
Smith and the anti-Realist O'Brien. In the end, there is only one
question that can be addressed to the anti-Realist: How does your
position differ from O'Brien's?[22]

By contrast, Richard Rorty contends that O'Brien is no antirealist
mouthpiece and Winston is no proxy for realism, and that the
point of their dialogue is to get us to see that nothing but chance
precludes our world being ruled by persons like O'Brien and to pre-
pare as best we can.[23] In contrast to van Inwagen, Rorty commends
reading Orwell as a pragmatist primarily interested in answering
questions like "will human life be better in the future if we adopt
this belief, this practice, this institution?,"[24] not a realist about truth
or anything else.

If philosophers have not come to any consensus about how to understand Orwell, neither has anyone else. Incompatible and mixed
characterizations of Orwell are legion: he has been called "an extreme intellectual and a violent anti-intellectual";[25] a "moral hero"[26]
but a "foolish idealist";[27] a "Tory anarchist"[28] but an "ambivalent"
and "unsophisticated"[29] one; a "half Tory, half Socialist";[30] "the secular prophet of socialism" albeit a "failed" one;[31] a revolutionary in

[22] Peter van Inwagen, *Metaphysics*, 3rd ed. (London: Avalon, 2009), p. 159. For a slight
modification, see Peter van Inwagen, "Was George Orwell a Metaphysical Realist?,"
Philosophia Scientae, Vol. 12 (2008), pp. 161–185.
[23] Richard Rorty, *Contingency, Irony, and Solidarity* (Cambridge: Cambridge
University Press, 1989), pp. 185.
[24] Richard Rorty, *Pragmatism and Anti-Authoritarianism* (Cambridge, MA: Harvard
University Press, 2021), p. 12.
[25] Victor Gollancz, "Foreword," in *The Road to Wigan Pier* (V: 221).
[26] John Wain, *A House for Truth* (London: Macmillan, 1972), p. 1.
[27] Henry Miller, "The Art of Fiction," *Paris Review*, Vol. VII (Summer 1962), p. 146.
[28] Rayner Heppenstall, *Four Absences* (London: Barrie and Rockcliff, 1960), p. 32.
[29] George Woodcock, *The Crystal Spirit: A Study of George Orwell* (New York: Shocken,
1984), p. 28.
[30] Ibid., pp. 136–137.
[31] George P. Eliot, "A Failed Prophet," *The Hudson Review*, Vol. 10, No. 10 (1957),
p. 149.

love with the past[32]—at least, a revolutionary in love with 1910[33]—
as well as "a revolutionary personality"[34] and a revolutionary pa-
triot,[35] but also a libertarian radical[36] and a sentimental liberal.[37]
He has been said to resemble Don Quixote, John the Baptist, Oscar
Wilde, Charles Dickens, William Morris, Bertrand Russell, Simone
Weil, Jonathan Swift, Voltaire, Hamlet, Candide, Samuel Johnson,
George Gissing, George Bernard Shaw, G. K. Chesterton, D. H.
Lawrence, Robinson Crusoe, Aldous Huxley, Charlie Chaplin, and
still more. These characterizations can't *all* be right. No wonder so
many of Orwell's commentators have found him terminally inconsistent[38] or contradictory.[39] More damningly, some readers suggest that he was someone to everyone and thus no one at all, that
"Because of Orwell's vagueness in his political philosophy, he can
be stretched across a wide spectrum of political opinion,"[40] that
"people of almost any political persuasion can find some of their
beliefs expressed in Orwell's work,"[41] and that "since everyone,

[32] John Rossi, "'My Country, Right or Left': Orwell's Patriotism," in *The Cambridge Companion to George Orwell*, edited by John Rodden (Cambridge: Cambridge University Press, 2007), p. 88.

[33] Cyril Connolly, *Horizon* (September 1945), p. 215.

[34] Irving Howe, "Orwell as a Moderate Hero," *Partisan Review* (Winter 1954–1955), pp. 105–106.

[35] Bernard Crick, *Orwell: A Life* (Boston: Little, Brown and Company, 1980), p. 272.

[36] Richard Rees, *George Orwell: Fugitive from the Camp of Victory* (Carbondale: Southern Illinois University Press, 1961), p. 25.

[37] Samuel Hynes, *20th Century Interpretations of Nineteen Eighty-Four*, p. 3.

[38] Anthony Burgess, *1985* (Boston: Little, Brown and Company, 1978), p. 39; Stephen Ingle, *Orwell Reconsidered* (New York, Routledge, 2020), p. 130.

[39] Gordon Bowker, *Inside George Orwell*, pp. 62 and 427; Crick, *Orwell: A Life*, p. xvii; Robert Colls, *George Orwell: English Rebel* (Oxford: Oxford University Press, 2013), p. 9; Tosco R. Fyvel, *George Orwell: A Personal Memoir* (New York: Macmillan, 1982), p. 209; Rayner Heppenstall, as quoted in Richard Bradford, *Orwell: A Man of Our Time* (London: Bloomsbury, 2020), p. 107; Christopher Hitchens, *Orwell's Victory* (London: Penguin, 2003), pp. 9 and 44; Samuel Hues, *The Auden Generation: Literature and Politics in England in the 1930s* (New York: The Viking Press, 1972), p. 277; Ben Plimott, "Introduction," in *Orwell's England*, edited by Peter Davison (New York: Penguin, 2001), p. xix; Patrick Reilly, *George Orwell: The Age's Adversary* (New York: Macmillan, 1986), pp. 197–198; Woodcock, *The Crystal Spirit*, p. 5 and 55.

[40] Scott Lucas, *Orwell* (London: Haus Publishing, 2003), p. 135.

[41] D. A. N. Jones, "Arguments against Orwell," in *The World of George Orwell*, edited by Miriam Gross (New York: Simon and Schuster, 1971), p. 158.

Left, Right, and Centre, can and does hijack the wretched man [i.e., Orwell] for every conceivable political purpose, the net result is almost exactly nil."[42] The worry has got to be that from such crooked timber no straight thing could be made and any attempt to systematize Orwell's philosophical sympathies is a fool's errand.

It is easy to overstate things here. Orwell, having written more than two million words,[43] surely changed his mind about some things just as Plato, Kant, and Nietzsche did, yet we still speak of Platonic, Kantian, and Nietzschean ethics. And some trends are discernible throughout his corpus. Michael Walzer points to "a broad continuity not only of moral character, but also of social identity" throughout Orwell's work.[44] And in his celebrated essay, "Why I Write," Orwell explains that "Every line of serious work that I have written since 1936 has been written, directly or indirectly, *against* totalitarianism and *for* democratic Socialism, as I understand it" (XVIII: 319). While a commitment to democratic Socialism—he always spelled it with a lower case 'd' and an upper case 'S'[45], and I have tried to mirror his spelling—is one of the ethical commitments that span his corpus, I argue in Chapter 8 that he was led to embrace it because of other ethical commitments that are evident even in his early work. Much of what follows is an attempt to identify those ethical commitments that were always there.

Orwell was no tough-minded realist who saw politics and morality invariably at odds. He had some faint praise for the now-defunct Common Wealth Party's slogan "What is morally wrong cannot be politically right," noting the "strong ethical tinge" (XV:109) of its propaganda.[46] And in his review of Hayek's *The Road to Serfdom*, he hopes that "the concept of right and wrong is

[42] Paul Johnson, *The Spectator*, 7 January 1984.
[43] D. J. Taylor, *Orwell: The Life* (New York: Henry Holt and Company, 2003), p. 1.
[44] Michael Walzer, "George Orwell's England," in *George Orwell*, edited by Graham Holderness, Bryan Loughrey, and Nahem Yousaf (New York: St. Martin's Press, 1988), p. 185.
[45] Crick, *Orwell: A Life*, p. xiv.
[46] In fairness, he also calls it an "astonishingly feeble slogan" (XVI: 312).

restored to politics" (XVI: 150), leading one of his biographers to conclude that politics without morality was, for Orwell, "the great modern evil."[47] Yet one gets the sense from Orwell's commentators that if his "instinctive approach to literary topics was moral,"[48] it was *merely* instinctive. Many commentators regard him as a moralist[49] albeit a "naive moralist"[50] with only "a vague moralistic hankering . . . which lacked intellectual coherence and analytical depth."[51] What he meant when he used words like 'decency' and 'evil,' two of his favorites, was never clear[52] or at least not clearly stated. Orwell's early editor, Victor Gollancz, felt obligated to preface *The Road to Wigan Pier* with the observation that "Orwell does not once define what he *means* by Socialism . . . nor even what he understands by the words 'liberty' and 'justice'" (V: 224), the sort of thing a naïve moralist would do.

True, Orwell was no professional philosopher, and he did not write like one. But, and this is the primary thesis of *The Ethics of George Orwell*, philosophy can help to better our understanding of Orwell's ethics and those conceptions of right action, happiness, humanism, personal identity, equality, liberty, and justice that he sometimes only hinted at. That philosophy might be useful in understanding him will surprise some, however, given a stubborn interpretation of Orwell favored by some of his most influential commentators. If *the inerudite interpretation* is correct, Orwell was no philosopher, outsider or otherwise, and the utility of using

---

[47] Bowker, *Inside George Orwell*, p. 428.
[48] Meyers, *Orwell: Life and Art*, p. 177.
[49] See, for example, Bowker, *Inside George Orwell*, p. 421; Crick, *Orwell: A Life*, p. xvi; J. R. Hammond, *A George Orwell Companion: A Guide to the Novels, Documentaries and Essays* (London: Macmillan Press, 1982), p. 48; Christopher Hollis, *A Study of George Orwell: The Man and His Works* (Delaware: Racehorse Publishing, 2017), p. 125; Ingle, *Orwell Reconsidered*, p. 131; John Rodden, *The Unexamined Orwell* (Austin: University of Texas Press, 2011), p. 79; Woodcock, *The Crystal Spirit*, p. 192.
[50] Craig L. Carr, *Orwell, Politics, and Power* (New York: Continuum Books, 2010), p. 29.
[51] Stephen Ingle, *George Orwell: A Political Life* (New York: Manchester Press, 1993), p. 107.
[52] Ian Slater, *Orwell: The Road to Airstrip One* (New York: W. W. Norton, 1985), p. 87.

philosophy to understand him must surely be in doubt. I turn to that interpretation next.

Against the Inerudite Interpretation

On some understandings of him, Orwell was not especially erudite when it came to philosophy: on a weak version of the inerudite interpretation he was profoundly disinterested in philosophy; on a stronger version he was positively hostile to it.

A striking number of his commentators suggest sympathy with the weak version of the inerudite interpretation. For example, Richard Rees, Orwell's longtime friend and literary executor, thought that Orwell's "chief limitation . . . was his lack of interest in philosophy and psychology," adding that he was "indifferent to linguistic and logical analysis" and "equally unimpressed by the existentialist philosophies" that were then in vogue.[53] George Woodcock thought "One cannot imagine him attempting to compose . . . massive philosophical treatises to explain the themes which appear in another form in his novels."[54] More recently, we are told that Orwell "was simply not interested in schools of philosophy and had no great capacity for philosophical thought,"[55] that "Orwell had little patience with literary theory, let alone high-flown philosophical speculation or linguistic analysis,"[56] and that he suffered from an "inability or unwillingness to ask philosophical questions."[57] But the most influential proponent of the inerudite interpretation is surely Bernard Crick, the first of Orwell's biographers to be

[53] Rees, *Fugitive from the Camp of Victory*, p. 8.
[54] Woodcock, *The Crystal Spirit*, p. 232.
[55] Stephen Ingle, *The Social and Political Thought of George Orwell: A Reassessment* (New York: Routledge, 2006), p. 124.
[56] John Rodden, *The Unexamined Orwell*, p. 253. Literary theorists, for their part, haven't been much interested in Orwell either: see Alex Woloch, *Or Orwell*, p. xvii.
[57] David L. Kubal, *Outside the Whale: George Orwell's Art and Politics* (Notre Dame: Notre Dame University Press, 1972), p. 49.

given access to his estate and archives. Crick argued that Orwell "would . . . have been incapable of writing a contemporary philosophical monograph, scarcely of understanding one"[58] and that he was able to say things of significance "without being precisely philosophical."[59] At greater length:

> Apparently innocent of reading either J.S. Mill or Karl Popper, Orwell had reached the same conclusions for himself. . . . But there was no explicit philosophical grounding for his characteristic views on politics and ethics, only the invocation of "conscience" and "traditional moral code." He left off where philosophers should begin, but unlike many of them he did get to the right starting point.[60]

Orwell, Crick thought, simply lacked the "philosophical ability to resolve" a philosophical problem, even if "he had the literary genius to go right to the heart of the problem."[61]

Crick seems to have convinced Rorty that Orwell read no philosophy,[62] but the best evidence for the strong version of the inerudite interpretation seems to be supplied by Orwell himself. In a letter to Rees, Orwell explains that he is working through Bertrand Russell's *Human Knowledge: Its Scope and Its Limits*, a book he "Tried & failed" to complete (XX: 219). Struggling with a point about categorical logic, Orwell concludes, "I can never follow that kind of thing," adding, "It is the sort of thing that makes me feel that philosophy should be forbidden by law" (XX: 52). Things get worse, somehow. In *The Lion and the Unicorn*, Orwell announces that the English "feel no need for any philosophy or systematic

---

[58] Crick, *Orwell: A Life*, p. xx–xxi.

[59] Ibid., p. xix.

[60] Crick, *Orwell: A Life*, p. 351.

[61] Bernard Crick, "*Nineteen Eighty-Four*: Context and Controversy," in *The Cambridge Companion to George Orwell*, edited by John Rodden (Cambridge: Cambridge University Press, 2007), p. 157.

[62] See Rorty, *Contingency, Irony, and Solidarity*, p. 173, ffn. 9.

'world-view'" (XII: 393) and records "the lack of philosophical faculty, the absence in nearly all Englishmen of any need for an ordered system of thought or even for the use of logic" (XII: 399). Similarly, in "Lear, Tolstoy, and the Fool" he explains that "most Englishmen" have "no philosophical faculty" (XII: 492) and in *The English People* he explains that "England has produced poets and scientists rather than philosophers" and that "an inability to think logically" is one of the "abiding features of the English character" (XVI: 204). "The English," he thinks, "will never develop into a nation of philosophers" (XVI: 227).

If Orwell had affection for the unphilosophical English, he had only venom for the philosophical French. Reviewing Jacque Maritain, Orwell complained about "those cloudily abstract passages which seem to be so common in present-day French literature" (XVII: 175). He twice called John-Paul Sartre "a bag of wind" (XIX: 457 and 461) who produced "baffling fantasy" (XVII: 406); *No Exit* may be "a powerful play," Orwell allows, but "whether it has any meaning that is relevant from the point of view of living human beings is more doubtful" (XVII: 408). Rayner Heppenstall, Orwell's flatmate and BBC producer, remembers that Orwell was incredulous that Sartre "had seriously gone into the question whether other people existed or not," and concluded that Sartre was "an ass."[63] And passing remarks like "There is no need to get bogged up in metaphysical discussions about the meaning of 'reality'" (X: 500) and "There is only one way of avoiding thoughts, and that is to think too deeply" (XI: 104) don't sound much like the Socratic aphorism that the unexamined life is not worth living.

Note too that the philosophical drunk is an Orwellian trope: in *A Clergyman's Daughter*, the rakish Mr. Warburton indulges regularly and dares the protagonist, Dorothy Hare, to show him "a philosophy of life that isn't hedonism" (III: 285); in *Keep the Aspidistra Flying*, the novel's protagonist, Gordon Comstock, begins to feel

---

[63] Heppenstall, *Four Absences*, p. 173.

"more philosophic" only after his beer goes to his head (IV: 99) and, having gotten soused, drunkenly ponders his damnation "with a sort of philosophic interest" (IV: 192); in *Coming Up for Air*, it is only after a couple of pints that George Bowling "All of a sudden . . . felt kind of thoughtful and philosophic" (VII: 25); in *Nineteen Eighty-Four*, the old man that Winston interrogates in a boozer speaks "with a tolerant, philosophical air" but only after a half-liter of beer (IX: 96). None of this suggests Orwell had much use for philosophical thinking, certainly not sober philosophizing.

This project is not doomed if the inerudite interpretation is correct: philosophy might help us to better understand Orwell's thought even if he hated it. Still, I regard the case for the inerudite interpretation as wildly overblown and feel obligated to put the thing to bed. Someone should.

Begin with Crick. For a biography about someone ostensibly disinterested in philosophy, Socrates shows up a lot: Crick notes that Orwell's classmates compared him to Socrates, "the spokesman of this skeptical, rationalist tradition."[64] Cyril Connolly confirms that an Etonian would have read at least some of the Platonic dialogues,[65] which explains Orwell's familiarity with Plato's parting words to Socrates in the *Phaedo* (XV: 318). Crick allows that Orwell was prone to asking "Socratic questions,"[66] calling him a "Socratic gad-fly,"[67] and alludes to other philosophers to characterize Orwell as needs be: Orwell apparently shared Locke's views about land and labor[68] and, like Rousseau, idealized outdoor outings while disliking the artificiality of cities;[69] *Nineteen Eighty-Four* is akin to Hobbes's *Leviathan*,[70] although it is in *Animal Farm* that

[64] Crick, *A Life*, p. 50. Gordon Bowker refers to a young Orwell as "the aloof cynic and Socratic disputer of all things sacred" and suggests that Orwell took up "his old Socratic role" while stationed in Burma. See Bowker, *Inside George Orwell*, p. 64 and 86.
[65] Connolly, *Enemies of Promise*, p. 217.
[66] Crick, *A Life*, p. 186.
[67] Ibid., p. 304.
[68] Ibid., p. xvii.
[69] Ibid., pp. 12 and 198.
[70] Ibid., p. 398.

Major explains that animal life is "miserable, laborious, and short" (VIII: 3), and Orwell, like Hobbes, sought to be buried in sacred ground.[71] While Crick thought Orwell philosophically inerudite, he weirdly finds utility in appealing to philosophers to explain him.

For Rees's part, if he thought Orwell uninterested in, indifferent to, and unimpressed with philosophy, he also thought that Orwell "probably had a gift" for it[72], adding, "I did not say that his mind is ill-equipped for dealing with these subjects."[73] Others who knew Orwell remember him as attuned to the discipline: Christopher Hollis, a fellow Etonian who served with Orwell in Burma, suggests that "Such, Such Were the Joys" "is mainly valuable because of its philosophic reflections"[74] while Jacintha Buddicom, Orwell's youthful beloved, remembers him as having "a quite unusually calm and philosophical temperament" and thought of him as a "literary guide-philosopher-and-friend," comparing him to Bertrand Russell.[75]

Russell's influence on Orwell should not be understated,[76] and his throwaway line about making philosophy illegal betrays the fact that, *pace* Crick, Orwell *did* read philosophical monographs, including Russell's. At the time of his death, Orwell's library seems to have included Russell's *The History of Western Philosophy*, multiple editions of *Mysticism and Logic and Other Essays*, *Philosophy and Politics*, *The Practice and Theory of Bolshevism*, and *Roads to Freedom* (XX: 296).[77] Orwell's reviews of Russell's books noted Russell's "essentially decent intellect" and that "In a time of universal panic and lying he is a good person to make contact with"

[71] Ibid., p. 405.

[72] Rees, *Fugitive from the Camp of Victory*, p. 8.

[73] Ibid., p. 110.

[74] Hollis, *A Study of George Orwell*, p. 9.

[75] Jacintha Buddicom, *Eric & Us: A Remembrance of George Orwell* (London: Leslie Frewin Publishers, 1974), p. 20, 87, and 47.

[76] For discussion, see David Dwan, *Liberty, Equality, and Humbug* (Oxford: Oxford University Press, 2018) and my "Orwell and Bertrand Russell," in *The Oxford Handbook of George Orwell*, edited by Nathan Waddell, forthcoming.

[77] Davison cautions that some of these books may have not been Orwell's (XIX: 296).

(XI: 312), and he singled out *Freedom and Organisation* and *The Practice and Theory of Bolshevism* for praise (XIX: 128).[78] He also sometimes borrowed from Russell. In a 1947 article, Orwell explained that:

> The greatest difficulty of all is the apathy and conservatism of people everywhere, their unawareness of danger, their inability to imagine anything new—in general, as Bertrand Russell put it recently, the unwillingness of the human race to acquiesce in its own survival. (XIX: 164)[79]

Orwell thought Russell was eminent among philosophers: if A. J. Ayer was "a great friend," Russell was "the chief star in the constellation" (XVIII: 242). And I strongly suspect that Orwell did Russell a great honor in *Nineteen Eighty-Four*: Winston's struggle against O'Brien's logic quietly references Russell's critique of idealism without naming him.[80]

As Winston is being tortured, O'Brien, "the Party philosopher,"[81] engages him in a philosophical tête-à-tête where "there is scarcely an important philosophical question they do not examine."[82] After O'Brien tells Winston that "Nothing exists except through human consciousness," Winston struggles to recall:

[78] Orwell gets the title wrong, reversing 'Theory' and 'Practice' (XIX: 128), although to my ear his ordering is more natural.

[79] Russell claimed that "the difficulty is to persuade the human race to acquiesce in its own survival": see Bertrand Russell, "The Atomic Bomb and the Prevention of War," *Bulletin of the Atomic Scientists*, Vol. 2, No. 7–8 (1946), p. 21. Something like this quote from Russell is included in the communications of League for the Dignity and Rights of Man contained in the George Orwell Archive. There, the quote attributed to Russell reads, "The difficulty to-day is to persuade the human race to acquiesce in its own survival." Russell's last name is misspelled 'Russel.'

[80] For an extended discussion, Peter Brian Barry, "Bertrand Russell and the Forgotten Fallacy in *Nineteen Eighty-Four*," forthcoming in *George Orwell Studies* (2022).

[81] Rees, *Fugitive from the Camp of Victory*, p. 93.

[82] William Steinhoff, *George Orwell and the Origins of 1984*, p. 221.

The belief that nothing exists outside your own mind—surely there must be some way of demonstrating that it was false? Had it not been exposed long ago as a fallacy? There was even a name for it, which he had forgotten. (IX: 279)

Orwell doesn't always seem to regard O'Brien's reasoning as fallacious or even wrong: in *A Clergyman's Daughter*, one of Orwell's early novels, Dorothy regards the proposition that "all real happenings are in the mind" as a "truism" (III: 272). So somewhere along the line Orwell became suspicious that O'Brien's fallacy had been exposed. But who exposed it? And where?

In *The History of Western Philosophy*—again, a book Orwell seems to have owned—Russell considers the arguments of Bishop Berkeley, who defended a version of idealism according to which "material objects only exist through being perceived."[83] Russell accuses Berkeley of a modal scope fallacy, and while he never names it as such, it is clear Russell thought Berkeley was guilty of *some* fallacy: "The fallacy involved is a very common one," Russell explains.[84] And while there is no record of Orwell and Russell discussing, say, Berkley's idealism over lunch, one biographer supposes that the temptation to do so "must have been irresistible."[85] We *do* know that Orwell was greatly interested in Russell's opinion of *Nineteen Eighty-Four* and hoped that Russell would author a blurb (XIX: 487–488) and a review (XX: 95). And it is in his review of Russell's *Power* that Orwell worries, "It is quite possible that we are descending into an age in which two and two will make five when the Leader says so" (XI: 311), the first time he published anything like the infamous "2 + 2 = 5." I contend that the unnamed fallacy in *Nineteen Eighty-Four* is the one Russell identified in his

[83] Bertrand Russell, *The History of Western Philosophy* (New York: Simon and Schuster, 1945), p. 647.
[84] Ibid., p. 652.
[85] Bowker, *Inside George Orwell*, p. 347

critique of Berkeley: Winston cannot recall its name *because Russell never named it*.

At this point, the defender of the inerudite interpretation is bound to play her trump card: didn't no less than A. J. Ayer say that Orwell was philosophically inerudite? Some of Orwell's biographers seem to think so: Crick understands Ayer as thinking that Orwell "had no interest in philosophy whatsoever"[86] and Gordon Bowker understands Ayer as thinking that Orwell "gave no impression of caring much for philosophy."[87] But that *is simply not what Ayer said.* Here, I quote Ayer at some length:

> Orwell and I shared a common outlook—politically, for one thing. We were both radicals, but he wasn't interested in academic philosophy in the very least. I think he thought it was rather a waste of time, that if people were going to philosophize they ought to apply their philosophy to political and social questions. I think the kind of abstract philosophy I went in for didn't appeal to him, and we didn't much talk about it. And he didn't hold it against me that I indulged in it![88]

Ayer is clear that Orwell wasn't interested in *academic* philosophy, that *abstract* philosophy had little appeal for him.[89] Bowker's suggestion that Orwell was "suspicious of metaphysics"[90] is consistent with Ayer's recollection, but so is Orwell's being greatly interested in less abstract and academic matters like ethics and social and political philosophy, which Ayer alludes to. Orwell's complaint, recorded by Ayer, reads less like an outright dismissal of philosophy and more like a call for philosophers to do more applied philosophy.

[86] Crick, *Orwell: A Life*, p. 325. He still allows that Ayer influenced Orwell "at least somewhat": p. 325. See also Colls, *English Rebel*, p. 211.

[87] Bowker, *Inside George Orwell*, p. 324.

[88] See Wadham, *The Orwell Tapes*, p. 205.

[89] Woodcock is careful to state only that Orwell "was not philosophically inclined, at least not in an academic sense": see Woodcock, *The Crystal Spirit*, p. 285.

[90] Bowker, *Inside George Orwell*, p. 202.

Russell is again relevant here: undoubtedly Orwell had little interest in Russell's influential theory of descriptions, for example, yet he read and reviewed Russell's public philosophy, the sort of thing the inerudite interpretation suggests he would not or could not do.

Worse for the inerudite interpretation, Orwell *did* display an interest in academic and abstract philosophy, Ayer's remarks notwithstanding. At least, he sometimes indulged in speculation about old philosophical chestnuts: he hypothesized a relationship between illness, blood flow, and intelligent thought (XIX: 307) suggesting sympathy with a physicalist reduction of mental states; he lamented that "our language is practically useless for describing anything that goes on inside the brain" (XII: 128) and that "every individual has an inner life, and is aware of the practical impossibility of understanding others or being understood" (XII: 129), hinting at an interest in solipsism; he acknowledged that he has many beliefs that he cannot demonstrably prove—say, that the earth is not flat—but retained them based on trust in others and the absence of emotional disturbance (XIII: 77), an epistemological thesis.

He also appears to be aware of particular philosophers or at least their aphorisms, including Nietzsche, whom he channels often: in a review of P. G. Wodehouse, Orwell explains that the great charm of one character is that "he is beyond good and evil," even dropping Nietzsche's name (X: 446); in a letter to Humphry House, Orwell attributes to Nietzsche (he misspells it 'Nietzche') a view about Christianity quoted from memory that "if you are all right inside you don't have to be *told* that it is putrid. You can smell it—it stinks" (XII: 141); on more than one occasion, Orwell channels Aphorism §146 from *Beyond Good and Evil*, cautioning those who hunt dragons to avoid becoming dragons themselves, sometimes attributing the thought to Nietzsche explicitly (XI: 113 and XVI: 387), sometimes not (XI: 167).[91] Nietzsche's discussion

---

[91] On Kaufmann's translation, Nietzsche warns that "Whoever fights monsters should see to it that in the process he does not become a monster." See Friedrich Nietzsche,

of the will to power might help make sense of what Orwell says about power[92]—more about that in Chapter 4—and, if it matters, at least one friend thought that Orwell in his final days looked like Nietzsche on his deathbed.[93]

Let me end this assault on the inerudite interpretation with one more observation. In a 1945 piece titled "What Is Science?" Orwell worried that "scientific education for the masses will do little good, and probably a lot of harm, if it simply boils down to more physics, more chemistry, more biology." As a corrective, he proposes:

> Clearly, scientific education ought to mean the implanting of a rational, sceptical, experimental habit of mind. It ought to mean acquiring a *method*—a method that can be used on any problem that one meets—and not simply piling up a lot of facts. (XVII: 325)

What discipline is Orwell commending here? At the risk of self-indulgency, I submit that if there is a single discipline apt for developing rational, skeptical, and experimental habits of mind, it is philosophy.

If the inerudite interpretation is largely bankrupt, where does its popularity come from? Orwell's readers who doubt his philosophical acumen should recall that "philosophy-bashing" is "an ancient and very British sport in which many philosophers themselves gamely partook."[94] Biographers partake too. Michael Shelden, who assures us that Orwell had too much faith in common sense to study any philosophical system,[95] explains that Maurice Merleau-Ponty, French philosopher and former beau of Orwell's second wife,

Beyond Good and Evil: Prelude to a Philosophy of the Future, translated by Walter Kaufmann (New York: Vintage, 1989), p. 89.

[92] Meyers, *Wintry Conscience of a Generation*, p. 116.

[93] D. J. Taylor, *Orwell: The Life* (New York: Henry Holt and Company, 2003), p. 417.

[94] Dwan, *Liberty, Equality, and Humbug*, p. 5.

[95] Michael Shelden, *Orwell: The Authorised Biography* (London: Heinemann, 1989), p. 411.

Sonia Brownell, was "a good philosopher": he told her "I love you, I think."[96] That Orwell should have a bit of fun with us is no surprise: everyone else does. But the jokes are funnier when you get the punchline, and that requires having some clue what philosophers are talking about. Orwell did. I also suspect that readers who doubt Orwell's philosophical acumen conceive of a philosopher as an *academic*, someone formally trained in the discipline and employed in it. Even today, most serious candidates for the title of 'philosopher' are members of the academy who teach and research philosophy for a living. Orwell, of course, had no formal training and never held an academic post in higher education. So, if philosophers must be professional academics, Orwell doesn't make the cut. Yet Orwell, for his part, did *not* clearly conceive of the philosopher as an academic. At least, he seems to have thought that someone could be a *kind of philosopher* without being an academic, characterizing Mark Twain as "a species of philosopher" (XVI: 6).[97] I am similarly tempted to regard Orwell as a species of philosopher and only an unduly restrictive semantics of 'philosopher,' one that Orwell rejected, demands thinking otherwise.

The inerudite interpretation poses no obstacle to a study of Orwell's ethics. But for other reasons, some may find a study of Orwell's ethics misguided. In the final section of this chapter, I consider Orwell's habit of producing offensive speech and his preferred response to it, a response that has probably been misconstrued.

Canceling Orwell

As we approach the seventy-fifth anniversary of the publication of *Nineteen Eighty-Four* and Orwell's death, interest in Orwell will surely surge and a new generation of readers will learn of his sins.

---

[96] Ibid., p. 479.
[97] Shakespeare "was not a philosopher," alas (XIX: 64).

He has been accused, sometimes credibly, of being misogynistic, anti-Semitic, homophobic, cruel, and still more. He was a man of his time, and many of his views are what you would expect of a man of his time—that is, offensive by contemporary standards. I will have more to say about Orwell's misogyny in Chapter 6, but many contemporary readers will conclude that, in our contemporary parlance, Orwell *was not woke*. Worse, as a young man, Orwell seems to have sexually assaulted Jacintha Buddicom, his crush and the subject of some of his forlorn poetry. Jacintha's remembrance of their time together contains no trace of the event, but a postscript to the 2006 edition by Dione Venables, Jacintha's cousin, recalls finding Guiny, Jacintha's sister, looking "unusually grim" after finding a draft of a letter to Orwell, né Eric. One "furious letter" dated September 1921 detailed Jacintha's "disgust and shock that he should try and FORCE her to let him make love to her." Apparently, during the course of one of their regular daily walks, he "had attempted to take things further and make SERIOUS love to Jacintha. He had held her down . . . and though she struggled, yelling at him to STOP, he had torn her skirt and badly bruised a shoulder and her left hip." Guiny, who had a "hazy memory of Jacintha rushing in with a torn skirt and a tear-stained face," did not think that the eighteen-year-old and six foot four Orwell raped the twenty-year-old and five foot Jacintha, and a family friend suggests that the offending event "sounds more like a botched seduction,"[98] but one of Orwell's biographers regards him as lucky for having served her Majesty's empire in Burma and not having served time in Wandsworth Prison.[99]

What then should we do with Orwell? Should we continue to read him, praising those parts of his thought that merit praise while regrettably acknowledging those that do not? Should he be

---

[98] Kathryn Hughes, "Such Were the Joys," *The Guardian*, 17 February 2007, https://www.theguardian.com/books/2007/feb/17/georgeorwell.biography.

[99] John Sutherland, *Orwell's Nose: A Pathological Biography* (London: Reaktion Books, 2016), p. 87.

ignored or purged from the literary canon? Should we spend any time at all debating his ethics? Again, invoking the parlance of our time: Should Orwell be *canceled*? That I do not bring my discussion of Orwell's ethics to a halt presently should give some indication of what I think the answer to these questions is, but my goal in this section is not to answer them. Rather, I hope to consider what Orwell himself might have said. Orwell reflected on the link between ethics and language in a series of essays in the 1940s, and he had much to say about what should be done in response to offensive speech which may help us to determine what we ought to do when confronted with it.

Orwell's name is sometimes invoked when events are scratched, speakers deplatformed, guests disinvited, and projects terminated among other responses to offensive speech that collectively fall under the umbrella of "cancel culture." Steven Pinker, the Harvard psychology professor and bestselling author, has claimed he is the target of an "Orwellian" attack after several hundred academics signed a letter calling for his fellowship at the Linguistics Society of America to be terminated, following events documented in an article titled "Cancel Culture Is Orwellian."[100] After former President of the United States, Donald J. Trump, was banned from Twitter for violating its terms of service, his son, Donald Trump Jr., seemingly oblivious to the irony, tweeted "We are living Orwell's 1984. Free-speech no longer exists in America. It died with big tech and what's left is only there for a chosen few."[101] The working assumption appears to be that Orwell would be hostile to cancel culture, an assumption that is not entirely baseless. Orwell found it difficult to secure a publisher for *Animal Farm*—perhaps as many as twenty editors turned it down[102]—either because they thought it impolitic

---

[100] Damian Whitworth, "Steven Pinker: I Had to Speak Out: Cancel Culture Is Orwellian," *The Times*, 9 July 2020, https://www.thetimes.co.uk/article/steven-pinker-i-had-to-speak-out-cancel-culture-is-orwellian-sr2q03nh6 (Last accessed 30 September 2021).

[101] https://twitter.com/donaldjtrumpjr/status/1347697226466828288?lang=en

[102] Rodden, *Scenes from an Afterlife*, p. 51.

to publish a work that openly mocked the Soviets or because they were outright Soviet sympathizers. Orwell explained that "Because I committed the crime known in France as *lèse-Staline* I have been obliged at times to change my publisher, to stop writing for papers which represented part of my livelihood, to have my books boycotted in other papers, and to be pursued by insulting letters . . . and even threats of libel action" (XVIII: 442). In "The Freedom of the Press," an essay he intended to preface *Animal Farm*, he quoted a publisher who explained that after consultation with the Ministry of Information:

> I can see now that it might be regarded as something which it was highly ill-advised to publish at the present time. If the fable were addressed generally to dictators and dictatorships at large then publication would be all right, but the fable does follow, as I see now, so completely the progress of the Russian Soviets and their two dictators, that it can apply only to Russia, to the exclusion of the other dictatorships. Another thing: it would be less offensive if the predominant caste in the fable were not pigs. I think the choice of pigs as the ruling caste will no doubt give offence to many people, and particularly to anyone who is a bit touchy, as undoubtedly the Russians are. (VIII: 99)

Orwell concluded that "This kind of thing is not a good symptom" (VIII: 99) and, in a related essay, "The Prevention of Literature," insisted that "there can be no question about the poisonous effect of the Russian *mythos* on English intellectual life" (XVII: 373).

Orwell doesn't blame "this kind of thing" only on leftist Soviet-sympathizers; he was at least as concerned about wealthy conservatives unduly influencing free expression. In "Freedom of the Press," he worried that the British press is "owned by wealthy men who have every motive to be dishonest on certain important topics" (VIII: 100). In "The Prevention of Literature," he noted that one of the things working against English journalists is "the concentration of the Press in the hands of a few rich men" (XVII: 371). In "Boys' Weeklies" he insisted that "*All* fiction from the novels in the mushroom libraries downwards is censored in the interests of the ruling class" (XII: 76). Orwell's conclusion that "A genuinely unfashionable opinion is almost never given a fair hearing, either in the popular press or in the highbrow periodicals" (VIII: 100) finds fault with conservative media moguls and liberal literati alike.

How should all this inform a conclusion about what Orwell would think of cancel culture were he alive today and were other things equal? It is tempting to play a round of "What Would George Orwell Do?," a game that "has its illicit darker sides: mantle-stealing, body-snatching, and political grave-robbing . . . whereby the participants move Orwell's coffin to the left or right."[103] It might seem obvious to contemporary readers that Orwell would be hostile to cancel culture and that those who regard Orwell as their moral lodestone should condemn it with equal hostility. But things are not that simple.

Orwell, of course, offered robust defenses of free speech and expression, and often hinted that he would tolerate morally dubious speech however much he disliked it. As he praised freedom of expression in Britain during wartime, he added that "I want that to remain true, and by sometimes giving a hearing to unpopular opinions, I think we help it to do so" (XVI: 306). In "Benefit of Clergy: Some Notes on Salvador Dali," he found Dali to be both "a good draughtsman and a disgusting human being" (XVI: 237) and concluded that Dali's work ought not to be suppressed, adding the curious "Short of the dirty postcards that used to be sold in Mediterranean seaport towns, it is doubtful policy to suppress anything" (XVI: 238). He is aware that Charles Dickens acted badly to his wife but insisted that this fact "no more invalidates his work

---

[103] John Rodden, *Scenes from an Afterlife: The Legacy of George Orwell* (Wilmington, DE: ISI Books), p. 203.

than the second-best bed invalidates *Hamlet*" and that "a writer's literary personality has little or nothing to do with his private character" (XII: 21). A more dramatic example occurred during his travels to England's North, when Orwell attended a speech by Oswald Mosley, leader of the British Union of Fascists, that Orwell found "the most unutterable bollox" (X: 473). Some of Orwell's contemporaries thought that he took Mosley too lightly, including Tommy Degnan, Orwell's handler in Barnsley, who attended the same speech and earned some rough handling by Mosley's goons. Orwell complained that Degnan was wrong to disturb the meeting, mumbling something about being British and fair play,[104] anticipating his much-celebrated comment in "Freedom and the Press" that "If liberty means anything at all it means the right to tell people what they do not want to hear" (VIII: 108) and described calls for Mosley to be outlawed as "shameful" (XIX: 254). Even Fascists, apparently, should not be canceled.

Yet Orwell also clearly regarded some speech as worth correcting because it is offensive. As a younger man, he embraced the use of 'Scotchman' just because it annoyed and vexed. He praised Anthony Powell in a personal letter for "calling them 'Scotchmen,' not 'Scotsmen' as they like to be called," adding "I find this a good way of annoying them" (X: 484).[105] He used the word in his early novels: in *Burmese Days*, Orwell has John Flory explain that "The British Empire is simply a device for giving trade monopolies to the English—or rather to gangs of Jews and Scotchmen" (II: 38); in *Keep the Aspidistra Flying*, 'Scotchman' shows up four times, as does Gordon Comstock's complaint about "the Scotchification of England" (IV: 39); it shows up in the very first chapter of in *The Road to Wigan Pier* (V: 7). But in a 1945 *As I Please* (AIP) column,

---

[104] See Crick, *Orwell: A Life*, p. 191.

[105] Orwell's animus could manifest in other ways. Kay Ekevall recalls that Orwell would refuse invitations from Edwin Muir and crossed the street to avoid being introduced to him because Muir was Scottish: see *Orwell Remembered*, edited by Audrey Coppard and Bernard Crick (London: Ariel Books, 1984), p. 96.

he explained that he was going through the proofs of *Burmese Days* and substituting 'Chinese' for 'Chinaman' on the grounds that it had become "a deadly insult," and similarly commended that authors "avoid using insulting nicknames," a "small precaution which is not too much trouble," in the hope that they could "perhaps do a little to mitigate the horrors of the colour war" (XVI: 24). And in another AIP column, published only a week after he referenced "the absurdity of the rules governing literary censorship in Britain" (XIX: 46), he wondered "is it really necessary, in 1947, to teach children to use expressions like 'native' and 'Chinaman'?," adding:

> It is no use answering that it is childish for an Indian or an African to feel insulted when he is called a "native." We all have these feelings in one form or another. If a Chinese wants to be called a Chinese and not a Chinaman, if a Scotsman objects to being called a Scotchman, or if a Negro demands his capital N, it is only the most ordinary politeness to do what is asked of one. (XIX: 51)

Orwell's official position may be that liberty demands the right to tell people what they don't want to hear, but he clearly *also* thought there are sometimes morally sound reasons to refrain from saying it.

For his part, Orwell seems to have been responsive to moralized pleas for him to correct his morally offensive speech. While he called anti-Semitism "an essentially magical doctrine" (XVI: 83) and an "irrational thing" (XVII: 65), Orwell is sometimes labeled "mildly anti-Semitic"[106] (a phrase I have heard nowhere outside the secondary literature on Orwell). He merely repeats someone else's nasty invective in *Down and Out in Paris and London*, when he recalls the odd proverb "Trust a snake before a Jew and a Jew

[106] Crick, *Orwell: The Life*, p. 307; John Rodden, *Scenes from an Afterlife: The Legacy of George Orwell*, p. 197; John Newsinger, "Orwell, Anti-Semitism and the Holocaust," in *The Cambridge Companion to George Orwell*, edited by John Rodden (Cambridge: Cambridge University Press, 2007), pp. 112 and 123.

before a Greek, but don't trust an Armenian" (I: 72), but uses of 'the Jew' pop up uncomfortably often in that work. His personal correspondence is also distressing, especially his "War-time Diary," which includes the observation that there were "a higher proportion of Jews than one would normally see in a crowd of this size"— that is, the crowd gathered to shelter in various Underground stations—and the unprompted thought that "What is bad about Jews is that they are not only conspicuous, but go out of their way to make themselves so" (XII: 278). Orwell indignantly suspected that some of his contemporaries regarded him as an anti-Semite: he "had no doubt" that Tosco Fyvel, his friend and successor as editor of *Tribune*, thought that Orwell was anti-Semitic, clucking that "Some people go around smelling after antisemitism all the time" (XIX: 461). Fyvel's memoir largely defends Orwell against this charge but he recalls chastising Orwell, asking what was the "point in referring to this particular man throughout the article simply as 'the Jew'—'the Jew' did this, 'the Jew' did that, or worse, 'the little Jew' did the other?," and so forth. Fyvel recalls that Orwell was initially astonished but took his point and "never again referred to anyone simply as 'the Jew.' "[107] Having been criticized for his offensive speech, he knocked it off. If Orwell is supposed to be a moral exemplar, the lesson might be to follow suit.

The best reason to be skeptical about Orwell's supposed hostility to cancel culture is suggested in "The Freedom of the Press," where Orwell identifies the primary threat to free expression. It is not "censorship that can sometimes be enforced by pressure groups," which Orwell regards as "harmless" and "understandable" (VIII: 102). Nor is it state censorship during wartime which, here and elsewhere, he thinks "has not been particularly irksome" (VIII: 99). Instead, he names as "The sinister fact about literary censorship in England" that "it is largely voluntary" (VIII: 99–100). Orwell's concern is less

---

[107] Tosco Fyvel, *George Orwell: A Personal Memoir* (New York: Macmillan Publishing, 1982), p. 180.

that authors will be censored by the state or activist groups, more that authors will save themselves time and expense *by censoring themselves* out of timidity or lack of nerve. Orwell suggests that "the worst enemy a writer or journalist has to face" is "intellectual cowardice" (VIII: 99), a point noted by Orwell's poet friend, Paul Potts, who understood "The Freedom of the Press" as "a blast against self-censorship" (VIII: 97). Orwell's concern about self-censorship is also detectable in "Prevention of Literature," when he points out that "it is the peculiarity of our age that the rebels against the existing order . . . are also rebelling against the idea of individual integrity" (XVII: 371). Here too, Orwell is especially hostile, not to forces external to an author, but to internal forces that would lead her to quietism.

Some selective readers might note Orwell's claim in "Politics vs. Literature" that "public opinion . . . is less tolerant than any system of law," which seems to make public opinion, the weapon of choice of those who would cancel speech, a graver threat to free speech and expression than civil or criminal law. But consider the full text of that passage where Orwell discusses Swift's Houyhnhnms from *Gulliver's Travels*, who are "never *compelled* to do anything . . . merely 'exhorted' or 'advised' ":

> This illustrates very well the totalitarian tendency which is explicit in the anarchist or pacifist vision of Society. In a Society in which there is no law, and in theory no compulsion, the only arbiter of behaviour is public opinion. But public opinion, because of the tremendous urge to conformity in gregarious animals, is less tolerant than any system of law. (XVIII: 424)

Public opinion, if it has a stultifying effect, has power only given the understandable urge to conform, an urge that is not shared by all to equal degrees and can be counterbalanced. Orwell knew that "To exercise your right of free speech you have to fight against economic pressure and against strong sections of public opinion"

(XVII: 379), but also that "To write in plain, vigorous language"—
that is, Orwell's preferred style—"one has to think fearlessly"
(XVII: 376). This is, after all, the author who recalled the hymn that
challenged us: "Dare to be a Daniel, / Dare to stand alone; / Dare to
have a purpose firm, / Dare to make it known" (XVII: 371). A genuine Daniel does not whimper about supposed oppression by social media outlets: he stands alone.

The correct response to the moral coercion of public opinion, as
I read Orwell, is to develop an immunity to it, to cultivate a personality largely free from the desire to conform which is not the same
thing as becoming unresponsive to moral reasons to act better nor
tolerating all morally heinous speech no matter how much one
dislikes it. If that's right, Orwell's supposed hostility to cancel culture may be seriously overstated. In actual practice, Orwell was
happy to cancel some associations and dialogue out of a sense of
disgust and approbation: he refused to even shake the hand of
Randall Swingler, a Communist author who attacked Orwell in
print, for example.[108] Even Orwell had his limits.

Conclusion

In this opening chapter, I have suggested that philosophy can be
useful in understanding Orwell and his work, primarily by helping
to identify and critically examine those ethical concepts and principles implicit in Orwell's work. I argued that the inerudite interpretation is seriously flawed, but the best way to show the poverty of
the inerudite interpretation is to highlight the nuances of Orwell's
ethical thought and put them on display. Again, Orwell was no professional philosopher but a philosophical outsider, and he never
explicated his favored ethical commitments and sympathies in
the manner that a professional philosopher might. The task for

[108] Bowker, *Inside George Orwell*, p. 331.

professional philosophers, then, is to ferret out those commitments and sympathies and put them on display, to make them discernable as if they were behind a clear windowpane.

In the next chapter, I begin my discussion of Orwell's ethics in earnest, and I start with some basics. It is common among ethicists to distinguish between *deontic* and *axiological* concepts: the former concern right action, the latter concern value. If there is such a thing as Orwell's ethics, we should be able to answer basic deontic questions: what, according to Orwell, makes an action the right thing to do? How do we distinguish right from wrong? We should also be able to answer basic axiological questions: what, according to Orwell, makes our lives go well? What things are good and what is worth doing? What is it to be good in the first place? I try to answer these and other questions in Chapter 2.

2

George Orwell

The Age's Advocate

Some readers, noting the "adversarial cast of Orwell's mind,"[1] portray him as an adversary, not an advocate. Some suggest that "as a writer Orwell was primarily stimulated by negative impulses: He needed to write *against* something,"[2] which is consistent with lacking any impetus to write *for* something. Others explain that while "we always know unequivocally what he is *against*, we are never as certain about what he was *for*."[3] If he were only an adversary, not an advocate, there will be little chance of saying what his ethics are, only what he was against. But the thesis that Orwell was only an adversary is seriously overstated for at least two reasons. First, knowing what a thinker is against enables some sound inferences about what they are for. His satirical later novels, for example, make it clear that he was for equality and democracy *because* he was against authoritarianism and totalitarianism, that he was for clarity of language and honest expression *because* he was against the corruption of language by lies and sloppiness, and so forth.[4] Second, Orwell is hardly shy about his advocacy, a point that is easily missed if one only reflects on his most famous

[1] Alok Rai, *Orwell and the Politics of Despair: A Critical Study of the Writings of George Orwell* (Cambridge: Cambridge University Press, 1990), p. 73.

[2] Daphne Patai, *The Orwell Mystique: A Study in Male Ideology* (Amherst: University of Massachusetts Press, 1984), p. 7.

[3] Ian Slater, *Orwell: The Road to Airstrip One* (New York: W. W. Norton, 1985), p. 244.

[4] Rebecca Solint, *Orwell's Roses* (New York: Viking, 2021), p. 47.

George Orwell. Peter Brian Barry, Oxford University Press. © Oxford University Press 2023.
DOI: 10.1093/oso/9780197627402.003.0002

novels, *Animal Farm* or *Nineteen Eighty-Four*, the cardinal sin of Orwell scholarship. In this chapter, I make that case that Orwell has a great deal to say about ethics especially in his essays, commentary, reviews, and correspondence, even if what he says requires some unpacking. The goal of this chapter is make the case that Orwell was not merely an adversary but an advocate for various ethical theses that collectively constitute a surprisingly comprehensive theory of ethics.

I divide this chapter into three sections. First, I consider Orwell's humanism and make the case that he counts as a humanist not only because he rejected some familiar antihumanist doctrines but also because he endorsed a conception of goodness that makes goodness a function of facts about what is good for human beings. Second, I discuss what Orwell had to say about well-being, what makes our lives go well and permits us to flourish. I discuss Orwell's favored conception of well-being and I tend to some problems in the secondary literature. While Orwell's opposition to hedonism has often been noted, his use of the term is ambiguous and some of his stated opposition isn't really opposition to hedonism, properly understood, a point many readers have missed. And if there is consensus that Orwell opposed hedonism, there is little discussion of what conception of well-being he would replace it with. I make the case that what he says about human needs suggests he favors an objective list theory of well-being. Third, I discuss Orwell's normative ethics. Orwell has been characterized often enough as an anticonsequentialist, but his strongest case against consequentialism has been largely missed in lieu of other arguments that aren't really arguments against consequentialism, and, here too, there has been little discussion of what conception of right action he would replace it with. I argue that Orwell's best argument against consequentialism emerges from his discussion of moral sainthood, is grounded in his favored conception of well-being, and depends on the moral significance of agent-relative reasons for action. I then argue that Orwell is well understood as a threshold deontologist, which may leave his status as an anticonsequentialist more unsettled than some might be comfortable with.

Obviously, Orwell did not state his favored positions in terms utilized by professional philosophers, but by the end of the chapter it will hopefully be clear that Orwell was an advocate for a remarkably comprehensive ethical theory that will ground much more that he says about ethics.

Orwellian Humanism

In "Rudyard Kipling," Orwell states that "A humanitarian is always a hypocrite" (XIII: 153), which feels like a throwaway line if he was "first and foremost, a humanist"[5] and "his personal and political qualities were based on an individual form of secular humanism."[6] Orwell, an avowed democratic Socialist, affirmed that "The basis of Socialism is humanism" (XVII: 61). But what does his humanism commit him to? How did he understand it?

Orwell, Humanist?

Humanism is often understood in contrast to something else—say, the Renaissance project of replacing God with human beings as the subject of academic interest or Darwinism and the rejection of literal readings of religious texts[7]—and humanists are often understood as rejecting religious, theistic, and Christian beliefs.[8] Orwell

[5] Vernon Richards, "Orwell the Humanist," in *George Orwell at Home (and among the Anarchists): Essays and Photographs* (London: Freedom Press, 1998), p. 9.

[6] Nicolas Walter, "Orwell and Anarchism," in *George Orwell at Home (and among the Anarchists): Essays and Photographs* (London: Freedom Press, 1998), p. 74.

[7] Alan Lacey, "Humanism," in *The Oxford Companion to Philosophy*, edited by Ted Honderich (Oxford: Oxford University Press, 1993), pp. 375–376.

[8] Andrew Copson, "What Is Humanism?," in *The Wiley Blackwell Handbook of Humanism*, edited by Andrew Copson and A. C. Grayling (London: John Wiley & Sons, 2015), p. 2.

is sometimes understood as a humanist given he rejects religion,[9] belief in immortality,[10] and the need for external resources for salvation,[11] but also because he opposes tyranny.[12] But his humanism might seem "vague," "platitudinous," or "completely empty"[13] if he only opposes and never advocates. He does suggest a positive conception of humanism he affirms that "Humanism assumes that man is the measure of all things" (XVII: 176), a dictum that should be familiar to philosophers. But could Protagoras's dictum—that is, that man is the measure of all things—really be the basis for Orwell's humanism? That might seem unlikely if not inconsistent with doctrines typically associated with him.

In the *Theaetetus*, Socrates identifies the thesis that "knowledge is only perception" with the dictum of "Protagoras, wisest of all men, that man is the measure of all things."[14] If knowledge is only perception, then *perceiving* something amounts to *knowing* that it's the case, a result seemingly at odds with Orwell's assurance in "Looking Back on the Spanish War" that "however much you deny the truth, the truth goes on existing, as it were, behind your back" (XIII: 505). It is also a little too close to the subjectivism about truth expressed by O'Brien in *Nineteen Eighty-Four* when he affirms that "Reality exists in the human mind, and nowhere else" and that "Whatever the Party holds to be the truth, *is* truth" (IX: 261). Worse, if the Protagorean dictum commits Orwell to subjectivism about truth, it also commits him to subjectivism about *moral* truth, an intolerable result for those who find in Orwell "strong confidence in the existence of universal moral norms."[15] Orwell's turn toward Protagoras

[9] Bernard Crick, *Orwell: A Life* (Boston: Little, Brown, 1980), p. 143.

[10] Patrick Reilly, *George Orwell: The Age's Adversary* (New York: Macmillan, 1986), p. 69.

[11] Alan Sandison, *The Last Man in Europe: An Essay on George Orwell* (New York: Barnes and Noble Books, 1974), p. 25.

[12] Douglas Kerr, *George Orwell* (Horndon, UK: Northcote House, 2003), p. 87.

[13] David Dwan, *Liberty, Equality, and Humbug* (Oxford: Oxford University Press, 2018), p. 88.

[14] From *Plato: Complete Works*, edited by John M. Cooper (Indianapolis, IN: Hackett, 1997), p. 179.

[15] Dwan, *Liberty, Equality, and Humbug*, p. 15.

might seem wrong from the start. If this is what Protagorean humanism yields, who wants it?

Man Is the Measure(ment)

But have we understood Orwell here? The Protagorean dictum can be disambiguated in a way that makes his humanism less counterintuitive and more consistent with what he says elsewhere. It is only on a subjectivist reading of the Protagorean dictum that truth is a function of our perceptions: man is the measure of all things, on this reading, insofar as *our measurements* are deemed authoritative and we are the authoritative *measurers* of things. But the Protagorean dictum admits of another, more pragmatic reading. On this pragmatic reading, whether something is morally good or bad is a function of whether it makes our lives go well or go poorly. So understood, man is the measure of all things, not because our perceptions or judgments are especially authoritative, but because, roughly *we are the unit of measurement*. Much like, on a folk conception of measurement, whether something is or is not a meter long is a function of its relation to the Parisian meter bar, the platinum bar placed in the French National Archives, on the pragmatic reading, whether something is good or bad, for example, is a function of its relations to human beings and what enhances or diminishes our well-being. Man is the measure on the pragmatic reading, not because we are measurers, but because we are *the measurement*: among other things, it affirms that what is good is *what is good for human beings*.

The pragmatic reading does not make Orwell a defender of Party orthodoxy: it does not affirm that whatever human beings *hold* to be good is good but that what is, in fact, good for us is good, and as such the pragmatic reading is compatible with pervasive mistaken beliefs about what is good for us. Nor does it commit him to supposing that only human beings are of moral value or that only we can be wronged. The pragmatic reading is consistent with supposing, for example, that abusing nonhuman animals and poor stewardship of the environment are bad. Suppose, following Kant, that cruelty to nonhuman animals makes us vicious and vicious-ness is bad for us.[16] Cruelty to nonhuman animals, therefore, is bad for us. Similarly, suppose that failing to be good stewards of nature inflates our self-importance and destroys our humility.[17] Being poor stewards of nature, therefore, is bad for us. And since both are bad for us, the pragmatic reading implies that both are bad simpliciter. The pragmatic reading, since it grounds moral good-ness in facts about what enhances human well-being, cannot make sense of the thought that nonhuman animals or good stewardship of nature are good in and of themselves; perhaps whales have a complaint. But in that respect the pragmatic reading is no worse off than Kantian ethics.

I attribute the pragmatic reading to Orwell given what he says about goodness. In a book review, he explains that:

> Even in the animal world, the gregarious and peaceful creatures are usually the most successful. The sheep will outlive the wolf. Among human beings, almost every quality looked upon as "good" is a quality tending to make it possible for men to live to-gether in communities: or else it is a relic of some earlier attitude which was once supposed to have a utilitarian purpose, such as warding off the vengeance of jealous gods. (XVII: 449)

Almost everything we regard as good, apparently, either has fa-vorable consequences for human well-being or is thought to. This tight connection between the referent of "good" and what has (or

[16] See Matthew C. Altman, *Kant and Applied Ethics: The Uses and Limits of Kant's Practical Philosophy* (Malden, MA: Wiley-Blackwell, 2011), pp. 13–44.
[17] Thomas Hill Jr., "Ideals of Human Excellence and Preserving Natural Environments," *Environmental Ethics*, Vol. 5 (1983), pp. 211–224.

is thought to have) utility for human beings is not exactly the pragmatic reading, admittedly, and might be better read as a thesis about the origins of the meaning of "good," something that might interest metaethicists reading Orwell. Still, astute readers should watch for more cases in which Orwell seems to understand moral facts and properties as a function of natural facts and properties about human beings and human well-being. There will be more on display.

Attributing the pragmatic reading to Orwell does have implications for how he might be understood. Surely what is good for human beings can change; Orwell agreed, explaining that human nature is "capable of indefinite development" (XVIII: 62). If what is good for human beings can change, then what is good can change and the pragmatic reading amounts to a mild version of moral relativism. But this result need not disturb Orwell's readers who hope for objective ethics in Orwell: if we can say that "Human beings are bipedal" is an objective fact even allowing that our progeny might not be, we can affirm that "Freedom is good" is an objective fact even allowing that freedom may not be good for our progeny with a radically different nature.

Humanism, Orwell thought, is captured by the Protagorean dictum that "Man is the measure of all things." I submit that the best and most consistent reading of the Protagorean dictum is embodied in the pragmatic reading of it, one that Orwell seems at least sympathetic with, and entails that what is good is that which is good for us, that is, that which enhances our well-being. But what does human well-being consist in? What did Orwell think it consists in?

(Or)Well-Being

Orwell admired Henry Miller, praising "the rhythmic quality of your English" and the fact that he "dealt with facts well known to everybody but never mentioned in print" (X: 495). Yet, Orwell thought, Miller wrote with "no moral purpose" (XII: 92) and with a "non-moral" voice (XII: 96). He was "a completely negative, unconstructive, amoral writer, a mere Jonah, a passive accepter of evil" (XII: 112). Here, Orwell invokes the metaphor that gives rise to the title of the essay in which he discusses Miller, "Inside the Whale":[18]

> All his best and most characteristic passages are written from the angle of Jonah, a willing Jonah. Not that he is especially introverted—quite the contrary. In his case the whale happens to be transparent, only he feels no impulse to alter or control the process that he is undergoing. He has performed the essential Jonah act of allowing himself to be swallowed, remaining passive, *accepting*. (XII: 107)

Miller favors an "attitude of the completest indifference, no matter *what* happens" (XII: 107). And why shouldn't Miller stay inside the whale, well insulated from the sound and fury outside? If he prefers debauchery to antifascist resistance, why isn't amoral loafing best for Miller?

In this section, I try to answer these questions on Orwell's behalf. To anticipate, Orwell seems to have thought that Miller and the rest of us would be *happier* outside the whale, his own observation in "Politics versus Literature" that "Happiness is notoriously difficult to define" (XVIII: 427) notwithstanding. To explain I turn to Orwell's implicit discussion of happiness. In particular, I reconstruct his case against hedonism and for an objective list theory of well-being.

---

[18] Miller references whales too, if only to ruminate on the size of the whale phallus. See Henry Miller, *Tropic of Cancer* (New York: Grove Press, 1961), p. 3.

Three Theories of Well-Being

In his influential *Reasons and Persons*, Derek Parfit identifies three theories that purport to answer questions like "What would be best for someone, or would be most in this person's best interests, or would make this person's life go, for him, as well as possible?" Parfit distinguishes the following triad:

> On *Hedonistic Theories*, what would be best for someone is what would make his life happiest. On *Desire-Fulfillment Theories*, what would be best for someone is what, throughout his life, would best fulfill his desires. On *Objective List Theories*, certain things are good or bad for us, whether or not we want to have the good things, or to avoid the bad things.[19]

Parfit's construction of hedonism is novel, since hedonism has traditionally been explicated by formulas like "Pleasure alone is intrinsically good" and "Pleasure is the only thing worth seeking for its own sake,"[20] which can mislead if pleasure is understood as having a distinctive phenomenological feel, a claim most hedonists reject.[21] Hedonists typically understand pleasure to include all manner of pleasant feelings and experiences, some of which have an especially salient phenomenology (like ecstasy, elation, and euphoria), some of which need not (like satisfaction, contentment, and enjoyment). Parfit considers the example of Freud who, at the end of his life, refused pain-killing drugs preferring clear but tormented thinking to confused euphoria.[22] Perhaps it strains everyday language to suggest that Freud found clear-headed torment

---

[19] Derek Parfit, *Reasons and Persons* (Oxford: Clarendon Press, 1984), p. 493.

[20] Fred Feldman, *Utilitarianism, Hedonism, and Desert: Essays in Moral Philosophy* (Cambridge: Cambridge University Press, 1997), p. 80.

[21] For discussion, see Andrew Moore, "Hedonism," *Stanford Encyclopedia of Philosophy* (Winter 2019 edition), edited by Edward N. Zalta, https://plato.stanford.edu/archives/win2019/entries/hedonism/.

[22] Parfit, *Reasons and Persons*, p. 494.

more pleasant, but on the hedonist's view, clear-headed torment was more pleasant for Freud because it made him happiest. Orwell's readers who suppose that hedonists must suppose that we ought to always avoid pain and suffering[23] are in error; the hedonist need only suppose that what makes our lives go, for us, as well as possible is what makes us happiest.

To be sure, Orwell's corpus is littered with hostile comments about "hedonism" and sometimes he even offers something like a critique of it. But much of what he says is not actually about he-donism, the theory of well-being, and thus can't be part of an argu-ment against it. I consider some of his failed critiques of hedonism before reconstructing his best argument against it.

Some Failed Arguments against Hedonism

Orwell thought his friend and coauthor Arthur Koestler was a he-donist, something Orwell "disapproved of because he wasn't at all like that."[24] Some of Orwell's characters were like that, including Mr. Warburton, the rakish libertine of A Clergyman's Daughter, who sexually assaults Dorothy Hare, the self-punishing daughter of a local reverend.[25] Eventually, he worms his way back into her com-pany, explaining that "to me, it seems the merest common sense to have a bit of fun while the going's good." She objects "That's just he-donism," and he replies:

[23] Cf. John Atkins, George Orwell: A Literary and Biographical Study (New York: Frederick Ungar, 1954), p. 116.

[24] As quoted in Remembering Orwell, edited by Stephen Wadhams (New York: Penguin, 1984), p. 165. Rayner Heppenstall recalls Orwell saying, "The chink in Koestler's armour is his hedonism," adding for his own part that "I don't think that hedonism in itself, if it is only an additional thing to a basic pursuit in life, is to be condemned, but George did condemn it": see Orwell Remembered, edited by Audrey Coppard and Bernard Crick (London: Ariel Books, 1984), p. 169.

[25] In the final version, he begins "making love to [Dorothy], violently, outrageously, even brutally" (III: 41). In the original draft, Orwell is clear that Warburton "tried to rape Dorothy" (III: 299).

> My dear child, can you show me a philosophy of life that isn't
> hedonism? Your verminous Christian saints are the biggest
> hedonists of all. They're out for an eternity of bliss, whereas we
> poor sinners don't hope for more than a few years of it. Ultimately
> we're all trying for a bit of fun; but some people take it in such
> perverted forms. (III: 285)

Whatever they say, apparently, even saints *really* want bliss, albeit
bliss in the next world, a hermeneutic of suspicion Orwell invokes
elsewhere.[26] Warburton is at least honest when he explains that
"When I eat my dinner I don't do it to the greater glory of God . . .
I do it because I enjoy it" (III: 275). His more general claim is that
we're *all* trying for a bit of fun even those who won't admit it.

Here, Orwell frames hedonism as a theory of human motivation: all human actions are motivated by an intrinsic desire for
pleasure. But this thesis, *psychological hedonism*, is not a theory
of well-being and its falsity would leave hedonism, the theory
of well-being, untouched: even if we sometimes act for other intrinsic desires besides the intrinsic desire for pleasure, our well-
being might still be maximized only if our lives are sufficiently
pleasurable.

Orwell confuses hedonism with other doctrines elsewhere too.
In a review of Aldous Huxley's *Brave New World*, Orwell explains
that "hedonistic societies do not endure" because "a ruling class
which thought principally in terms of a 'good time' would soon lose
its vitality" (XII: 211). Orwell hints that *thinking* like a hedonist—
that is, thinking principally in terms of a good time—will lead to
unfortunate results. But the hedonist can agree with Orwell that

---

[26] In "Lear, Tolstoy, and the Fool," he says that "it is the Christian attitude which is self-
interested and hedonistic, since the aim is always to get away from the painful struggle
of earthly life and find eternal peace in some kind of Heaven or Nirvana" in contrast to
"The humanist attitude . . . that the struggle must continue and that death is the price of
life" (XIX: 64).

"Men can only be happy when they do not assume that the object of life is happiness" (XVI: 399). Most do.[27]

A different objection to hedonism is suggested by David Dwan, who, noting Bertrand Russell's influence on Orwell, recalls Russell's assurance that those "acts to be recommended from the point of view of the hedonist are on the whole the same as those to be recommended by the sane moralist"[28] and wonders why righteousness and enjoyment must overlap.[29] Dwan's complaint echoes a familiar objection that hedonism entails that all pleasures, even evil pleasures like those of the rapist, have moral value.[30] This objection rests on a different sort of confusion: hedonism only implies that what is best for someone is what makes them happiest, not that pursuing or securing what makes them happiest is right. The life of a serial killer might go, for him, as well as possible even if such a life is seriously unjust. Maybe righteousness and enjoyment don't overlap; the hedonist never said they did. But if hedonism is a failure, it is not a failure for *that* reason.

If hedonism merits rejection, it must be rejected on its own terms and shown deficient *as a theory of well-being*. It must be demonstrated that pleasure need not be best for someone, in their best interests, or otherwise make their life go, for them, as well as possible. Alternatively, it must be shown that something *besides* pleasure is best for someone, in their best interests, or otherwise makes their life go, for them, as well as possible. Orwell hints at the right sort of argument, albeit one that needs reconstruction.

---

[27] For discussion of a similar point, see Peter Railton, "Alienation, Consequentialism, and the Demands of Morality," *Philosophy and Public Affairs*, Vol. 13, No. 2 (1984), pp. 140–141.

[28] Bertrand Russell, *The Conquest of Happiness* (New York: Liveright, 1996), p. 190.

[29] Dwan, *Liberty, Equality, and Humbug*, p. 179.

[30] John Harsanyi, "Morality and the Theory of Rational Behaviour," in *Utilitarianism and Beyond*, edited by Amarata Sen and Bernard Williams (Cambridge: Cambridge University Press, 1982), p. 56.

Getting Outside the Whale: Orwell's Case
against Hedonism

One of Orwell's readers suggests that he "mainly objected to hedonism because it makes us soft" and "saps manly virtues like
courage and fortitude."[31] Orwell does seem to speak highly of certain "manly virtues" in this passage from *The Road to Wigan Pier*:

> All mechanical progress is towards greater and greater efficiency;
> ultimately, therefore, towards a world in which nothing goes
> wrong. But in a world in which nothing went wrong ... in a world
> from which physical danger had been banished—and obviously
> mechanical progress tends to eliminate danger—would physical
> courage be likely to survive? Could it survive? And why should
> physical strength survive in a world where there was never the
> need for physical labour? As for such qualities as loyalty, gener-
> osity, etc., in a world where nothing went wrong, they would be
> not only irrelevant but probably unimaginable. The truth is that
> many of the qualities we admire in human beings can only func-
> tion in opposition to some kind of disaster, pain, or difficulty; but
> the tendency of mechanical progress is to eliminate disaster, pain,
> and difficulty. (V: 180)

But in his melancholic essay "Such, Such Were the Joys" he strikes a
very different tone:

> Virtue consisted in winning: it consisted in being bigger, stronger,
> handsomer, richer, more popular, more elegant, more unscru-
> pulous than other people—in dominating them, bullying them,
> making them suffer pain, making them look foolish, getting the
> better of them in every way. Life was hierarchical and whatever

---

[31] David Ramsay Steele, *Orwell Your Orwell: A Worldview on the Slab* (South Bend, IN: St. Augustine's Press, 2017). p. 129.

happened was right. There were the strong, who deserved to win and always did win, and there were the weak, who deserved to lose and always did lose, everlastingly. (XIX: 378).

This hardly reads like an endorsement of traditionally masculine virtues, much less like a critique of hedonism.

A better critique is discernable in Orwell's repeated suggestion that modern life risks making us "soft." Orwell disparaged the "depth of softness" in middle-class life (XII: 104), worried that mechanical progress tends to make our environment and our lives "safe and soft" (V: 181), and affirmed that "softness is repulsive" (V: 182). More probingly, in his essay "Pleasure Spots," Orwell asked various philosophical questions—e.g., "What is man?" and "What are his needs?"—and explained:

Man needs warmth, society, leisure, comfort and security: he also needs solitude, creative work and the sense of wonder. If he recognised this he could use the products of science and industrialism eclectically, applying always the same test: does this make me more human or less human? He would then learn that the highest happiness does not lie in relaxing, resting, playing poker, drinking and making love simultaneously. And the instinctive horror which all sensitive people feel at the progressive mechanisation of life would be seen not to be a mere sentimental archaism, but to be fully justified. For man only stays human by preserving large patches of simplicity in his life, while the tendency of many modern inventions—in particular the film, the radio and the aeroplane—is to weaken his consciousness, dull his curiosity, and, in general, drive him nearer to the animals. (XVIII: 32)

Leisure, comfort, and security get identified as human needs and plausibly so, but so do less standard candidates like solitude, creative work, and a sense of wonder. Similarly, in *The Road to Wigan*

Pier, he objected to what tends "to frustrate the human need for effort and creation" (V: 186), adding:

> The truth is that when a human being is not eating, drinking, sleeping, making love, talking, playing games, or merely lounging about—and these things will not fill up a lifetime—he needs work and usually looks for it, though he may not call it work. Above the level of a third- or fourth-grade moron, life has got to be lived largely in terms of effort. For man is not, as the vulgarer hedonists seem to suppose, a kind of walking stomach; he has also got a hand, an eye, and a brain. Cease to use your hands, and you have lopped off a huge chunk of your consciousness. (V: 183–184)

Orwell's shot at the "vulgarer hedonists" is a straw man, but his worry about lopping off a chunk of one's consciousness is telling. The problem with modern comforts, apparently, is that they deprive us of what we need: "Much of what goes by the name of pleasure is simply an effort to destroy consciousness" (XVIII: 32). And whatever else Orwell means by "consciousness," it surely includes those distinctively human psychological faculties named above. We might find it pleasant to indulge in modern comforts and prefer them to creative work, but indulgence will frustrate our needs and make us worse off, as suggested in Orwell's complaint that the working class "has been plundered of all they really need . . . by cheap luxuries which mitigate the surface of life" (V: 83).

Two things follow from Orwell's talk of human needs. First, he implicitly endorsed an objective list theory of well-being: if we *need* time to ourselves, creative endeavors, and a capacity for imagination, these are nonoptional requirements for a good life whether or not we think they are.[32] Second, given our needs, indulgence

---

[32] "It is probable if not absolutely clear that Orwell believed that there were universal or quasi-universal prerequisites for a happy life": Dwan, *Liberty, Equality, and Humbug*, p. 175.

in certain pleasures is bad for us *even if indulgence is pleasant.* If—Orwell would say "since"—pleasure can deprive us of what is essential to a good life, pleasure is *not* intrinsically good and hedonism's central value thesis is false.

That Orwell endorsed an objective list theory of well-being helps explain what is wrong with Henry Miller and his wasted life. If we need creative work then even if Miller prefers a Jonah-like existence, more is needed for him to flourish and his passive acceptance is bad for him however pleasurable, since it deprives him of what he needs. Maybe Miller's amoral attitude toward life is "justified" if that only means that "Whether or not it is an expression of what people *ought* to feel, it probably comes somewhere near to expressing what they *do* feel" (XII: 110). But given his favored theory of well-being, Orwell should say that people ought to feel no such thing.

Even if Miller's loafing is bad for him, and thus bad simpliciter on the pragmatic reading, does Miller act *wrongly* when he climbs inside the whale? Again, a theory of well-being is not a theory of normative ethics and doing what is objectively bad for us need not be wrongful. What, for Orwell, makes an action right or wrong? I try to answer this question next.

Orwell's Normative Ethics

Consequentialism is a family of normative ethical theories that explains other moral properties, such as duty or virtue, in terms of promoting value.[33] On one influential formulation, consequentialist theories define right action as a function of that which *maximizes* the good.[34] Actions are right, on this view, just

---

[33] David O. Brink, "Some Forms and Limits of Consequentialism," in *The Oxford Handbook of Ethical Theory*, edited by David Copp (Oxford: Oxford University Press, 2006), p. 381.

[34] John Rawls, *A Theory of Justice*, Revised edition (Cambridge, MA: Belknap, 1999), pp. 22–23.

in case their consequences are optimific, that is, better than the consequences of any feasible alternative. No small number of British progressives and radicals were consequentialists, including Bentham and Mill, and during Orwell's day left liberals tended to be consequentialist.[35] By contrast, Orwell was probably not consequentialist and his readers who have said as much are probably not wrong.[36] But as with his case against hedonism, his supposed case against consequentialism has not been well understood and knowing what he was against does not reveal him as an advocate. In this section, I note some failed arguments against consequentialism and then identify what I take to be Orwell's best anticonsequentialist argument. I then make the case that Orwell is best understood as a threshold deontologist and note a small caveat.

Ends, Means, Greatest Numbers, Lesser Evils

Orwell sometimes distanced himself from slogans associated with consequentialism. For example, in *The English People* he praises the English for having "failed to catch up with power politics, 'realism,' *sacro egoismo* and the doctrine that the end justifies the means" (XVI: 206).[37] The doctrine that the end justifies the means was endorsed by some Communists in Orwell's day. Stephen Spender, describing his support for Communism in the 1930s, wrote that "One did not have to consider, except from the point of view of their effectiveness, the means which were used nor the fate of individuals."[38] Lev Zalmanovich Kopelev similarly recalls that "I

---

[35] Ben Jackson, *Equality and the British Left: A Study in Political Thought, 1900–1964* (Manchester: Manchester University Press, 2007), p. 66.

[36] David Dwan, "Orwell's Paradox: Equality in *Animal Farm*," *ELH*, Vol. 79, No. 3 (2012), p. 661.

[37] Dwan takes this passage as evidence that Orwell rejects consequentialism: see Ibid., p. 681, ffn. 36.

[38] Stephen Spender, in *The God That Failed*, edited by Richard Crossman (New York: Columbia University Press, 1950), p. 235.

firmly believed that the ends justified the means" and that "Our great goal was the universal triumph of Communism, and for the sake of that goal everything was permissible."[39] The anti-Communist Orwell, by contrast, complained of national movements that have "adopt[ed] the theory that the end justifies the means" (XVI: 190) and insisted "I don't hold with all this stuff that boils down to saying 'Anything is right which advances the cause of the Party'" (XI: 256). Perhaps the most dramatic case in which Orwell denied that the ends justify the means emerges in *Nineteen Eighty-Four*, where "the logic of ends-justifies-means is pushed to the brink of absurdity and beyond."[40] As Winston and Julia are being sized up for membership in The Brotherhood, O'Brien queries "In general terms, what are you prepared to do?" to which Winston replies, "Anything that we are capable of" (IX: 179). Winston affirms they will give their lives, murder innocents, throw acid in the face of a child, and "do anything which is likely to cause demoralisation and weaken the power of the Party" (IX: 179–180). But when O'Brien asks, "You are prepared, the two of you, to separate and never see one another again?," Julia, thus far ignored, exclaims "No!" (IX: 180).[41] Julia is sometimes understood as a morally vapid caricature of a female character,[42] but her refusal to do anything to bring down Big Brother stands in stark relief to Winston's fanaticism.

[39] Lev Zalmonvich Kopelev, *No Jail for Thought*, translated by Anthony Austin (London: Secker and Warburg, 1977), pp. 11–12.

[40] Alex Zwerdling, *Orwell and the Left* (New Haven, CT: Yale University Press, 1974), p. 24.

[41] Bernard Crick regards Winston and Julia as agreeing to do the unthinkable here, noting "*their* mutual willingness to throw sulfuric acid into a child's face" and what "*they* have agreed to do to a child": Bernard Crick, "Reading *Nineteen Eighty-Four* as Satire," in *Reflections on America, 1984: An Orwell Symposium*, edited by Robert Mulvihill (Athens: University of Georgia Press, 1986), pp. 31 and 42, emphasis added. But Orwell's text only indicates that Winston answers O'Brien's questions and makes clear that O'Brien "almost ignored Julia, seeming to take it for granted that Winston could speak for her" (IX: 179). There is no *they* there.

[42] See, for example, Beatrix Campbell, *Wigan Pier Revisited: Poverty and Politics in the Eighties* (London: Virago Press, 1984), p. 147 and Daphne Patai, *The Orwell Mystique: A Study in Male Ideology* (Amherst: University of Massachusetts Press, 1984), p. 244. Cf. Loraine Sanders, *The Unsung Artistry of George Orwell: The Novels from "Burmese Days" to "Nineteen Eighty-Four"* (New York: Routledge, 2021), p. 93.

Does it follow that Orwell rejected consequentialism? The problem is that consequentialists need not accept that the ends justify the means, at least not without qualification. Since consequentialism only affirms that acts with optimific results are right, it does not imply that the ends justify the means, full stop. Here, Peter Singer clarifies:

> I do think that the end justifies the means. I think that that's the point, in a way, that, of course, bad ends don't justify means. And if the means involve harming people and there are other means that you could have taken, then you should take those other means. But if the only way to prevent something very bad happening is to do something which would itself be bad but not as bad as the very bad thing that you're trying to prevent happening, then you're justified in doing the lesser evil rather than allowing the greater evil to occur.[43]

Singer is clear that ends do not justify the means if the end is not good enough—that is, if some other end would be even better. Further, ends do not justify means if some other means would be cheaper, more efficient, less costly, or whatever. Since the doctrine that the ends justify the means places no constraints on which ends and means are morally salient while consequentialism does, they should not be identified and rejecting the former does not entail rejecting the latter.

Orwell is hostile to other slogans sometimes associated with consequentialism. In his 1940 review of *Mein Kampf*, he explained that:

> After a few years of slaughter and starvation "Greatest happiness of the greatest number" is a good slogan, but at this moment "Better an end with horror than a horror without end" is a winner.

[43] Transcript from "Justifying the Means: What It Means to Treat All Suffering Equally," *NPR*, June 1 2020, https://www.npr.org/transcripts/866768837.

Now that we are fighting against the man who coined it, we ought not to underrate its emotional appeal. (XII: 118)

The slogan "Greatest happiness of the greatest number" is derived from the eighteenth-century thinkers who defined utilitarianism,[44] but it is better read as a slogan and not identified with the doctrine it expresses: producing optimific results which the consequentialist does regard as constitutive of right actions does not necessarily produce the greatest happiness for the greatest number. Suppose that a subject can either push a button or refrain from pushing it; if he refrains, a thousand people will receive a modest reward that will make each of them happier but a single person will be tormented so heinously that their aggregate happiness plummets; if he pushes, no one is tormented, no one is rewarded, and aggregate happiness remains constant. The greatest happiness for the greatest number is realized only if he pushes the button, since more are not tortured and benefit than tortured and put in agony, but pushing does not maximize overall happiness. So they ought not be identified. If consequentialism is identified with bringing about the greatest happiness for the greatest number, there could be no justification for preventing the serious agony of a minority of persons, an absurd result for the consequentialist. Here too, consequentialism is wrongly identified with a supposed slogan.

Worse, if Orwell rejects some consequentialist slogans, he sometimes seems *sympathetic* with others. Consider this passage from "Writers and Leviathan":

most of us still have a lingering belief that every choice, even political choice, is between good and evil, and that if a thing is necessary it is also right. We should, I think, get rid of this belief, which belongs in the nursery. In politics one can never do more

[44] Joseph Persky, *The Political Economy of Progress: John Stuart Mill and Modern Radicalism* (Oxford: Oxford University Press, 2016), p. 26.

than decide which of two evils is the lesser, and there are some situations from which one can only escape by acting like a devil or a lunatic. (XIX: 292)

Talk of choosing among evils is commonplace for Orwell: he justified war with Germany on the grounds that "You can let the Nazis rule the world, that is evil; or you can overthrow them by war, which is also evil" (XIII: 43); he explained that "I know enough of British imperialism not to like it, but I would support it against Nazism or Japanese imperialism, as the lesser evil" (XVI: 191)[45]; he speculated that "the choice before man is always a choice of evils" (XVI: 400); one of his better poems is titled "The Lesser Evil" (X: 92–93). Nothing wrong with all this, but talk of choosing the lesser of two evils seems like consequentialist talk.

The case for reading Orwell as an anticonsequentialist is imperiled presently. Still, a case can be made. To explain, I consider Orwell's critique of sainthood, one that should seem familiar to philosophers.

Saints and other Inhumans

In *Keep the Aspidistra Flying*, Gordon Comstock recalls the aphorism that "the modern world is only habitable by saints and scoundrels" (IV: 267). Orwell offers a more damnable assessment of saints in "Reflections on Gandhi," where he explained that "Saints should always be judged guilty until they are proved innocent" (XX: 5), that "sainthood is . . . a thing that human beings must avoid" (XX: 8), and that we ought to "reject sainthood as an ideal" (XX: 10). Much has been made of Orwell's attack on sainthood, yet it has seemingly gone unnoticed that a challenge to

---

[45] Sometimes Orwell claims that British imperialism is worse than Nazism (XVI: 306), sometimes that it is not quite as bad (XVI: 330).

consequentialism emerges from it. It may be that in his "yogi-ridden age, it is . . . assumed that 'non-attachment' is not only better than a full acceptance of earthly life, but that the ordinary man only rejects it because it is too difficult," but Orwell insisted that "It is doubtful whether this is true" (XX: 8). Understanding why Orwell rejected an ethics of nonattachment is crucial to understanding his critique of Gandhi and sainthood but also his best argument against consequentialism.

Orwell's assessment of Gandhi is not uniformly negative: he praises Gandhi's "physical courage" and persistent belief in "better nature" of other people (XX: 6). Yet Orwell rejects the "other-worldly, anti-humanist tendency of his doctrines," adding:

> [O]ne should, I think, realize that Gandhi's teachings cannot be squared with the belief that Man is the measure of all things and that our job is to make life worth living on this earth, which is the only earth we have. They make sense only on the assumption that God exists and that the world of solid objects is an illusion to be escaped from. (XX: 7)

Orwell doubts that Gandhi's "teachings can have much for those who do not accept the religious beliefs on which they are founded" (XX: 7) and Gandhi's conception of a fulfilled life, which requires goods like transcendence and spiritual liberation, probably isn't open to a humanist.[46] But while Orwell objected to Gandhian dietary restrictions and prohibitions against sexual intercourse and desire, he found what Gandhi says about close friendships and exclusive loves especially problematic:

> Close friendships, Gandhi says, are dangerous, because "friends react on one another" and through loyalty to a friend one can be

---

[46] Anthony J. Parel, *Pax Gandhiana: The Political Philosophy of Mahatma Gandhi* (Oxford: Oxford University Press, 2016), p. 7.

led into wrong-doing. This is unquestionably true. Moreover, if one is to love God, or to love humanity as a whole, one cannot give one's preference to any individual person. This again is true, and it marks the point at which the humanistic and the religious attitude cease to be reconcilable. To an ordinary human being, love means nothing if it does not mean loving some people more than others. (XX: 7–8)

He continued:

The essence of being human is that one does not seek perfection, that one is sometimes willing to commit sins for the sake of loyalty, that one does not push asceticism to the point where it makes friendly intercourse impossible, and that one is prepared in the end to be defeated and broken up by life, which is the inevitable price of fastening one's love upon other human individuals. (XX: 8)

No wonder Orwell assured us in "Lear, Tolstoy, and the Fool" that the difference between saints and ordinary human beings "is a difference of kind and not of degree" (XIX: 63). Perhaps saints can flourish without such things, but actual human beings would be doomed to unhappy lives. Consistent with his humanism, Orwell thought that sainthood is bad because it is bad for us.

Orwell's attack on sainthood greatly resembles Susan Wolf's influential critique of moral sainthood.[47] Wolf too worries that, since moral saints are not motivated by ideals of personal attachment, moral saintliness does not "constitute a model of personal wellbeing towards which it would be particularly rational or good or desirable for a human being to strive."[48] But if Gandhian sainthood

[47] See Kristian Williams, *Between the Bullet and the Lie: Essays on Orwell* (Chico, CA: AK Press, 2017), pp. 41–75.
[48] Susan Wolf, "Moral Saints," *Journal of Philosophy*, Vol. 79, No. 8 (1982), pp. 419.

is morally dubious because of its antihumanist demand that we abandon human attachments, consequentialism is dubious for the same reason, or so goes a familiar challenge to consequentialism.

Attachment and Agent-Relative Reasons for Action

I have no particular conception of friendship or love to defend, but I take it that any plausible conception allows that friendly and loving relationships give rise to *agent-relative* reasons for action, reasons that make an essential reference to the person who has them.[49] Common-sense morality has it that personal attachments are the source of many of our reasons, but also that agent-relative reasons have considerable moral weight. Intuitively, agent-relative reasons are always morally significant and often decisive. They also arguably make trouble for consequentialism.

Agent-relative reasons are rivaled by *agent-neutral* reasons, that is, reasons that do not make an essential reference to the person that has them. Consequentialism, insofar as it gives each of us the common aim to maximize overall goodness, supplies each of us with an agent-neutral reason: all of us, and no one in particular, has reason to maximize the good. Consequentialists can acknowledge that I have a reason to help someone in need if no one else can and if helping that person would be morally maximally good. But in that case, my agent-relative reason to help is derived from the more general, agent-neutral reason to maximize overall goodness. What consequentialists cannot acknowledge, as the argument goes, is that "some agent-relative considerations are *underivatively* relevant ... not merely in virtue of their serving some further purpose."[50] If underivative agent-relative reasons exist in abundance

[49] Parfit, *Reasons and Persons*, p. 27.
[50] David McNaughton and Piers Rawling, "Deontology," in *Ethics and Practice*, 3rd edition, edited by Hugh LaFollette (Malden, MA: Blackwell Publishing, 2007), p. 34. See also Samuel Scheffler, "Introduction," in *Consequentialism and Its Critics*, edited by Samuel Scheffler (New York: Oxford University Press, 1988), pp. 1–2.

and consequentialism suggests otherwise, so much the worse for consequentialism.

Orwell's rejected Gandhi's ethics as antihumanist because it did not recognize the widespread existence of certain morally significant irreducible agent-relative reasons. But if that is a reason to reject Gandhi's ethics, *it is also a reason to reject consequentialism* if consequentialism cannot tolerate the existence of such reasons. Orwell never made this argument explicitly, of course, but it follows quickly from an argument he did make. On this line of argument, consequentialism gets the basics of morality wrong and should be rejected for that reason.

I do not pretend that consequentialists have no rebuttal to this argument.[51] But if Orwell hinted at any plausible argument against consequentialism, this is it. So we have good reason to think he opposed consequentialism. But what ethical theory did he advocate for? If he rejected consequentialism, what would he replace it with?

Orwell's Threshold Deontology

In his "Through a Glass, Rosily," Orwell wondered "can the cause of progress be served by lies, or can it not?," noting that "Anglo-Russian relations are more likely to prosper if inconvenient facts are kept in the dark" (XVII: 397). Having observed that "the advantages of a lie are always short-lived" he concluded that "genuine progress can only happen through . . . the continuous destruction of myths" (XVII: 398). But Orwell did not think that there is an absolute obligation to truth-telling, nor did he act as though there was. He spent "two wasted years" from 1941 to 1943 working in the Indian section of the BBC's Eastern Division as a Talks Producer encouraging support for Allied efforts, work that "conflicted wildly with his belief in

---

[51] Railton, "Alienation, Consequentialism, and the Demands of Morality," pp. 134–171.

telling the truth at all times."[52] His introduction to the BBC took the form of a six-week course nicknamed "the Liars' School,"[53] and his responsibilities included the production of wartime propaganda, the very thing that he identified as lies (XIII: 503).[54] He acknowledged "I am regularly alleging in my newsletters that the Japanese are plotting to attack Russia," adding, "I don't believe this to be so" (XIII: 229).

Yet if Orwell knew he was lying, he did not think he acted wrongly, explaining that "I don't think this matters so long as one knows what one is doing, and why" (XIII: 229). He also hinted at a justification of his work when he referenced "the ethics of b'casting" in a letter to George Woodcock, pointing out that he "kept our propaganda slightly less disgusting than it otherwise might have been" (XIV: 214). A more compelling defense emerges in a June 1944 AIP column:

> Everyone who has ever had anything to do with publicity or propaganda can think of occasions when he was urged to tell lies about some vitally important matter, because to tell the truth would give ammunition to the enemy. (XVI: 253)

Orwell's case for lying is strongest when, for example, telling the truth ensured that troops would refuse to fight for a just cause (VI: 162). He also seems to think that lying, in some cases, is not merely permissible but morally required: when he says that "In fighting against Fascism you cannot always be bound by the Marquess of Queensbury rules, and sometimes a lie is almost

---

[52] Tanya Agathaocleous, *George Orwell: Battling Big Brother* (Oxford: Oxford University Press, 2000), p. 65.

[53] William Empson, "Orwell at the BBC," in *The World of George Orwell*, edited by Miriam Gross (New York: Simon and Schuster, 1971), p. 94.

[54] He also wrote in his "War-time Diary," "All propaganda is lies, even when one is telling the truth" (XIII: 229). A reader might have thought that *All lies are false* is a necessary truth.

unavoidable" (XVII: 20), I am inclined to substitute "obligatory" for "unavoidable."

Orwell's position concerning our obligation to tell the truth is suggestive of *threshold deontology*, the ethical theory that recognizes moral norms requiring or forbidding some action but allows that they are overridden when, but only when, compliance yields consequences that are not merely bad but *horrendous*.[55] In such cases, moral norms are overridden and the right thing to do is defined in consequentialist terms.[56] Understanding Orwell as a threshold deontologist renders his overall position with respect to lying consistent: he can allow that there are moral norms requiring truth-telling and that propaganda is not wrongful if but only if telling the truth would result in horrendous consequences—say, the victory of Fascists or totalitarians.

If Orwell is a threshold deontologist, then Woodcock is unfair when he attributes to Orwell the view that "we can have freedom when it is convenient, but at moments of crisis freedom is to be stored away for the return of better days."[57] Orwell should not be understood as agreeing that any supposed crisis overrides moral norms, only the prospect of horrendous consequences. True, the distinction between merely bad and outright horrendous consequences is difficult to articulate, but Orwell seems to recognize one. In his response to James Burnham's panicky argument for suppressing the American Communist Party, Orwell allowed that:

> [T]here are times when it is justifiable to suppress a political party. If you are fighting for your life, and if there is some organization which is plainly acting on behalf of the enemy, and is

[55] Michael Moore, *Placing Blame: A General Theory of the Criminal Law* (Oxford: Oxford University Press, 1997), p. 721.

[56] Larry Alexander, "Deontology at the Threshold," *San Diego Law Review*, Vol. 37 (2000), pp. 893–912, see p. 894.

[57] George Woodcock, "George Orwell, 19th Century Liberal," in *George Orwell: The Critical Heritage*, edited by Jeffrey Meyers (London: Routledge, 1975), pp. 244–245. Originally published in *Politics*, December 1946, pp. 384–388.

strong enough to do harm, then you have got to crush it. But to suppress the Communist Party *now*, or at any time when it did not unmistakably endanger national survival, would be calamitous. (XIX: 103)

Suppression of political association and free expression are sometimes justifiable, apparently, but only when national survival is at stake. Otherwise, norms governing free association and expression prohibit suppression. No surprise, then, that Orwell wrote in "Freedom of the Press" that "In 1940 it was perfectly right to intern Mosley," leader of the British Union of Fascists, "whether or not he had committed any technical crime," since "We were fighting for our lives and could not allow a possible quisling to go free" (VIII: 108) but also that "To keep him shut up, without trial, in 1943 was an outrage" (VIII: 106). Whether or not Orwell was correct, the thought is presumably that horrendous consequences loomed in 1940 if the liberties of Mosley and his brood were not curtailed, but not in 1943, such that what was otherwise morally forbidden was morally right.

Orwell's threshold deontology is also evident in his discussion of wartime ethics. Sometimes, his views about civilian immunity seem perfectly conventional: he regards the "mass bombing of civilians" as a "new and especially horrifying development" (XVIII: 221). But his assurance that "one must not kill children if it is in any way avoidable" is tempered by his declarations that "all talk of 'limiting' or 'humanizing' war is sheer humbug" (XVI: 193) and that "The immunity of the civilian, one of the things that have made war possible, has been shattered. . . . I don't regret that" (XVI: 194). This is the same Orwell who would not shoot at a pantsless enemy soldier because "a man who is holding up his trousers isn't a 'Fascist,' he is visibly a fellow-creature" (XIII: 501).[58] Some philosophers

[58] Orwell does not draw any moral conclusions from his reflections on this incident. It a memory "not proving anything in particular" (XIII: 501).

have understood Orwell as rejecting norms governing civilian immunity,[59] but I am not sure that is the conclusion to draw. Some of what Orwell says about killing in war sounds like bombast, including this:

> [I]f someone drops a bomb on your mother, go and drop two bombs on his mother. The only apparent alternatives are to smash dwelling houses to powder, blow out human entrails and burn holes in children with lumps of thermite, or to be enslaved by people who are more ready to do these things than you are yourself; as yet no one has suggested a practicable way out. (XI: 113)

Yet passages like these are fraught with urgency: the "only apparent alternatives" are horrible but better and more just than being enslaved by those who would do still more horrible things. I am inclined to read Orwell as endorsing nonabsolute moral norms governing noncombatant immunity and killing in war generally that can be overridden when, but *only when*, abiding by them yields horrendous consequences.

A final, less loaded example adds some nuance. In "Politics and the English Language," Orwell famously proposes a series of rules that promise to keep language from concealing or preventing thought:

(i) Never use a metaphor, simile, or other figure of speech which you are used to seeing in print.

(ii) Never use a long word where a short one will do.

---

[59] See Jeff McMahan, *Killing in War* (Oxford: Oxford University Press, 2009), pp. 210–212; Michael Walzer, *Just and Unjust Wars* (New York: Basic Books, 2006), p. 262. For a metered defense of Orwell's rejection of the doctrine of civilian immunity, see Victor Tadros, "Orwell's Battle with Brittain: Vicarious Liability for Unjust Aggression," *Philosophy and Public Affairs*, Vol. 42, No. 1 (2014), pp. 42–77.

(iii) If it is possible to cut a word out, always cut it out.

(iv) Never use the passive where you can use the active.

(v) Never use a foreign phrase, a scientific word, or a jargon word if you can think of an everyday English equivalent.

(vi) Break any of these rules sooner than say anything outright barbarous. (XVII: 430)

Some of Orwell's readers suggest these rules "should be carved in stone above every writer's desk."[60] Others complain about their "absolute nature," noting "The first five all include either a 'never' or an 'always,' "[61] an odd complaint, since the final rule makes it clear that the others are *not* absolute. Rule (vi) identifies a threshold: the previous rules should be followed unless following them yields "barbarous" consequences. True, barbarous writing is probably not a horrendous result, but this is no reason to think that his threshold deontology is confused. Here is some plausible guidance:

There are two varieties of threshold deontology worth distinguishing. On the simple version, there is some fixed threshold of awfulness beyond which morality's categorical norms no longer have their overriding force. Such a threshold is fixed in the sense that it does not vary with the stringency of the categorical duty being violated. The alternative is what might be called "sliding scale threshold deontology." On this version, the threshold varies in proportion to the degree of wrong being done—the wrongness of stepping on a snail has a lower threshold (over which the wrong can be justified) than does the wrong of stepping on a baby.[62]

---

[60] Jeffrey Meyers, *Orwell: Life and Art* (Champaign: University of Illinois Press, 2010), p. 182. Meyers also, correctly, notes that "it is possible to obey all these rules . . . yet still be an outrageous liar" (182).

[61] R. J. B., "Johnson: Those Six Little Rules," *The Economist*, 20 July 2013, https://www.economist.com/prospero/2013/07/29/johnson-those-six-little-rules.

[62] Larry Alexander and Michael Moore, "Deontological Ethics," *Stanford Encyclopedia of Philosophy* (Winter 2020 edition), edited by Edward N. Zalta, https://plato.stanford.edu/archives/win2020/entries/ethics-deontological/.

On the latter sliding scale version of threshold deontology, the threshold for absconding from norms governing political writing is lower than that for absconding from norms governing civilian immunity since the degree of wrong caused by producing doggerel is lesser than the degree of wrong done by targeting innocents. Orwell, quite reasonably, has different thresholds for overriding different norms, a move consistent with the threshold deontologist's gambit.

Understanding Orwell as a threshold deontologist does mean abandoning a conception of him as an absolutist about political morality, a conception some commentators think is "essential."[63] But is it? Orwell's reputation for honesty is a bit mythic,[64] but consider honesty, the virtue. On a traditional conception of the virtues, someone lacks the virtue of honesty if she is too little disposed to tell the truth, a deficiency that marks the liar, the timid, and the milquetoast. But someone *too* disposed to tell the truth also lacks virtue: such people do not simply lack tact; they are bound to offend and hurt and wrong and are dubiously regarded as virtuous. The honest person is sensitive to context and circumstance and recognizes that truth-telling can have seriously grave consequences. They will agree with Orwell that some lies are "less pernicious" than others (XII: 76), as he suggested in "Boys' Weeklies," but also that some lies are less pernicious than some truths. In short, honesty, the virtue, is not absolutely opposed to some well-motivated

[63] Alan Sandison, *The Last Man in Europe: An Essay on George Orwell* (New York: Barnes and Noble Books, 1974), p. 67. Cf. Gordon Bowker, who references Orwell's "old Catholic enemy, the doctrine of Absolutism": Bowker, *Inside George Orwell*, p. 226.

[64] "At all times he was wonderfully brave, as patient, decent, honest, and fair-minded as a human being could be": Herbert Matthews, in *Nation*, 27 December 1952, p. 597; "Orwell is 'the most honest writer alive'": V. S. Pritchett, "1984," in *Nineteen Eighty-Four to 1984: A Companion to Orwell's Classic Novel*, edited by C. J. Kupping (New York: Carroll and Graf Publishers, 1984), p. 151; "England never produced a novelist more honest, more courageous, more concerned with the common man—and with common sense": James Stern, *New Republic*, 20 February 1950, p. 18.

falsehoods. Insofar as he allowed that norms governing truth-telling are not absolute, the gambit of the threshold deontologist, Orwell's status as honest can be maintained without supposing he is a moral absolutist about truth-telling.

But reading Orwell as a nonabsolutist might have some unwanted implications. His hatred of empire and imperialism motivates essays like "A Hanging" and "Shooting an Elephant," and his first novel, *Burmese Days*, exposes the fiction that "there was, or indeed, could conceivably be, any ethics in the running of an empire."[65] It is tempting to read Orwell as supposing that there are absolute moral norms opposing imperialism which he often called "evil" (X: 501; X: 508; XVI: 186). But that move is closed if Orwell is a threshold deontologist who denied that moral norms, at least many of them, are absolute. One consequence of regarding Orwell as a threshold deontologist is that some moral norms that seemed essential to his ethics may not have the absolute status that more romantic understandings of him take for granted.

That said, romantic understandings of Orwell are probably terminal anyway. Orwell is reasonably regarded as a great hater of empire, but his feelings toward the Burmese, for example, are not those of a saint: in "Shooting an Elephant," he describes the British Raj as "an unbreakable tyranny, as something that clamped down . . . upon the will of prostrate peoples" and that "the greatest joy in the world would be to drive a bayonet into a Buddhist priest's guts" (X: 502). Supposing that Orwell, the man, lacked vice altogether is unrealistic hero-worship; supposing that he thought the norms of political morality are absolute, admitting of no exceptions, is not that far off.

---

[65] Rosinka Chaudhuri, "Introduction," in George Orwell, *Burmese Days* (Oxford: Oxford University Press, 2021), p. xv.

Conclusion

I have attempted to clarify some basic themes in Orwell's ethics, having argued that his humanism consists in the pragmatic reading of the Protagorean dictum that moral goodness is a function of what is good for human beings, that he endorses an objective-list conception of well-being, that his humanism grounds his rejection of consequentialism, and that he endorses threshold deontology. But this is not quite the end of the story. Those readers committed to regarding Orwell as an anticonsequentialist might worry that some philosophers contend that threshold deontology *is* a consequentialist theory, that threshold deontology "must rest ultimately on consequential analysis, comparing one set of consequences (badness resulting from obeying the constraint) with another (badness of violating the constraint itself, given by the threshold)."[66] If Orwell's threshold deontology collapses into consequentialism, then he is caught by the consequentialist snare after all. Those readers who would deny that Orwell is a consequentialist thus have a surprising bit of philosophy to do: they must show that threshold deontology does not reduce to consequentialism.

In the next chapter, I change course a bit. Orwell advocates for more than just the ethical theses that I articulate above; he also has much to say about free will and moral responsibility. In Chapter 3, I consider and attempt to render coherent what Orwell has to say about free will and moral responsibility. What emerges is a surprisingly complicated theory that resembles an influential contemporary account of the latter and a historically prominent example of the former.

---

[66] Amartya K. Sen, "Rights and Agency," *Philosophy and Public Affairs*, Vol. 11, No. 1 (1982), p. 7.

3

Orwell on Free Will and Moral Responsibility

During his time at Eton, Orwell sometimes contributed to *College Days*, a literary magazine he helped produce. His contributions, which show "no sign of literary genius . . . only of cheerful endeavor,"[1] include a short one-act ironically titled "Free Will," given that almost nothing happens (X: 68–69). This was not the last time that he would reference free will: in *Coming Up for Air*, he has George Bowling explain that during World War I "You'd no sense of acting of your own free will, and at the same time no notion of trying to resist" (VII: 115); in *Nineteen Eighty-Four*, O'Brien explains to Winston that the Party is "not content with negative obedience, nor even with the most abject submission," and that his forthcoming surrender "must be of your own free will" (IX: 267).

Arguably, "lack of free will"[2] is one of the themes of *Nineteen Eighty-Four* even if Oceania is a world in which "Freedom and justice are illusions."[3] But it is worth noting just how little agency Winston exercises in that novel. Just after he is invited to O'Brien's home, Winston reflects on the events that eventually doom him:

> He knew that sooner or later he would obey O'Brien's summons. Perhaps tomorrow, perhaps after a long delay—he was

---

[1] Bernard Crick, *Orwell: A Life* (Boston: Little, Brown, 1980), p. 70.

[2] John Bowen, "Introduction," in George Orwell, *Nineteen Eighty-Four* (Oxford: Oxford University Press, 2021), pp. ix.

[3] Judith N. Shklar, "*Nineteen Eighty-Four*: Should Political Theory Care?," *Political Theory*, Vol. 13, No. 1 (February 1985), p. 11.

George Orwell. Peter Brian Barry, Oxford University Press. © Oxford University Press 2023.
DOI: 10.1093/oso/9780197627402.003.0003

not certain. What was happening was only the working-out of a process that had started years ago. The first step had been a secret, involuntary thought, the second had been the opening of the diary. He had moved from thoughts to words, now from words to actions. The last step was something that would happen in the Ministry of Love. He had accepted it. (IX: 166)

The process that started with an "involuntary thought" is not described in terms that suggest that Winston was in control: he "was not conscious of wanting" the diary for any purpose when he first bought it (IX: 8); when he tries to write he finds that he "lost the power of expressing himself" and was "only imperfectly aware of what he was setting down" (IX: 10); he "discovered that while he sat helplessly musing he had also been writing, as though by automatic action," learning after the fact that he wrote "DOWN WITH BIG BROTHER" (IX: 20). And, of course, given that Winston was tortured and manipulated in the last third of the novel, there must be good reason to doubt that he was free, even as the Party holds him responsible.

In what follows, I argue that Orwell, like the Party, does not shirk from holding persons morally responsible even in the face of powerful reasons to deny the existence of free will. To explain, I split this chapter just about in two. First, I argue that Orwell appears sympathetic with compatibilism about moral responsibility, and I appeal to Harry Frankfurt's influential work to explain. Second, I argue that he also appears sympathetic with hard incompatibilist skepticism about free will, and I appeal Friedrich Nietzsche to explain. What emerges is an *Orwellian* position about free will and moral responsibility: morally responsible agency is possible even if there are good reasons to doubt that free will exists. I conclude with some thoughts about how this Orwellian position is related to Orwell's thought generally.

Orwellian Compatibilism about
Moral Responsibility

One of Orwell's readers characterizes him as an English Kierkegaard and explains that, for Orwell, "An act . . . has no ethical quality whatever unless it be chosen out of several all equally possible."[4] Yet Orwell so often highlights the *absence* of choice even as he exercises the reactive attitudes, those sentiments that we naturally express following perceived expressions of good or ill will.[5] Closer to the mark is the suggestion that Orwell joined the Spanish antifascist resistance "not for political reasons, but, as in all his subsequent acts, from an innate feeling that it was the only thing he could do."[6] Indeed, it is striking just how often Orwell denies, sometimes explicitly, any supposed connection between moral obligation and alternative possibilities, a familiar refrain of compatibilists about moral responsibility, or so I argue in this section. First, I recall Harry Frankfurt's attack on a famous principle of moral responsibility and note that some of Orwell's vignettes greatly resemble Frankfurt's counterexamples. I then note an argument that Orwell implicitly offers a counterexample to Frankfurt-style compatibilism, and that he is sometimes read as making trouble for it. I try to disarm that argument and correct that reading by appealing to Frankfurt's later work. If the argument of this section is successful, Orwell will appear to be a Frankfurt-style compatibilist about moral responsibility.

[4] Sant Singh Bal, *George Orwell: The Ethical Imagination* (New Delhi: Arnold-Heinemann, 1981), p. 95.

[5] Peter Frederick Strawson, "Freedom and Resentment," in his *Freedom and Resentment and Other Essays* (London: Routledge, 2008), pp. 1–28. See also John Martin Fischer and Mark Ravizza, *Responsibility and Control: A Theory of Moral Responsibility* (Cambridge: Cambridge University, 1998), pp. 6–8.

[6] George Mayberry, in *New Republic*, 23 June 1952, p. 21.

Frankfurt's Attack on the Principle of Alternative Possibilities

As Orwell wrote, several compatibilist philosophers made their case, including A. J. Ayer, Orwell's "great friend" (XVIII: 242), who defended a conditional analysis of freedom where someone is free to do one thing rather than another so long as it is true that she would have done that other thing if, counterfactually, she chose to, a truth not imperiled by determinism.[7] I know of nowhere that Orwell suggests sympathy with or even awareness of Ayer's conditional analysis, but he does seem to anticipate another influential compatibilist.

In a now-classic paper, Harry Frankfurt critiques a principle that has played "A dominant role in nearly all recent inquiries into the free-will problem," although it is cast as a principle about moral responsibility:

> The Principle of Alternative Possibilities (PAP): a person is morally responsible for what she has done only if she could have done otherwise.[8]

Frankfurt ultimately rejects PAP, based partly on some clever thought experiments involving a neuroscientist, Black, who wants an agent, Jones, to act. Here is a slightly modified variant of Frankfurt's original thought experiment:

> Suppose someone—Black, let us say—wants Jones to perform a certain action. Black is prepared to go to considerable lengths to get his way, but he prefers to avoid showing his hand

---

[7] A. J. Ayer, "Freedom and Necessity," in *Free Will*, edited by Gary Watson (Oxford: Oxford University Press, 1981), p. 22.

[8] Harry G. Frankfurt, "Alternative Possibilities and Moral Responsibility," in his *The Importance of What We Care About: Philosophical Essays* (Cambridge: Cambridge University Press, 1988), p. 1.

unnecessarily. So he waits until Jones is about to make up his mind what to do, and he does nothing unless it is clear to him (Black is an excellent judge of such things) that Jones is going to decide to do something other than what he wants him to do. If it does become clear that Jones is going to decide to do something else, Black takes effective steps to ensure that Jones decides to do, and that he does do, what he wants him to do. Whatever Jones's initial preferences and inclinations, then, Black will have his way.[9]

Crucially, we are to imagine that Black never actually intervenes because Jones, for reasons of his own, decides to and does the very thing that Black wants him to do. Intuitively, Jones could not have done otherwise but, Frankfurt insists, it is quite unreasonable to refrain from blaming or praising Jones just because Black, who did nothing in the actual sequence of events, would have intervened if things had gone differently. Jones appears to be morally responsible but could not have done otherwise, a putative counterexample to PAP.

I take no position about the validity of Frankfurt's counterexamples, nor the cottage industry that has emerged in response to them.[10] But Orwell, unintentionally of course, supplies his own vignettes that, like Frankfurt's counterexamples, seem to suggest that PAP is false.

Orwell's Attack on PAP

In a letter, Orwell posed an odd request to Anthony Powell: he asked, "If you happen to see Graham Greene, could you break

[9] For the original, see ibid., p. 6.
[10] For a helpful summary, see David Robb, "Moral Responsibility and the Principle of Alternative Possibilities," *Stanford Encyclopedia of Philosophy* (Fall 2020 edition), edited by Edward N. Zalta, https://plato.stanford.edu/archives/fall2020/entries/alternative-possibilities/.

the news to him that I have written a very bad review of his novel for the New Yorker," adding, "I couldn't do otherwise—I thought the book awful" (XIX: 393). That Orwell thought he needed to apologize indicates that he felt guilt, a first-person analogue of resentment. This would not be the only time that he held himself responsible while denying that he could have done otherwise.[11]

For example, in "Why I Write," Orwell spoke about writing as something he could not but do: he explained that his "true nature" ensured that he would settle down and write books (XVIII: 316); he recalled that, as a young writer, he used flowery description "almost against my will, under a kind of compulsion from outside" (XVIII: 317); he suggested that no one would write a book "if one were not driven on by some demon whom one can neither resist or understand" (XVIII: 320). In an especially remarkable moment, he recalled a long chapter from *Homage to Catalonia* full of newspaper quotations he feared "must ruin the book" and a critic who asked, "Why did you put in all that stuff?" adding "You've turned what might have been a good book into journalism" (XVIII: 320). Orwell responded that:

---

[11] I am aware of two instances in which Orwell seems to refrain from exercising the reactive attitudes when someone *else* could not have done otherwise, though I doubt that either undermines the argument that follows.

First, in the Introduction to the Ukrainian edition of *Animal Farm*, he writes that "I would not condemn Stalin and his associates merely for their barbaric and undemocratic methods. It is quite possible that, even with the best intentions, they could not have acted otherwise under the conditions prevailing there" (VIII: 111). That said, he only declines to condemn Stalin and his ilk "merely" for their barbaric and undemocratic methods; he might still condemn them for other reasons.

Second, Orwell "cannot blame" a middle-class Socialist who "living within the framework of capitalist society ... has got to go on earning his living, and ... clings to his bourgeois economic status" (V: 125). Perhaps Orwell does not understand "has got to go on earning his living" as a modal claim suggesting that the middle-class Socialist literally cannot do otherwise, only that the oppressive conditions produced by capitalism provide him with a good excuse for clinging to his class status. Maybe he was just especially hard on himself.

What he said was true, *but I could not have done otherwise.*
I happened to know, what very few people in England had been
allowed to know, that innocent men were being falsely accused. If
I had not been angry about that I should never have written the
book. (XVIII: 320, emphasis added)

Orwell regards himself as blameworthy for having produced "a
failure" (XVIII: 320) even as he denies that he could have done
otherwise.

In "Such, Such Were the Joys," the brooding remembrance of
his school days, Orwell revealed "the great, abiding lesson of my
boyhood": he lived "in a world where it was *not possible* for me to
be good," that is, "where the rules were such that it was actually
not possible for me to keep them" (XIX: 359).[12] As an example,
he explained that "Soon after I arrived at St. Cyprian's . . . I began
wetting my bed" (XIX: 356) and offered a striking assessment of
his transgression: "There was no volition about it, no consciousness. . . . You did not properly speaking *do* the deed: you merely
woke up in the morning and found that the sheets were wringing
wet" (XIX: 357). Yet he blamed himself:

I knew the bed-wetting was (a) wicked and (b) outside my control. The second fact I was personally aware of, and the first I did
not question. It was possible, therefore, to commit a sin without
knowing that you committed it, without wanting to commit it,
and without being able to avoid it. Sin was not necessarily something that you did: it might be something that happened to you.
(XIX: 359)

He continued:

---

[12] Hollis similarly surmises that time at school "seemed to teach him that he both was
wicked and could not help being wicked." See Christopher Hollis, *A Study of George
Orwell: The Man and His Works* (Delaware: Racehorse Publishing, 2017), p. 10.

All through my boyhood I had a profound conviction that I was no good, that I was wasting my time, wrecking my talents, behaving with monstrous folly and wickedness and ingratitude— and all this, it seemed, *was inescapable*, because I lived among laws which were absolute, like the law of gravity, *but which it was not possible for me to keep*. (XIX: 366, emphasis added)

Again, Orwell regarded himself as morally responsible but unable do have done otherwise.

Finally, in "Shooting an Elephant" Orwell recalled the essay's eponymous event and again produced a vignette that resembles Frankfurt's counterexamples. Having been warned of a rampaging elephant, Orwell, rifle in tow, found it at rest a few hundred yards away. He "had no intention of shooting the elephant," "did not in the least want to shoot him," and "knew with perfect certainty" that he ought not to shoot (X: 503). But the gathered crowd eggs him on, and "suddenly I realized that I should have to shoot the elephant after all" (X: 504). A crucial moment is documented here:

[I]t was at this moment, as I stood there with the rifle in my hands, that I first grasped the hollowness, the futility of the white man's dominion in the East. Here was I, the white man with his gun standing in front of the unarmed native crowd—seemingly the leading actor of the piece; but in reality I was only an absurd puppet pushed to and fro by the will of those yellow faces behind. I perceived in this moment that when the white man turns ty- rant it is his own freedom that he destroys. He becomes a sort of hollow, posing dummy, the conventionalized figure of a sahib. For it is the condition of his rule that he shall spend his life in trying to impress the "natives" and so in every crisis he has got to do what the "natives" expect of him. He wears a mask and his face grows to fit it. *I had got to shoot the elephant*. (X: 504, em- phasis added)

He considered marching away but concluded "no—that was impossible" (X: 504) finding "only one alternative" (X: 505). He regarded his conduct as shameful, explaining that "It seemed to me that it would be murder to shoot him" (X: 504). So once again, he regarded himself as morally responsible, yet unable to do otherwise.

If he never targeted PAP explicitly, Orwell, like Frankfurt, produced putative counterexamples to PAP, a reason to regard Orwell as a Frankfurt-style compatibilist about moral responsibility.

Is Orwell a Frankfurt-Style Compatibilist?

But not so fast. Orwell's vignettes are arguably *unlike* Frankfurt's counterexamples in at least two important ways. Worse, he may have produced a devastating counterexample to Frankfurt-style compatibilism.

Note that Frankfurt's counterexamples include a counterfactual intervener, someone who ensures that Jones will act as Black wishes. There is no such counterfactual intervener in Orwell's vignettes, a difference that seems to matter: absent some counterfactual intervener's influence, why should Orwell be taken at his word? He *had* to review Greene poorly? He could not *but* ruin his own book? He *must* shoot the elephant?

The difference is not fatal. In his original counterexample, Frankfurt is ambivalent about how Black ensures Jones's compliance—hypnosis or a microchip or whatever—so long as *some* mechanism ensures Jones's compliance.[13] While there is no counterfactual intervener in Orwell's vignettes, there are mechanisms that arguably ensured that he will act: perhaps his immersion in British imperialism generated a self-conception that, paired with the powerful urgings of the crowd, guaranteed that he

---

[13] Frankfurt, "Alternative Possibilities and Moral Responsibility," p. 7.

would shoot;[14] perhaps his exceptional honesty compelled him to hurt Greene's feelings; and so on. If Orwell's vignettes lack a counterfactual intervener, they do include mechanisms that could ensure his inability to do otherwise.

The second dissimilarity is more problematic. Crucially, in Frankfurt's counterexamples, Jones seems in *control* of what he does: he acts for his own reasons, purposes, desires, or whatever.[15] But Orwell is less clearly in control in his vignettes. He doesn't act for reasons at all when he wets the bed, and the reasons for which he shoots—he shot "solely to avoid looking a fool" (X: 506)— are not *his* reasons. In "Shooting an Elephant," Orwell warns of imperialism's awful consequences for oppressors, explaining that "when the white man turns tyrant it is his own freedom that he destroys (X: 504),[16] a Hegelian result in which the master becomes perversely dependent on the slave.[17] So understood, he seems to lack the control needed for moral responsibility.

All is not lost. Orwell only needs one counterexample to render PAP terminal, and other vignettes might do the trick. Orwell's habit of harshly reviewing his friends' work[18] suggests a strong disposition to tell hard truths, a disposition he seems unalienated from

---

[14] "[T]he imperial policeman is part of a myth of such momentum that he is not a free agent. . . . imperial power has to be enacted in the form of dominance over the natural world": Douglas Kerr, *Orwell and Empire* (Oxford: Oxford University Press, 2022), p. 33. Kerr goes on to conclude that "The elephant has to die" and that Orwell "has no choice" (33).

[15] Carolina Sartoria, *Causation and Free Will* (Oxford: Oxford University Press, 2016), p. 17.

[16] In Burma, Orwell arguably "lost his freedom from political responsibility": Ruth Ann Lief, *Homage to Oceania: The Prophetic Vision of George Orwell* (Columbus: Ohio University Press, 1969), p. 21.

[17] Orwell sounds Hegelian in other places too, as in his "War-time Diary" when he suggests that "A revolution starts out with wide diffusion of the ideas of liberty, equality, etc. Then comes the growth of an oligarchy which is as much interested in holding onto its privileges as any other governing class. Such an oligarchy must necessarily be hostile to revolutions elsewhere, which inevitably re-awaken the ideas of liberty and equality" (XII: 196).

[18] Tosco R. Fyvel, *George Orwell: A Personal Memoir* (New York: Macmillan, 1982), p. 146.

and may have ensured he could not but author a review of Greene's new book that calls for apologia.

Still, all is not well, as evidenced by the fact that Orwell is sometimes read as a problem for the Frankfurt-style compatibilist. For example, Susan Wolf suggests that *Nineteen Eighty-Four* makes trouble for "The Real Self View"[19] (RSV), a compatibilist conception of moral responsibility she attributes to Frankfurt.[20] The RSV implies that only a proper subset of an agent's psychological attitudes constitutes her real self, "the self with which the agent is to be properly identified," in contrast to her "alienated self" with which she is not.[21] To distinguish attitudes that constitute a real self, proponents of the RSV might distinguish an agent's motivational and valuational systems, where the former consists of whatever psychological attitudes move her to act and the latter of those psychological attitudes that, when combined with factual beliefs, yield judgments about what should be done.[22] On the RSV, someone is morally responsible for what she does just when "she is at liberty (or able) both to govern her behavior on the basis of her will and to govern her will on the basis of her valuational system" but not if "something inhibits, interferes with, or otherwise prevents the effective exercise of these abilities."[23]

Crucially, the RSV requires only that "an agent *have* a real self, and that she be able to govern her behavior in accordance with it."[24] It matters not how her valuational system came to be the way it is, a problem since:

[19] Susan Wolf, *Freedom within Reason* (Oxford: Oxford University Press, 1990), p. 371.

[20] Susan Wolf, "Sanity and the Metaphysics of Responsibility," in *Responsibility, Character, and the Emotions*, edited by Ferdinand Schoeman (Cambridge: Cambridge University Press, 1987), p. 51.

[21] Wolf, *Freedom within Reason*, p. 30.

[22] Gary Watson, "Free Agency," *Journal of Philosophy*, Vol. 72 (April 1975), pp. 205–220.

[23] Wolf, *Freedom within Reason*, p. 33.

[24] Ibid., p. 35.

[W]e sometimes do question the responsibility of a fully developed agent event when she acts in a way that is clearly attributable to her real self. For we sometimes have reason to question an agent's responsibility *for* her real self. That is, we may think it is not the agent's fault that she is the person she is—in other words, we may think it is not her fault that she has, not just the desires, but also the values that she does. . . . whether or not hypnosis is necessarily limited to transient effects on a mere portion of an agent's psyche, we can easily envision other forms of psychological conditioning (consider, for example, Orwell's *1984*) that could make more permanent and pervasive changes in the most central features of a person's self.[25]

Focusing on the details of 1984—the Americanized title of Orwell's final book—helps explain the problem. Its final line reveals that Winston "loved Big Brother" (IX: 311), a recent alteration to his valuational system since just prior to being taken to Room 101 Winston *hated* Big Brother (IX: 293). Winston's newfound love may, at the time, reflect his real self, but that self is so obviously the product of O'Brien's manipulation that Winston is not plausibly understood as morally responsible. If the RSV implies otherwise, so much the worse for it.

It is at least odd to read Orwell as endorsing Frankfurt-style compatibilism and the author of a fatal counterexample to it, so some response is called for. I argue that the Frankfurt-style compatibilist need not affirm that Winston is morally responsible at the end of *Nineteen Eighty-Four* and that Frankfurt's later work explains why.

---

[25] Ibid., p. 37.

Wholeheartedness, Satisfaction, and Aspidistras

Frankfurt articulated his conception of moral responsibility in another now-classic paper in which he holds that "It is in securing the conformity of his will to his second-order volitions . . . that a person exercises freedom of the will."[26] Blurring some details, he suggested that a person exercises the sort of freedom of the will necessary for moral responsibility when she has the will that she wants to have, that is, when she wants some desire to lead her to act and that desire nondeviantly results in the desired action. And then came the objections.[27] In later work partly motivated by these objections, Frankfurt explained that that we ought "construe the freedom of someone's will as requiring . . . that he be wholehearted in it," that is, that he have "no endogenous desire to be volitionally different than he is."[28] Later, he explains that wholeheartedness is a function of being *satisfied* with one's will, with the "absence of restlessness or resistance."[29] At greater length:

> [I]s a matter of simply *having no interest* in making changes. What it requires is that psychic elements of certain kinds *do not occur*. But while the absence of such elements does not require either deliberate action or deliberate restraint, their absence must nonetheless be reflective. In other words, the fact that the person is not moved to change things must derive from his understanding and evaluation of how things are with him. Thus, the essential non-occurrence is neither deliberately contrived nor wantonly unselfconscious. It develops and prevails as an unmanaged consequence of the person's appreciation of his psychic condition.[30]

[26] Harry Frankfurt, "Freedom of the Will and the Concept of a Person," in his *The Importance of What We Care About: Philosophical Essays* (Cambridge: Cambridge University Press, 1988), p. 20.

[27] For a summary, see McKenna and Pereboom, *Free Will*, pp. 208–210.

[28] Harry Frankfurt, "The Faintest Passion," in his *Necessity, Volition, and Love* (Cambridge: Cambridge University Press, 1999), p. 101.

[29] Ibid., p. 103.

[30] Ibid., p. 105.

Wholeheartedness requires more than consistency of desires: it requires that, after reflection, an agent lacks pangs of regret, feelings of shame, stubborn misgivings, a guilty conscience, and still more. A wholehearted agent has the will that she wants to have, but she also lacks any psychological state expressive of *dissatisfaction* with her will. On his developed view, moral responsibility requires not just conformity of desires but wholehearted satisfaction with one's will.

Frankfurt's developed view can, I think, respond to the sort of objection offered by Wolf and others, one that makes much of the *ahistorical* nature of Frankfurt style-compatibilism, that is, the fact that it is insensitive to historical considerations that intuitively undermine moral responsibility. True, adding that a morally responsible agent must be wholehearted doesn't save the day if *wholeheartedness itself* arises from historical considerations that undermine responsibility. Frankfurt has defended the ahistoricity of his conception with admirable consistency:

> Briefly, it seems to me that if someone does something because he wants to do it, and if he has no reservations about that desire but is wholeheartedly behind it, then—so far as his moral responsibility for doing it is concerned—it really does not matter how he got that way.[31]

But it seems to me that Frankfurt is mistaken about his own view: it *does* matter how someone got that way, and *he says as much*. Frankfurt is clear that we cannot simply examine a time-slice of an agent's psychological economy and infer that she is wholehearted since the happy state of wholeheartedness *must be the product of reflection* and reflection is diachronic. Further,

---

[31] Harry Frankfurt, "Reply to John Martin Fischer," in *Contours of Agency: Essays on Themes from Harry Frankfurt*, edited by Sarah Buss and Lee Overton (Cambridge, MA: MIT Press, 2002), p. 27.

his discussion of wholeheartedness, noted above, makes clear that it only arises when certain kinds of reflection have successfully been undertaken: the wholehearted person must understand and evaluate how things are with her, her noninterest in making changes must be neither deliberately contrived nor wantonly unselfconscious, she needs to appreciate her psychic condition, and so forth. Whatever he thought in his influential early work, Frankfurt's developed conception of moral responsibility, the one that incorporates wholehearted satisfaction, *is* historical and how a person got that way *is* relevant to determining whether she is morally responsible.

With this correction in place, the Frankfurt-style compatibilist can deny that *Nineteen Eighty-Four* supplies a fatal counterexample. True, at the end of *Nineteen Eighty-Four*, Winston loves Big Brother, but, again, prior to being taken to Room 101 he *hated* Big Brother, so this profound change to his valuational system must be fairly recent. Indeed, "the final, indispensable, healing change had never happened, until this moment" (IX: 311)—that is, two paragraphs before Winston's newfound love is announced in the novel's final line. And it isn't clear that Winston *can* reflect by the novel's end. When Winston begins to trace "2 + 2 = 5" in the dust of his table—and there is *serious* debate about what Orwell intended here[32]—he does so "Almost unconsciously" (IX: 303). And recall that O'Brien assured Winston that he will be made "incapable of . . . curiosity" (IX: 269): the incurious are hardly reflective. Since nothing suggests that Winston has or can undergo the reflection necessary for

[32] In the original typescript, the corrected proofs, and the first printing of *Nineteen Eighty-Four* along with all US editions, Winston traces "2 + 2 = 5." In almost all UK editions published between the Secker & Warburg first edition and 1987 Winston traces "2 + 2 =" with nothing on the right side of the identity symbol. The former suggests that Winston is broken, the latter suggests that hope is not lost. For a compelling account of "one of the most consequential typographical anomalies in the history of English literature," see Dennis Glover's "Introduction" to *Nineteen Eighty-Four* (Carlton, Australia: Black, Inc., 2019), pp. vii–xxiv.

wholeheartedness, the Frankfurt-style compatibilist can deny that he is morally responsible. The supposed counterexample fails.

Contrast Winston with Gordon Comstock, the moth-eaten protagonist of *Keep the Aspidistra Flying*. Gordon, at thirty years old, has abandoned a respectable job to continue work on his epic poem. He complains endlessly about the corrosive effect of money, much to the detriment of his social relations, especially with his endlessly patient girlfriend, Rosemary, and his contempt for bourgeois values seems a defining mark of his personality. Equally defining is that, in the Comstock family, "*nothing ever happened*" (IV: 41), that is, they didn't have children (IV: 66). By contrast, Gordon thinks, "Really vital people, whether they have money or whether they haven't, multiply almost as automatically as animals" (IV: 41), and he praises the broke factory lad who "puts his girl in the family way. . . . At least he's got blood and not money in his veins" (IV: 47). Gordon's lack of an heir is a symbol of, among other things, his failed agency.

When Rosemary becomes pregnant accidentally, Gordon still seems to have little by way of agency. They discuss the prospects of marriage and abortion, an exchange that is marked by themes of freedom and necessity: she assures him "You must decide for yourself" (IV: 252) and that "I want you to feel free. . . . Really and truly free" (IV: 256); he mumbles "We shall have to get married, I suppose" (IV: 252), lamenting that "If I marry you I shall have to turn respectable. . . . I shall have to get a proper job" (IV: 254). Gordon talks as if his choice is determined, that "he knew already what he was going to do" and "felt as though some force outside himself were pushing him" (IV: 263), and after some fatalistic talk about being "foredoomed" and "fulfilling his destiny" he resolves to "buckle to work, sell his soul and hold down his job" (IV: 266). In the novel's final pages, he insists that they have an aspidistra in their flat and we are advised that "once again things were happening in the Comstock family" (IV: 277).[33] Finally, Gordon is imbued with agency.

Is he also morally responsible? Gordon seems defeated, as having given in rather than having secured the will he wants. But after he capitulates, Gordon walks about stewing and his real self is revealed:

> Now that the thing was done he felt nothing but relief: relief that now at least he had finished with dirt, cold, hunger and loneliness and could get back to decent, fully human life. His resolutions, now that he had broken them, seemed nothing but a frightful weight that he had cast off. . . . And it was not merely because of Rosemary and the baby that he had done it. That was the obvious cause, the precipitating cause, but even without it the end would have been the same; if there had been no baby to think about, something else would have forced his hand. For it was what, in his secret heart, he had desired. (IV: 265)

Three things to note in this passage. First, Gordon is not "forced to embrace" capitalism;[34] what he *really wanted all along* was to lay down his sword and embrace middle-class decency. Second, after capitulating, he comes to feel relief, a feeling expressive of the absence of restlessness and resistance. Third, this happy condition is the product of reflection and emerged only after he thought things over. The moral of *Keep the Aspidistra* is emphatically *not* that "determination to live as one chose . . . was the very basis of freedom,"[35] at least not if determination involves making some decisive

---

[33] The ending "reinforces our sense of the text's status as one of Orwell's most irritating books": Benjamin Kohlmann, "Introduction," in George Orwell, *Keep the Aspidistra Flying* (Oxford: Oxford University Press, 2021), p. xxvii.

[34] Philip Bounds, *Orwell & Marxism: The Political and Cultural Thinking of George Orwell* (London: I. B. Tauris, 2009), p. 185.

[35] Dennis Glover, *The Last Man in Europe: A Novel* (New York: Overlook Press, 2017), p. 164.

commitment that resounds endlessly through one's psychological economy, as Frankfurt once put it.[36] Gordon becomes wholeheartedly satisfied with his will, not because he made a choice, but because he became wholehearted after a period of reflection. And that is why Gordon, but not Winston, is morally responsible.

But what if Winston *was* more reflective? What if, after reflecting on his love of Big Brother, he came to lack any feelings expressive of restlessness or resistance? Such an extension of *Nineteen Eighty-Four* is conceivable. Do we now have a counterexample that should trouble the Frankfurt-style compatibilist? Intuitions will vary here: for my part, if Winston's love of Big Brother survives the crucible of reflection, then his psychological economy is not *entirely* attributable to O'Brien's malign influence, and I am happier to regard him as morally responsible. But a better reply is available.

Inner Party members, like Winston, will find reflection difficult: enhanced telescreens, constant propaganda, pervasive fear and suspicion, the influence of Newspeak whose very purpose is to constrain thought, and still more features of Oceaniac life make thoughtful consideration of one's psychological economy almost impossible. Remaining satisfied must also be nigh impossible given the constant fear of inadvertently committing thoughtcrime. Winston's neighbor, Parsons, warns him that "Thoughtcrime is a dreadful thing, old man . . . . It's insidious. It can get hold of you without your even knowing it. Do you know how it got hold of me? In my sleep! Yes, that's a fact" (IX: 245), a worry that other Party members surely shared. Early in *Nineteen Eighty-Four*, Winston announces that "Nothing was your own except the few cubic centimetres inside your skull" (XIX: 29); the Party would deny him even that as would some actual regimes. In "The Prevention of Literature" Orwell explained that:

[36] Frankfurt, "Identification and Wholeheartedness," in his *The Importance of What We Care About*, p. 168.

There is no such thing as a genuinely non-political literature, and least of all in an age like our own, when fears, hatreds, and loyalties of a directly political kind are near to the surface of everyone's consciousness. Even a single tabu [sic] can have an all-round crippling effect upon the mind, because there is always the danger that any thought which is freely followed up may lead to the forbidden thought. It follows that the atmosphere of totalitarianism is deadly to any kind of prose writer. . . . And in any totalitarian society that survives for more than a couple of generations it is probable that prose literature, of the kind that has existed during the past four hundred years, must actually *come to an end*. (XVII: 375)

If totalitarians can undermine the capacity for thought necessary to write prose, they can undermine the capacity for reflective thought the Frankfurt-style compatibilist regards as necessary for moral responsibility. Politics and moral responsibility are tied together in at least that respect: so says Orwell.

I conclude that Orwell is well regarded as a Frankfurt-style compatibilist about moral responsibility. I do not conclude that Orwell is well regarded as a compatibilist about free will. I explain why in the next section.

Orwellian Skepticism about Free Will

In *The English People*, a work that Orwell regarded as "a piece of propaganda for the British Council" (XVII: 189) and wished to go out of print (XX: 226), he pondered philosophical questions like "Is there such a thing as 'the English character'?" and "Can one talk about nations as though they were individuals?," among others. In response to the question "Do such things as 'national cultures' really exist?," he explains that:

This is one of those questions, *like the freedom of the will* or the identity of the person, in which *all the arguments are on one side and instinctive knowledge is on the other*. (XVI: 203, emphasis added)

Which arguments did Orwell have in mind? And if all the arguments are on one side, which side are they on? Do they imply that free will exists? That it doesn't? We are not told, though we are given a clue that I exploit below. I contend that Orwell often says things that sound a great deal like things that avowed free will skeptics have said and insofar as anything like an argument emerges from his ruminations about free will it is a hard incompatibilist argument. An *Orwellian* take on free will, grounded in what he actually says, is a skeptical take.

Instinctive Knowledge and Free Will

That Orwell thought that arguments and instinctive knowledge are on opposite sides is telling given a long tradition in British philosophy of supposing that something like instinctive knowledge is evidence of free will. Orwell's dictum—"all the arguments are on one side and instinctive knowledge is on the other"—resembles Samuel Johnson's pronouncement that "All theory is against freedom of the will; all experience for it," and "Dr. Johnson," Samuel Johnson's title, is referenced in *the very paragraph* that Orwell opposes argument and instinctive knowledge (XVI: 204). The eighteenth- century Scottish philosopher Thomas Reid thought that we all possess a natural conviction of our acting freely and, absent proof to the contrary, no argument is necessary to secure that we are free.[37] Closer

---

[37] See William Rowe, *Thomas Reid on Freedom and Morality* (Ithaca, NY: Cornell University Press, 1993), esp. pp. 103–111.

to Orwell's day, Charles Arthur Campbell, another Scottish philosopher, pointed to our immediate experience of making an effort as reason to believe that free will is real.[38] Ayer and Russell were surely aware of this tradition[39] and it is hardly a stretch to imagine the topic coming up over lunch with Freddie or the old Earl. It seems likely, then, that Orwell would have thought that instinctive knowledge is on the side of free will. That means that all the arguments are *against* free will.

Which arguments? I cannot be certain which arguments Orwell actually contemplated, but given what he actually says it seems unlikely that he had an argument familiar to legions of philosophy undergraduates in mind. To explain, I consider what Orwell says about determinism.

On Hard Determinism

Incompatibilism is the thesis that free will is not metaphysically possible if determinism is true, while determinism is the thesis that facts about the remote past in conjunction with the laws of nature entail that there is only one unique future.[40] Incompatibilism and determinism can be united in a simple syllogism that yields an argument against free will:

1. Free will is metaphysically impossible if determinism is true.
2. Determinism is true.
3. Therefore, free will is metaphysically impossible.

[38] See Charles Arthur Campbell, *In Defence of Free Will* (London: Allen & Unwin, 1967).

[39] Russell questioned whether anyone could locate the mental experience of making an effort: see Bertrand Russell, *Religion and Science* (New York: Oxford University Press, 1961), p. 166.

[40] McKenna and Pereboom, *Free Will: A Contemporary Introduction*, p. 19.

Call this the *simple hard determinist argument*. Could this, or something like it, be among the arguments against free will that Orwell had in mind?

I doubt it, since I doubt that Orwell endorsed either incompatibilism or determinism. Of course, a philosophical outsider like Orwell would not have used the terminology, but he often says things indicating that he at least thought about these two theses. He comes close to affirming incompatibilism in an essay on Thomas Hardy where he says that "If one believes that the future is predetermined, no figure is so pitiful as the 'great' man, the man who a little more than others has the illusion of controlling his destiny" (XIV: 44). But incompatibilism should rule out the exercise of attitudes like pity if the future is (pre)determined, not encourage it, and pity is recommended only as a response to the great men, not all of us. As for determinism, Orwell sometimes talks as though *his* actions are determined: in *The Road to Wigan Pier*, he recounts "the silliest and worst-delivered lecture I have ever heard" and finding "it physically impossible to sit it out; indeed my feet carried me out, seemingly of their own accord, before it was halfway through" (V: 74). But he seems inclined to deny determinism generally. For example, in *The Lion and the Unicorn*, he allows that England along with the whole world "is changing" but he explains that "like everything else it can change only in certain directions. . . . That is not to say that the future is fixed, merely that certain alternatives are possible and others not" (XII: 393). Allowing that the future is circumscribed by past events and the laws of nature does not entail that it is determined by them. So it is unclear that Orwell endorsed either premise of the simple hard determinist argument.

What Orwell actually says suggests sympathy with a very different kind of skeptical argument. To explain, I turn to a philosopher Orwell was prone to quoting, Friedrich Nietzsche.

Nietzsche's Skepticism about Self-Creation

Martin Luther's famous "Here I stand, I can do no other," delivered at the Diet of Worms in 1521,[41] is sometimes invoked as a counterexample to PAP.[42] But, as Robert Kane observes, Luther might have been "responsible for making himself the sort of person he then was by virtue of other choices or actions in his life history," a prospect that allows the incompatibilist to maintain that Luther remains morally responsible even if he could not have done otherwise then.[43] Kane takes talk of "making oneself a sort of person" seriously, identifying free will with that "power of agents to be the ultimate creators or originators and sustainers of their own ends or purposes" and explaining that to "will freely" is "to be the ultimate creator (prime mover, so to speak) of your own purposes."[44] Kane says more about being an ultimate creator here:

> [W]hen we trace the causal or explanatory chains of action back to their sources in the purposes of free agents, these causal chains must come to an end or terminate in the willings (choices, decisions, or efforts) of the agents, which cause or bring about their purposes. If these willings were in turn caused by something else so that the explanatory chains could be traced back further to heredity or environment, to God, or fate, then the ultimacy would not lie with the agents but with something else.[45]

But how plausible is self-creation? How plausible is it that anyone is an ultimate creator?

---

[41] Alan Sandison repeatedly suggests that Orwell is a modern-day inheritor of Luther's Protestant ethic in *The Last Man in Europe: An Essay on George Orwell* (New York: Barnes and Noble Books, 1974). He does not note this similarity.

[42] Daniel Dennett, *Elbow Room* (Cambridge, MA: MIT Press, 1999), p. 133.

[43] Robert Kane, *The Significance of Free Will* (Oxford: Oxford University Press, 1998), p. 42.

[44] Ibid., p. 4.

[45] Ibid.

Nietzsche finds talk of self-creation and ultimate creators implausible when he mocks "the desire to bear the entire and ultimate responsibility for one's actions oneself . . . [to] pull oneself up into existence by the hair, out of the swamps of nothingness."[46] Here is an especially sharp attack:

> What alone can *our* teaching be?—That no one *gives* a human being his qualities: not God, not society, not his parents or ancestors, not he *himself*—(the nonsensical idea last rejected was propounded as "intelligible freedom" by Kant, and also perhaps Plato before him). *No one* is accountable for existing at all, or being constituted as he is, or for living in the circumstances and surroundings in which he lives.[47]

He regards the concept of free will as having a dubious pedigree, insisting that "We no longer have any sympathy today with the concept of 'free will'" and that "we know only too well what it really is—the most infamous of all the arts of the theologian."[48] Given remarks like these, Brian Leiter understands Nietzsche as endorsing "fatalism" that "appeals centrally to the role that physiology and unconscious drives play in determining action," not an ability to engage in self-creation.[49] Nietzsche's remark that "It is simply not possible that a human being should *not* have the qualities and preferences of his parents and ancestors in his body"[50] anticipates the view that character and personality traits are strongly heritable[51] although his fatalism does not imply that our

[46] Friedrich Nietzsche, *Beyond Good and Evil: Prelude to a Philosophy of the Future*, translated by Walter Kaufmann (New York: Vintage, 1989), p. 28.

[47] Ibid., p. 65.

[48] Friedrich Nietzsche, *Twilight of the Idols and The Anti-Christ*, translated by R. J. Hollingdale (New York: Vintage, 2003), p. 64.

[49] Brian Leiter, *Moral Psychology with Nietzsche* (Oxford: Oxford University Press, 2019), p. 116.

[50] Nietzsche, *Beyond Good and Evil*, p. 214.

[51] Leiter, *Moral Psychology with Nietzsche*, p. 167–169.

lives and actions are determined by those traits, only that "what we become is far more constrained, in advance, than we had ever realized."[52]

Nietzsche's fatalism suggests poor prospects for self-creation: if various drives and traits which we did not originate seriously circumscribe our options, then we probably lack the power to be originators and sustainers of our own ends. But Nietzsche's fatalism is not the only threat to free will that he identifies. His suggestion that no one is accountable for being constituted as he is nor for living in the circumstances and surroundings in which he lives suggests sympathy with situationism, the thesis that human behavior is primarily explained by situational facts, including facts about our circumstances and environment, and that dispositional traits, including character traits, explain very little.[53] Nietzsche's situationism is evident in his assertion that any "guilt that is being punished, even when it exists . . . lies in educators, parents, environment."[54] Facts about our situation are also facts that we usually lack substantial control to alter: no one controls the environment in which they developed nor the way that they were raised. Here too, if we are not accountable for our situation and our situation mostly explains who we are and what we do, then the prospects for self-creation look dim.

Note that neither fatalism nor situationism depend on the truth of determinism and might be true even if determinism is false. We are probably unable to alter facts about our traits and situation, when we are unable to alter them, for more mundane reasons: we were too young, not born yet, lack resources to genetic engineering, or whatever. Since Nietzschean skepticism about free will and

---

[52] Ibid., p. 125.

[53] For an extended discussion of situationism's philosophical implications, see John Doris, *Lack of Character: Personality and Moral Behavior* (Cambridge: Cambridge University Press, 2002).

[54] Friedrich Nietzsche, *Human; All Too Human: A Book for Free Spirits*, translated by R. J. Hollingdale (Cambridge: Cambridge University Press, 1986), p. 45.

self-creation does not depend on the truth of determinism, he is best understood as endorsing, not hard determinism, but *hard incompatibilism*,[55] the view that we lack free will whether determinism is true or not since we are bound to lack ultimate control in either case.[56]

Orwell never puts things this plainly, but he does often express sympathy with Nietzsche's fatalism and situationism. So if those two theses warrant the conclusion that Nietzsche was skeptical about the existence of free will independent of the truth of determinism, we have good reason to draw a similar conclusion about Orwell. In the next section, I make the case that Orwell was sympathetic with fatalism and situationism.

Orwell on Fatalism and Situationism

In a sketch for *Burmese Days*, Orwell writes that "To understand any act which a man performs, even the lighting of a cigarette, it is necessary to know his entire history from the moment of his birth, & beyond that the history of the entire universe" (X: 96). Orwell was wise to omit this speculation from his final draft. Knowing everything about someone's history requires knowing about various trivial Cambridge changes[57] they undergo that are irrelevant to understanding their actions: if I burn all my copies of *Animal Farm*, then you, gentle reader, are no longer reading something written by someone who owns that book, an alteration to your relational

---

[55] Leiter, *Moral Psychology with Nietzsche*, p. 117.

[56] For helpful discussion, see Derk Pereboom, *Living without Free Will* (Cambridge: Cambridge University Press, 2001) and Derk Pereboom, *Free Will, Agency, and the Meaning of Life* (Oxford: Oxford University Press, 2014). For a somewhat different skeptical argument, see Galen Strawson, "The Impossibility of Moral Responsibility," *Philosophical Studies*, Vol. 75, No. 1/2 (1994), pp. 5–24. Strawson appeals to Nietzsche explicitly (p. 15).

[57] "An object undergoes a Cambridge-change if there is any change in the true statements that can be made about this object": Derek Parfit, *Reasons and Persons* (Oxford: Oxford University Press, 1984), p. 494.

properties that plays no obvious role in explaining who you are and what you do.

Orwell's sympathy with fatalism and situationism are both on display in "Why I Write." He explains that "It seems to me nonsense, in a period like our own, to think that one can avoid writing of such subjects" and while he might have wrote naturalistic novels full of purple prose if he lived "in a peaceful age" he was "forced into becoming a sort of pamphleteer" (XVIII: 319), that is, because of his situation. Other artists too had their options seriously circumscribed by their situation: Salvador Dali suffered from "the perversion of instinct that has been made possible by the machine age" (XVI: 234) and if he was a morally appalling person that is because he "grew up into the corrupt world of the nineteen-twenties" (XVI: 240). No reason to suppose that you or I are any different: In "A Happy Vicar I Might Have Been," one of his better poems, Orwell makes clear that he was "born, alas, in an evil time" and closes with the lines "I dreamt I dwelt in marble halls, / And woke to find it true; / I wasn't born for an age like this; / Was Smith? Was Jones? Were you?" (X: 524). All of us are constrained by the time we live in, that is, our situation. But he also suggests that his drives are not open to him to create. Orwell identifies "four great motives for writing" that "exist in different degrees in every writer" (XVIII: 318) distinguished by the desires constitutive of them: first, "Sheer egoism," the desire to seem clever or to be talked about and remembered; second, "Esthetic enthusiasm," the desire to share an experience which one feels is valuable; third, "Historical impulse," the desire to see things as they are and record facts for posterity; fourth, "Political purpose," the desire to push the world in a certain direction and alter ideas about what is worth striving for (XVIII: 318). And if he is not responsible for the fact that he possesses these motives, neither is he responsible for their motivational valence: If "By nature," he is someone "in whom the first three motives would outweigh the fourth" he became most greatly moved by political purpose and became the writer we know him to be because of the time he lived in. Generally, "the proportions" of a writer's motives "will vary from time to time, according to the atmosphere in which he is living" (XVIII: 318–319). Orwell, like all of us, is the product of his psychology, physiology, and situation.

Like Nietzsche, Orwell does not quite say that who we are and what we do is determined. In this selection from a talk for the BBC Home Service about Samuel Butler, he explains that:

> A human being is what he is largely because he comes from certain surroundings, and no one ever fully escapes from the things that have happened to him in early childhood. To some extent your character depends on the way your parents treated you, and their character depends on the way theirs have treated them, and so on. . . . it is probably true that you can't give a really revealing history of a man's life without saying something about his parents and probably his grandparents. (XVII: 181)

If we never *fully* escape we may *partially* escape such that our character depends on how our parents treated us to *some* extent but not *entirely* on that situational factor. Even in "Why I Write," where he initially claims that a writer's "subject matter will be determined by the age he lives in," he concludes only that a writer "before he ever begins to write he will have acquired an emotional attitude from which he will never completely escape" (XVIII: 318). In "T. S. Eliot," he says of good writers that "the general direction of their development is determined" (XIV: 67) which may seriously circumscribe who they become and what they write without determining anything. Of Eliot himself, Orwell explained that "It is absurd . . . to imagine that he might have used his gifts in the cause of democracy and Socialism," yet he allowed that Eliot "could not have developed into a Socialist, but he might have developed into the last apologist of aristocracy" (XIV: 67). What is true of Eliot is apparently true of all of us: who we are and what we will do is seriously circumscribed without being determined.

I opened this section by noting that Orwell referenced arguments against free will. Whatever arguments he had in mind, he was clearly sympathetic with fatalism and situationism, two theses that suggest that the kind of self-creation some incompatibilists think is necessary for free will never occurs. Whether or not it was Orwell's argument, an *Orwellian* argument against free will is a Nietzschean hard incompatibilist argument that calls for deep skepticism about the very possibility of free will.

Conclusion: Orwell's Sort-of Semicompatibilism

In this chapter, I have discussed two theses that might seem to pair together poorly: Frankfurt-style compatibilism about moral responsibility and hard incompatibilism about free will. Together, they entail that morally responsible agency is possible but free will isn't, an odd result if free will is defined as the unique ability of persons to exercise the strongest sense of control over their actions necessary for moral responsibility.[58] Is the Orwellian position about free will and moral responsibility that I have sketched simply confused?

Not necessarily. My Orwellian is not alone in thinking that there is conceptual space between free will and moral responsibility. According to *semicompatibilism*, moral responsibility is compatible with determinism (since it does not require the power to do otherwise), whereas free will (which does require this power) is not.[59] Alternatively, it is the view that moral responsibility is compatible with the truth of determinism even if determinism is incompatible with freedom to do otherwise.[60] Neither statement is quite Orwell's view of things, but my Orwellian *does* think that morally

---

[58] McKenna and Pereboom, *Free Will*, p. 6.

[59] John Martin Fischer, Frankfurt-Type Examples and Semicompatibilism," in *The Oxford Handbook of Free Will*, 2nd edition, edited by Robert Kane (Oxford: Oxford University Press, 2011), pp. 243–264.

[60] John Martin Fischer, "Responsiveness and Moral Responsibility," in his *My Way: Essays on Moral Responsibility* (Oxford: Oxford University Press, 2006), p. 78.

responsible agency is not terminally threatened by that which terminally threatens free will. My Orwellian is a semicompatibilist,
sort-of. What is novel to my Orwellian is their motivation for
embracing sort-of semicompatibilism. Recall Ayer's suggestion
noted in Chapter 1 that Orwell thought we should apply philosophy to political and social questions if we are going to philoso-
phize at all. Permit me some speculation.

What the folk think about free will and its compatibility with
determinism is an empirical question; perhaps the folk are tacitly incompatibilist, perhaps they are compatibilists, perhaps they
are deeply confused. If the folk are confused, what should be done
about it? Should philosophers work hard to clean up their confusion? Would it matter? Peter Strawson famously contended that
the truth or falsity of determinism would have little impact on our
actual practices of holding ourselves and others responsible.[61] But
perhaps Strawson is wrong. Perhaps the folk, newly skeptical of
free will, would become hopelessly despondent, utterly negligent
in their dealings with others, and altogether worse off for it.[62] Even
philosophers impressed with hard incompatibilism have found
themselves interacting with other others in ways that suggest sympathy with compatibilism about moral responsibility.[63] If the folk
would react poorly in response to well-founded free will skepticism,

[61] Speaking of "the nature of the human commitment" to the exercise of the reactive
attitudes, Strawson explains that "it is *useless* to ask whether it would not be rational
for us to do what it is not in our nature to (be able to) do." See Strawson, "Freedom and
Resentment," p. 20. As Bobby Bingle reminded me, Strawson also thought that the answer to the question "What difference would it make?" upon learning that someone
lacked ultimate responsibility was "none," that "It is entirely irrelevant" with respect
to how we would or should exercise the reactive attitudes. See Peter Strawson, "Reply
to David Pears," in *The Philosophy of P. F. Strawson*, edited by Lewis Edwin Hahn
(Chicago: Open Court, 1998), p. 261.
[62] Galen Strawson has apparently received death threats and more than a little hostile correspondence given his publicly expressed skepticism about free will: see Oliver
Burkeman, "The Clockwork Universe: Is Free Will an Illusion?," *The Guardian* (27 April
2021), https://www.theguardian.com/news/2021/apr/27/the-clockwork-universe-is-
free-will-an-illusion.
[63] Shaun Nichols, *Bound: Essays on Free Will and Responsibility* (Oxford: Oxford
University Press, 2015), p. 141.

philosophers have a choice. Should we shout the truth from rooftops? Keep our dirty little secret to ourselves? Something else?

Deeply skeptical about free will, my Orwellian worries that popularizing these suspicions will do little to secure justice, liberty, and decency. And while she can't honestly declare her belief in free will, she can encourage a conception of moral responsibility that permits us to hold persons responsible even if they could not have done otherwise. How would that go? She could write about characters who faced impossible odds and struggled mightily against forces all but assured of victory. She might offer herself as tribute and intimate that she is an apt target for the reactive attitudes even in the face of serious social pressures and corrupting influences. She might encourage the exercise of reactive attitudes essential to bringing about what is conventionally regarded as justice, liberty, and decency while remaining quiet about the threats to free will. She would, in short, *operate very much as Orwell did*: she would engage in *compatibilist propaganda*, getting the folk to concentrate on more fruitful exercises of the reactive attitudes while preventing them from becoming preoccupied with the loss of ultimate control. This is not a confused mindset but a principled one that requires being silent about that which we are better off not speaking about.

My Orwellian sort-of semicompatibilist is thus deeply interested in moral psychology and regards it as essential to bringing about justice. So was Orwell. In Chapter 4, I explain that Orwell thought that the major problem of his time was an adamantly philosophical one that also requires noble propaganda to solve. Explaining what the major problem of his time was and why he thought it so urgently needed a solution requires considering Orwell's moral psychology. I turn to this task in my next chapter.

4

Orwellian Moral Psychology

I begin by recording something of a puzzle. During the 1940s,
Orwell repeatedly reflects on "the major problem of his time," one
identified toward the end of "Looking Back on the Spanish War":

> To raise the standard of living of the whole world to that of Britain
> would not be a greater undertaking than this war we are now
> fighting. I don't claim, and I don't know who does, that that would
> solve anything in itself. It is merely that privation and brute la-
> bour have to be abolished before the real problems of humanity
> can be tackled. *The major problem of our time is the decay of the be-*
> *lief in personal immortality*, and it cannot be dealt with while the
> average human being is either drudging like an ox or shivering in
> fear of the secret police. (XIII: 510, emphasis added)

Experience indicates that Orwell's readers typically think that he
would have identified something *else* as the major problem of his
day: ascendent totalitarians, heightened surveillance, repression
of liberty, growth of unchecked power, lousy writing, or whatever. In this vein, some commentators suggest that "the key question of Orwell's century" concerned "how to preserve the liberty
of the individual during an age when the state was becoming pow-
erfully intrusive into private life"[1] and that "the basic dilemma of
[Orwell's] time" was that "an end had unmistakably come to that

---

[1] Thomas E. Ricks, *Churchill and Orwell: The Fight for Freedom* (New York: Penguin,
2017), p. 3.

George Orwell. Peter Brian Barry, Oxford University Press. © Oxford University Press 2023.
DOI: 10.1093/oso/9780197627402.003.0004

optimistic belief in man's inevitable progress."[2] Yet he is clear: the major problem of his time implicated the decay of belief in personal immortality. But why? Of all the problems he considered, why is *this* the major one?

In this chapter, I argue that Orwell's special interest in the supposed decay of belief in personal immortality follows from his moral psychology. Talk of "Orwellian Moral Psychology" might confuse from the start. "Orwellian" is the most widely used adjective derived from the name of a modern writer, more common than "Kafkaesque" or "Dickensian."[3] It can connote crushing tyranny and fear and conformism[4] or the alienation of individuals who dare to rebel,[5] and still more.[6] I intend nothing so dramatic, referring only to a research project that studies ethical thought, motivation, and behavior informed by empirical research and moral philosophy. Orwellian moral psychology is also informed by what Orwell says about such matters.

In this chapter, I first recall what Orwell said about belief in personal immortality. I then identify some obviously British strains in his moral psychology, most notably his sympathy with some Humean theses about motivation and moral judgment and a Lockean conception of personal identity. Finally, I argue that these British strains jointly ensure that the major problem of his time will not be solved easily, his attempts to do just that notwithstanding. Allegedly, it is a problem "He never pretended to have

[2] Tosco R. Fyvel, *George Orwell: A Personal Memoir* (New York: Macmillan, 1982), p. 208.

[3] Geoffrey Nunberg, "Simpler Terms: If It's 'Orwellian,' It's Probably Not," *New York Times*, 22 June 2003, https://www.nytimes.com/2003/06/22/weekinreview/simpler-terms-if-it-s-orwellian-it-s-probably-not.html.

[4] Christopher Hitchens, *Orwell's Victory* (London: Penguin, 2003), p. 5.

[5] Peter Lewis, *The Road to 1984* (New York: Harcourt Brace Jovanovich, Publishers, 1981), p. 16.

[6] Michael Schur's excellent *How to Be Perfect: The Correct Answer to Every Moral Question* (New York: Simon and Schuster, 2022) offers a list of "What People Who Want to Sound Fancy Say" paired with "What They Mean." "Ironic" is paired with "Annoying," "Postmodern" with "recent," "Freudian" with "Penis-related," and so on. "Orwellian" is paired with "I got banned from Twitter for being racist": p. 209.

found a solution to"[7] despite the fact he affirmed that he did; his worry was not so much with finding a solution as implementing it. I explain below.

The Major Problem of Our Time

In the early 1940s, Orwell repeatedly expressed his conviction that belief in personal immortality was waning: "the most obvious case" of a doctrine "which no one seriously believes in," he thought, involves "immortality of the soul" (XIV: 66) and "few thinking people now believe in life after death, and the number of those that do is probably diminishing" (XVI: 399).[8] The decay of the belief in personal immortality was, Orwell thought, "as important as the rise of machine civilisation" (XVI: 112). But why? And what should be done about it?

On the Decay of a Belief

In a 1944 AIP column, Orwell explained that "I find it very rare to meet anyone, of whatever background, who admits to believing in personal immortality" although it is "quite likely" that "a fairly large number . . . would admit the possibility that after death there might be 'something' " (XVI: 152).[9] Does Orwell contradict himself here? Not clearly, given this elaboration:

[7] Valerie J. Simms, "A Reconsideration of Orwell's *1984*: The Moral Implications of Despair," *Ethics*, Vol. 84, No. 4 (July 1974), p. 293.

[8] Richard Rees cautions that while Orwell "does in fact use the word 'soul' a great deal more often than might be thought . . . to use that word might suggest that Orwell believed in immortality and a whole lot of other things that he didn't believe in." See in *Orwell Remembered*, edited by Audrey Coppard and Bernard Crick (London: Ariel Books, 1984), p. 96.

[9] Elsewhere, he explains that "the common people are without definite religious belief, and have been so for centuries" (XII: 394) and he references the "sort of frozen disgust that most people feel when they hear the word 'God'" (XIII: 159).

> Never, literally, in recent years, have I met anyone who gave me
> the impression of believing in the next world as firmly as he
> believed in the existence of, for instance, Australia. Belief in the
> next world does not influence conduct as it would if it were gen-
> uine. With that endless existence beyond death to look forward
> to, how trivial our lives here would seem! Most Christians profess
> to believe in Hell. Yet have you ever met a Christian who seemed
> as afraid of Hell as he was of cancer? (XVI: 152)

Here, he distinguishes what people affirm and what they *actually*
believe, a distinction implicit in *Coming Up for Air* when George
Bowling explains that "I've never met anyone who gave me the
impression of *really* believing in a future life" (VII: 111, emphasis
added). Similarly, in *A Clergyman's Daughter*, Warburton questions
whether Dorothy believes "in Hell as you believe in Australia,"
suggesting that she and other "religious people . . . [are] so deuc-
edly cold-blooded about your beliefs" (III: 71). All this suggests
that Orwell was sympathetic with a kind of behaviorism that
makes beliefs partly a function of a disposition to perform constitutive actions, a sympathy that shows up in "Lear, Tolstoy, and the
Fool" when Orwell claims that "the enormous majority of human
beings, if they understood the issue, would choose this world"
and that "They do make that choice when they continue working,
breeding and dying instead of crippling their faculties in the hope
of obtaining a new lease of existence elsewhere" (XIX: 64). As an
empirical matter, he clearly thinks that there is little behavioral evidence that such dispositions are widely manifest, even if it's not
clear that he has much besides anecdotal evidence to back his
conclusions.

The distinction noted in the previous paragraph helps to clear up
a biographical point that threatens to complicate my discussion of
Orwell's take on the major problem of his time. Jacintha Buddicom
recalls some correspondence from June 1949, since lost to time,
that "defined his faith in some sort of after-life. Not necessarily, or

even probably, a conventional Heaven-or-Hell, but the firm belief that 'nothing ever dies,' that we must go on *somewhere*." She notes too that her diary from that time records "Letter from Eric [Blair] about Nothing Ever Dies."[10] But Jacintha's recollections are pretty modest evidence of belief in anything like personal immortality for reasons Orwell offers: even if he is read as affirming that a person survives the death of the physical body, his repeated failure to act accordingly suggests that he doesn't *really* believe any such thing and that his affirmation that nothing ever dies is not the expression of a sincere belief. Jacintha herself proposes a more plausible explanation, surmising that he probably wrote it because she had intimated that her mother was ill.

What is clear is that Orwell did not think that the supposed decay in belief in personal immortality was an altogether bad thing. He did "not want the belief in life after death to return" (XVI: 113), and explained that:

It was absolutely necessary that the soul should be cut away. Religious belief, in the form in which we had known it, had to be abandoned. By the nineteenth century, it was already in essence a lie, a semi-conscious device for keeping the rich rich and the poor poor. The poor were to be contend with their poverty, because it would all be made up to them in the world beyond the grave. . . . [T]hrough the whole fabric of capitalist society there ran a similar lie, which it was absolutely necessary to rip out. (XII: 124)

Belief in immortality was, Orwell thought, a palliative used by those "who defend an unjust order of Society by claiming that this world cannot be substantially improved and only the 'next world' matters" (XVIII: 422). For example, the unjust pigs of *Animal Farm*

---

[10] Jacintha Buddicom, *Eric & Us: A Remembrance of George Orwell* (London: Leslie Frewin Publishers, 1974), p. 157.

tolerate Moses, the clever raven who contributes nothing, who palliates the other animals with tales of the next world:

> He would perch on a stump, flap his black wings, and talk by the hour to anyone who would listen. "Up there, comrades," he would say solemnly, pointing to the sky with his large beak—"up there, just on the other side of that dark cloud that you can see—there it lies, Sugarcandy Mountain, that happy country where we poor animals can rest for ever from our labours! He even claimed to have been there on one of his higher flights, and to have seen the everlasting fields of clover and the linseed cake and lump sugar growing on the hedges. Many of the animals believed him. Their lives now, they reasoned, were hungry and laborious; was it not right and just that a better world should exist somewhere else? (VIII: 78)

"Other-worldliness," Orwell quipped, "is the best alibi a rich man can have" (XVI: 35).

If Orwell did not think that the decay in belief in personal immortality was an altogether bad thing, he did allow that its loss incurred a cost. He sounds almost like an existentialist[11] when explaining that "With the breakdown of Christianity, and, above all, of belief in the immortality of the soul, the 'meaning' went out of European life, with the result that many of the best spirits of the nineteenth century were haunted by a sense of futility" (XII: 190). He also suggested a way to cope with this loss of meaning. At the end of A Clergyman's Daughter, Dorothy is again endlessly sewing costumes and faux jackboots, despairing that "Life, if the grave really ends it, is monstrous and dreadful. No use trying to argue it away" (III: 292). At her lowest point:

---

[11] Richard Rees thought Orwell "was in real life a better existentialist . . . than many philosophers whose existentialism exists mainly between the covers of a book": Rees, George Orwell: Fugitive from the Camp of Victory (Carbondale: Southern Illinois University Press, 1961), p. 9.

Her mind struggled with the problem, while perceiving that there was no solution. There was, she saw clearly, no possible substitute for faith; no pagan acceptance of life as sufficient to itself, no pantheistic cheer-up stuff, no pseudo-religion of "progress" with visions of glittering Utopias and ant-heaps of steel and concrete. It is all or nothing. Either life on earth is a preparation for something greater and more lasting, or it is meaningless, dark, and dreadful. (III: 293)

But as Dorothy reflects "there stole into her nostrils a warm, evil smell, forgotten these eight months but unutterably familiar—the smell of glue" (III: 295) which is, somehow, "the answer to her prayer ... the solution to her difficulty lay in accepting the fact that there was no solution; that if one gets on with the job that lies to hand, the ultimate purpose of the job fades into insignificance" (III: 295). Having gotten on with her job, "The problem of faith and no faith had vanished utterly from her mind" and she becomes "absorbed, with pious concentration, in the penetrating smell of the glue-pot" (III: 297). Dorothy isn't exactly a joyful Sisyphus endlessly pushing a rock up the hill having embraced the absurd task as his own, and Orwell's proffered solution—get on with your work and don't think too much about it—ensures that *A Clergyman's Daughter* is unsatisfying as philosophy or narrative.[12]

Still, the major problem of his time demanded some response since, while the best spirits of the nineteenth century were haunted by feelings of futility, a still greater problem was on the horizon.

[12] Nathan Waddell gets it right when he notes that "the narrative tone at the end of *A Clergyman's Daughter* is hard to judge." Is it commending "a genial maybe even a stoical return to normality"? Or, noting that the sky is darkening as Dorothy labors, is it hinting that "what lies at the heart of things is not some anodyne blank but a conceptual and existential void?" See Nathan Waddell, "Introduction," in George Orwell, *A Clergyman's Daughter* (Oxford: Oxford University Press, 2021), p. xxii.

The Humanist's Dilemma

In a 1940 "Notes on the Way" column, Orwell recalled:

> [A] rather cruel trick I once played on a wasp. He was sucking jam
> on my plate, and I cut him in half. He paid no attention, merely
> went on with his meal, while a tiny stream of jam trickled out
> of his severed esophagus. Only when he tried to fly away did he
> grasp the dreadful thing that had happened to him. It is the same
> with modern man. The thing that has been cut away is his soul,
> and there was a period—twenty years, perhaps—during which he
> did not notice it. (XII: 124)

Orwell first recalled his cruel trick in his 1935 review of Henry
Miller's *Tropic of Cancer*, explaining that "Modern man is rather
like a bisected wasp which goes on sucking jam and pretends that
the loss of its abdomen does not matter," adding that "One result
of the breakdown of religious belief has been a sloppy idealization
of the physical side of life" (X: 404–405). But breakdown in religious belief apparently had other unfortunate consequences too.
In a 1939 book review, he worried that, left to choose between a
Christian and Communist worldview, we would be left to suppose
that "Either this life is a preparation for another, in which case the
individual soul is all-important, or there is no life after death, in
which case the individual is merely a replaceable cell in the general body (XI: 322). But the gravest problem that decay in belief in
personal immortality threatened was one that Orwell returned to
repeatedly during the 1940s.

Orwell sometimes betrayed a dim view of human beings: in
the same "Notes on the Way" column noted above, he explained
that "if one assumes that no sanction can ever be effective except
the supernatural one, it is clear what follows," namely, "Wars and
yet more wars, revolutions and counter-revolutions, Hitlers and
super-Hitlers—and so downwards into abysses which are horrible

to contemplate" (XII: 125). In a 1944 AIP column, he contended that "There is little doubt that the modern cult of power-worship is bound up with the modern man's feeling that life here and now is the only life there is" and that "If death ends everything, it becomes much harder to believe that you can be in the right even if you are defeated" (XVI: 112). The worry is especially clear when he described "the dilemma of the humanist" in the conclusion of a 1945 book review:[13]

> As long as supernatural beliefs persist, men can be exploited by cunning priests and oligarchs, and the technical progress which is the prerequisite of a just society cannot be achieved. On the other hand, when men stop worshipping God they promptly start worshipping Man, with disastrous results. (XVII: 227)

Orwell's thought seems to be that belief in personal immortality, paired perhaps with fear of divine retribution, is the only moral bulwark against inclinations which would otherwise lead us to very dark places.

The humanist must either tolerate the existence of supernatural belief or reject it. Tolerating it ensures exploitation and injustice, but rejecting it leads to power-worship, the rise of totalitarianism and Fascism, war, and still more disasters. Since Orwell is on record as rejecting the first horn of the dilemma, he seems committed to being impaled on the latter: again, belief in personal immortality *must go*, even if we must settle for disaster.

That said, Orwell is impaled on the second horn of the humanist's dilemma only if he accepts a premise that he clearly rejects. Why assume that no sanctions can be effective except supernatural ones? Why suppose that only divinely promised consequences can be effective in motivating us? Orwell mocks this assumption elsewhere.

---

[13] The book was Erich Kahler's *Man Is the Measure* and was "concerned with the problems of humanism" (XVII: 225).

In his adaptation of an H. G. Wells play, the question "What induce-
ment is there to live decently if death ends everything?" earns the
reply "Oh, inducements! You religious people are always talking
about inducements. Can't a man seek after righteousness for its
own sake?" (XV: 258). Orwell's humanist should not simply reject
belief in personal immortality; she can reject it *and* replace it with
something else, something widely available to human beings sufficient to get us to act rightly and live peacefully. But what?

In a 1944 AIP column, Orwell proposed a candidate to replace
belief in personal immortality but noted a problem:

> Reared for thousands of years on the notion that the individual
> survives, man has got to make a considerable effort to get used
> to the notion that the individual perishes. He is not likely to sal-
> vage civilization *unless he can evolve a system of good and evil*
> which is independent of heaven and hell. *Marxism, indeed, does
> supply this, but it has never really been popularized.* (XVI: 113,
> emphasis added)

By "Marxism" Orwell surely meant democratic Socialism—more
on that in Chapter 8—but in any case, he is clearly optimistic
that, if popularized, it would also serve as a bulwark against those
inclinations that would otherwise lead us to disaster. The problem
is that it has never been popularized, a problem he laid at the feet
of his fellow socialists. Orwell complained about "Marxists . . .
[who] do not often bother to discover what is going on inside other
people's heads" (V: 173) and explained that "the main weakness of
Marxism" was "its failure to interpret human motives" (XII: 244).
What socialists need, apparently, is a better understanding of what
actually moves actual human beings. *That* is how we break the
humanist's dilemma: we encourage and cultivate the right kind of
moral psychology that, in lieu of fear of divine retribution, will suffice to get us to live in just peace.

What does the right kind of moral psychology look like? It should probably begin with an honest assessment of what actually motivates our actions and moral judgments, and apparently involves some theses derived from David Hume. In the next section, I explain Orwell's Humean sympathies, half of what ensured that the major problem of his time seemed so vexing.

Orwell's Humean Moral Psychology

Some of Orwell's readers reference his "plain-man Kantianism,"[14] but Orwell did not think, like Kant, that the faculty of pure practical reason is necessary to act rightly. He is closer to David Hume, not simply because, like Hume, Orwell is "Characteristically empirical in his thought,"[15] but because he often seems to endorse Hume's aphorisms like "Reason is, and ought only to be the slave of the passions, and can never pretend to any other office than to serve and obey them."[16] I contend that Orwell is best understood not as a Kantian, but as a Humean who endorsed at least two doctrines often associated with Humean moral psychology.

The Humean Theory of Motivation

Contemporary Humeans tend to endorse the *Humean theory of motivation* (HTM), stated formally here:

---

[14] Philip Bounds, *Orwell & Marxism: The Political and Cultural Thinking of George Orwell* (London: I. B. Tauris, 2009), p. 159.

[15] Richard J. Voorhees, "Orwell's Secular Crusade," *The Commonweal*, Vol. 61 (January 1955), p. 449.

[16] David Hume, *Treatise of Human Nature* (Buffalo, NY: Prometheus Books, 1992), p. 415.

> R at t constitutes a motivating reason of agent A to ϕ iff there is
> some ψ such that R at t consists of a desire of A to ψ and a belief
> that were he to ϕ he would ψ.[17]

The HTM affirms that motivation always requires desire although
Humeans tend to be catholic about what counts as a desire, in-
cluding emotions, hopes, wishes, sympathies, and still more. But
Humeans are united in their conviction that beliefs, including
moral beliefs, are never by themselves sufficient for motivation.
Moral motivation, like all motivation, requires desire.

Orwell's sympathy with the HTM is clearest in the following passage from "Wells, Hitler and the World State":

> The energy that actually shapes the world springs from
> emotions—racial pride, leader-worship, religious belief, love
> of war—which liberal intellectuals mechanically write off as
> anachronisms, and which they have usually destroyed so com-
> pletely in themselves as to have lost all power of action. (XII: 538)

He also emphasized the motivational salience of desire when he
riffed on some of his most familiar themes: when he diagnosed
the underlying motives of Socialists, he suggested that "what they
desire, basically, is to reduce the world to something resembling
a chessboard" (V: 166); seeing the working class in the saddle in
Barcelona made his "desire to see Socialism established much *more*
actual than it had been before" (VI: 84); he insisted that "The desire
for liberty, for knowledge, and for a decent standard of living has
spread far too widely to be killed by obscurantism or persecution"

[17] Michael Smith, "The Humean Theory of Motivation," *Mind*, Vol. 96, No. 381
(1987), p. 36.

(XI: 335); he worried that that "we are moving into a mechanised age in which human beings will lose all desire for contact with the soil" (XI: 414); he complained that nearly all progressive thought of his day "has assumed tacitly that human beings desire nothing beyond ease, security and avoidance of pain" (XII: 118); he affirmed that "greater social equality . . . is what the great mass of the English people desire" (XVI: 217). The protagonists of Orwell's novels are arguably moved "not only by social or political motives, but by frustrated passion."[18] That Orwell would have sympathy with the HTM should not be a surprise given that Bertrand Russell insisted that "Since all behaviour springs from desire, it is clear that ethical notions can have no importance except as they influence desire."[19] We know that Orwell reviewed Russell's *Power: A New Social Analysis*, where he explained that "Desires, emotions, passions . . . are the only possible causes of action" and that "Reason is not a cause of action but only a regulator."[20] Given Russell's influence on Orwell[21] noted in Chapter 1, it cannot be a surprise if Orwell agreed with the HTM too.

Two upshots of the HTM are worth recording. First, if our desires are not typically under our rational control then getting ourselves and others to be motivated in morally desirable ways will not typically be under our rational control. Second, if our desires are not typically under our rational control then some of them may well be morally perverse. Orwell, for his part, was more than a little worried that an especially perverse desire was taking hold.

---

[18] Gordon Bowker, *Inside George Orwell: A Biography* (London: Palgrave Macmillan, 2003), p. xii.

[19] Bertrand Russell, "What I Believe," in *Why I Am Not a Christian*, edited by Paul Edwards (New York: Simon and Schuster, 1957), p. 129.

[20] Russell, *Power*, p. 171.

[21] See Peter Brian Barry, "Orwell and Bertrand Russell," in *The Oxford Handbook of George Orwell*, edited by Nathan Waddell (Oxford: Oxford University Press, forthcoming).

The Power Fetish

One of Orwell's readers suggests that "we do not find much about his theory of power" in his novels.[22] Yet during the 1940s, he repeatedly worried that an intrinsic desire for power, a desire for power for its own sake, was increasingly common. I call this intrinsic desire for power "the power fetish," and he expressed his concerns about it in multiple essays, reviews, columns, and books although his most dramatic reflections were saved for his final novel.

In *Nineteen Eighty-Four*, Goldstein's treatise promises to reveal "the central secret . . . the original motive, the never-questioned instinct that first led to the seizure of power" (IX: 226). Winston, who wrote in his forbidden diary *"I understand HOW: I do not understand WHY"* (IX: 83), never finished Goldstein's treatise but still came to understand why the Party wants power. After chiding Winston's "stupid" suggestion that the Party rules for the good of the governed, O'Brien reveals the central secret:

> It is this. The Party seeks power entirely for its own sake. We are not interested in the good of others; we are interested solely in power. Not wealth or luxury or long life or happiness: only power, pure power. (IX: 275)

That "Power is not a means, it is an end" (IX: 276) is perhaps Orwell's "main thesis" in *Nineteen Eighty-Four*,[23] but the power fetish is hinted at elsewhere. In *Coming Up for Air*, George Bowling explained that:

> Old Hitler's something different. So's Joe Stalin. They aren't like these chaps in the old days who crucified people and chopped

---

[22] Robert Plank, *George Orwell's Guide through Hell: A Psychological Study of "1984"* (San Bernardino, CA: Borgo Press, 1994), p. 113.

[23] G. Wesley McCullough, *George Orwell: A Reader's Approach* (London: Athena Press, 2002), p. 73.

their heads off and so forth, just for the fun of it. They're after something quite new—something that's never been heard of before. (VII: 165)[24]

By contrast, in a 1946 AIP column, Orwell denied that the power fetish is new, although he allowed that it has reached "new levels of lunacy in our own age" (XVIII: 504).

Orwell's readership is divided about whether he thought that the power fetish is real and really explains aspiring totalitarians. Some readers are confident that he did.[25] Others suggest that he only meant to parody the power-hungry.[26] Isaac Deutscher, who counts the power fetish as "the oldest, the most banal, the most abstract, the most metaphysical, and the most barren of all generalizations," recounts that Orwell repeatedly muttered that the Yalta Conference participants "are all power-hungry."[27] But Orwell couldn't quite endorse James Burnham's realism that takes the power fetish for granted (XVIII: 282), and while he recorded that "All modern men" recognize the existence of the power fetish he added the noncommittal "I am not saying that this is a true belief" (XIII: 152). Still, whether it is actual, the power fetish is certainly *conceivable*. The characters of *No Orchids for Miss Blandish*—the pulpy crime novel in which "only one motive is at work throughout . . . the pursuit

---

[24] Bowling does not say that Hitler and Stalin intrinsically desire power, but that's how some readers understand him. See, for example, D. J. Taylor, *On "Nineteen Eighty-Four": A Biography* (New York: Abrams Press, 2019), p. 26.

[25] John Atkins, *George Orwell: A Literary and Biographical Study* (New York: Frederick Ungar, 1954), pp. 194 and 245; Hollis, *A Study of George Orwell*, p. 151; Ian Slater, *The Road to Airstrip One* (New York: Norton and Company, 1985), p. 190; Colin Ward, "Orwell and Anarchism," in *George Orwell at Home (and among the Anarchists): Essays and Photographs* (London: Freedom Press, 1998), p. 42; George Woodcock, *The Crystal Spirit: A Study of George Orwell* (New York: Schoken, 1984), p. 219; Alex Zwerdling, *Orwell and the Left* (New Haven, CT: Yale University Press, 1974), p. 27.

[26] Bernard Crick, *Orwell: A Life* (Boston: Little, Brown, 1980), p. 322 and 399; Stephen Ingle, *George Orwell: A Political Life* (Manchester: Manchester University Press, 1993), p. 97; Rees, *Fugitive from the Camp of Victory*, p. 104.

[27] Isaac Duetscher, "1984—The Mysticism of Cruelty," in *Twentieth Century Interpretations of "1984": A Collection of Critical Essays*, edited by Samuel Hynes (New Jersey: Prentice-Hall, 1971), p. 38.

of power" (XVI: 351)—don't live in a distant possible world but a nearby one. If an intrinsic desire for power is conceivable, then, supposing that conceivability implies possibility, the power fetish is possible. And any theory that denies its impossibility, including psychological hedonism and some versions of Marxism, will have to go.

Orwell seems to have thought that the power fetish is actual— he says it "seems to be much more dominant than the desire for wealth" (XVIII: 504)—and it led him to suspect the motives of others. He contended that pacifists were power-hungry (XIX: 656), adding that they were "objectively pro-Nazi" (XIII: 40) for good measure, hinted at a connection between pacifism and a desire for violence (XX: 203),[28] and savaged them in this passage from "Lear, Tolstoy, and the Fool":

> Creeds like pacifism and anarchism, which seem on the surface to imply a complete renunciation of power, rather encourage this habit of mind. For if you have embraced a creed which appears to be free from the ordinary dirtiness of politics—a creed from which you yourself cannot expect to draw any material advantage—surely that proves that you are in the right? And the more you are in the right, the more natural that everyone else should be bullied into thinking likewise. (XIX: 66)

Orwell is doubly Nietzschean here, engaging in hermeneutics of suspicion as he purports to have both debunked their alleged motivations and located their actual motives in something like the will to power. Nothing wrong with being Nietzschean, but Orwell

---

[28] Orwell later distanced himself from this view (XVI: 495). Weirdly, a younger Orwell, writing in 1940, affirmed that pacifism was "a tenable position, and at this moment an honourable one" (XII: 98). And before he suggested that pacifists were power-hungry, he intimated that nonpacifists were. In *Coming Up for Air*, George Bowling explains that the leftist lecturer who advocates war with Hitler suffered from a combination of fear and a sadistic urge for "smashing people's faces in with a spanner" (VII: 156).

here betrays just why the humanist's dilemma will be so hard to crack. More below, but first note that things are complicated by another Humean thesis that I ascribe to Orwell.

Ethical Sentimentalism

The HTM connects human motivation and desire. *Ethical sentimentalism* (ES) is a family of views unified by a conviction that ethical judgments should be analyzed in terms of human emotional responses.[29] ES implies that emotion, as much as reasoning, has a role to play in moral judgment and that blaming someone, finding something morally valuable, and regarding an action as the right thing to do all involve the exercise of an emotional state. There might be pale analogues of moral judgment lacking emotional response: an insincere Marxist might denounce the ill treatment of the working class while lacking sympathy or fellow feeling for them, which is good reason to doubt their sincerity. But emotions and genuine moral judgment simply cannot be pried apart, according to this Humean thesis.

Orwell's sympathy with ES is most obvious in an unpublished piece, "New Words":

> All likes and dislikes, all aesthetic feelings, *all notions of right and wrong* (aesthetic and moral considerations are in any case inextricable) *spring from feelings which are generally admitted to be subtler than words.* (XII: 129, emphasis added)

The assertion that all notions of right and wrong spring from feelings is pretty close to the sentimentalist's contention that

---

[29] For a comprehensive discussion of views variously understood as sentimentalist, see Antti Kauppinen, "Moral Sentimentalism," *Stanford Encyclopedia of Philosophy* (Winter 2018 edition), edited by Edward N. Zalta, https://plato.stanford.edu/archives/win2018/entries/moral-sentimentalism/.

all moral judgments depend on emotion, and Orwell's actual moralizing frequently invoked such feelings: in the introduction to the Ukrainian edition of *Animal Farm*, he explained that he was led to socialism out of his "disgust with the way the poorer section of the industrial workers were oppressed and neglected" (VIII: 110); a different account of his conversion is offered in *The Road to Wigan Pier*, when he explained that he had "a bad conscience" after his time serving an oppressive empire and "was conscious of an immense weight of guilt that I had got to expiate" (V: 138); in *Homage to Catalonia*, the bombastic "when I see an actual flesh-and-blood worker in conflict with his natural enemy, the policeman, I do not have to ask myself which side I am on" (VI: 104) made sympathy for the oppressed and hatred of oppressors the source of Orwell's loyalties; he later suggested that the best way to garner support against Fascism was to appeal to our natural sentiments of sympathy and hatred for tyranny (V: 202).

Without acknowledging it by name, some of Orwell's commentators hint that he endorsed ES: we are told that his work is marked by "an indignant repudiation of the warped and miserable lives [that] has been emotional and not rational" and that "he has set himself against the majority, because he has felt the horrors of oppression and exploitation, not (at any rate not primarily) because he has reasoned about them";[30] he joined the fight against Spanish fascists "not for political reasons, but, as in all his subsequent acts, from an innate feeling that it was the only thing he could do";[31] *The Road to Wigan Pier*, apparently, is "an essay in human sympathy";[32] Orwell had a "natural sympathy for the defeated"[33] and his is "a portrait of a man in whom limitless moral sympathy and outright

[30] Geoffrey Gorer, reprinted in *George Orwell: The Critical Heritage*, edited by Jeffrey Meyers (London: Routledge and Kegan Paul, 1975), p. 121.

[31] George Mayberry, reprinted in *George Orwell: The Critical Heritage*, edited by Jeffrey Meyers (London: Routledge and Kegan Paul, 1975), p. 142.

[32] Taylor, *Orwell: The Life*, p. 181.

[33] See *Orwell Remembered*, edited by Audrey Coppard and Bernard Crick (London: Ariel Books, 1984), p. 206.

physical disgust are uneasily contending";[34] "It was the feeling of resentment that first made him think in revolutionary terms";[35] his socialism is "emotional" and not "scientific" (V: 225); and so forth. My suggestion that Orwell is sympathetic with ES should be no surprise.

That said, some readers might hesitate. ES is often associated with a noncognitivist tradition in metaethics that denies that moral judgments are truth-apt. If moral judgments are nothing more than expressions of emotions or feelings, then morality might seem like an entirely subjective matter, while Orwell, who feared "that the very concept of objective truth is fading out of the world" (XIII: 504) and thought that totalitarianism "attacks the concept of objective truth" (XVI: 89), seems to understand morality as an objective matter. Could Orwell really endorse ES?

Three points about Orwell's metaethics should be made. First, Orwell's appeals to objective truth are more complicated than sometimes allowed. True, he praises the English because "such concepts as justice, liberty and objective truth are still believed in" but adds that "They may be illusions, but they are very powerful illusions" (XII: 397), a remark more suggestive of pragmatism or fictionalism than full-blooded moral realism. But suppose that Orwell is committed to the existence of widespread objective moral truths. Talk of objective moral truth, and this is the second point, is not necessarily closed to philosophers in the Humean tradition. Various contemporary philosophers have worked hard to develop metaethical theories that are broadly Humean yet consistent with talk of moral truth and objectivity, including moral expressivists who think that moral sentences are devices for expressing our approval of moral norms that permit the thing in question[36] and quasi-realists who

---

[34] Ibid., p. 110.

[35] George Woodcock, "George Orwell: 19th Century Liberal," reprinted in *George Orwell: The Critical Heritage*, edited by Jeffrey Meyers (London: Routledge and Kegan Paul, 1975), p. 237.

[36] Allan Gibbard, *Wise Choices, Apt Feelings: A Theory of Moral Judgment* (Cambridge, MA: Harvard University Press, 1990).

deny various metaphysical and epistemological theses often associated with moral realism while insisting on their right to talk about truth if only in a deflationary sense.[37] But suppose their efforts are doomed to fail. It remains possible, and this is the third point, that the Humean tradition is consistent with mind-*dependent* versions of moral realism even if it is inconsistent with mind-independent versions where moral truths are independent of what anyone thinks or feels about them. Perhaps there are moral propositions that are true in a nondeflationary sense but whose truth is a function of what human beings actually think and feel. For example, our capacity for sympathy might track reliably something objectively bad for human beings and incline us to act and feel in constitutive ways.[38] If so, then sympathy, a sentiment, can both generate motivation in the way that desires and subjective feelings do and give rise to truth-apt judgments about what is to be done. Here too, success is an open question, but contemporary metaethics has ample conceptual space to house Orwell's Humean sympathies and talk of objective truth.

Orwell's Humean sympathies do not exhaust his apparent sympathies with British philosophy. He also appears sympathetic with a conception of personal identity popularized by John Locke, or so I argue in the next section.

Orwell on Personal Identity

Questions like "Who am I?" and "Can I change?" run throughout Orwell's work.[39] They are present enough that Richard Rees asked,

[37] Simon Blackburn, *Ruling Passions* (Oxford: Oxford University Press, 1998).

[38] Peter Railton, "Sentimentalism and Realism in Epistemology and Ethics," in *Ethical Sentimentalism: New Perspectives*, edited by Remy Debes and Karsten R. Stueber (Cambridge: Cambridge University Press, 2017), pp. 107–132.

[39] Robert Colls, *George Orwell: English Rebel* (Oxford: Oxford University Press, 2013), p. 41.

"What, indeed, did Orwell mean—what does anybody mean—by personal immortality? Who, or what, is the 'person'? And can anyone really desire or conceive of the possibility of becoming an immortal person?"[40] Orwell had some answers. "Western civilization," he explained in a 1944 AIP column, "was founded partly on the belief in individual immortality" and our intellectual forebears thought that "Life on earth . . . was simply a short period of preparation for an infinitely more important life beyond the grave." However, he thought, "belief in survival after death—the individual survival of John Smith, still conscious of himself as John Smith—is enormously less widespread than it was" (XVI: 112). The independent clause of the previous sentence should grab the attention of no small number of philosophers as it all but paraphrases the influential conception of personal identity defended by John Locke, a philosopher Orwell references explicitly exactly once.[41]

Orwell and Locke on Personal Identity

In his *An Essay Concerning Human Understanding*, Locke explains that a person just is "a thinking intelligent Being, that has reason and reflection, and can consider itself as itself, the same thinking thing in different times and places," adding that personal identity consists in "the sameness of rational Being: and as far as this consciousness can be extended backwards to any past action or thought, so far reaches the Identity of that *person*; it is the same *self* now it was then and 'tis by the same *self* with this present one that now reflects on it, that that action was done."[42] It is famously difficult to articulate just

[40] Rees, *Fugitive from the Camp of Victory*, p. 126.

[41] The one entry to Locke in the index to the twenty-volume *The Complete Works of George Orwell* directs to Orwell's observation that "What is true in science for Newton and Locke is no longer true for Professors Blackett or Bernal" (XVIII: 433).

[42] John Locke, *An Essay Concerning Human Understanding*, abridged and edited by Kenneth Winkler (Indianapolis: Hackett, 1996), p. 138.

what Locke thinks consciousness is, but it seems to involve, first, a mental state inseparable from an act of perception by means of which we are aware of ourselves as perceiving, and second, the on-going self we are aware of in these conscious states.[43] Later, Locke offers the following:

> [I]f the same *Socrates* waking and sleeping do not partake of the same *consciousness*, *Socrates* waking and sleeping is not the same Person. And to punish *Socrates* waking, for what sleeping *Socrates* thought, and waking Socrates was never conscious of, would be no more of Right, than to punish one twin for what his brother-twin did, whereof he knew nothing, because their outsides were so like, that they could not be distinguished; for such twins have been seen.[44]

On Locke's conception, the Etonian who went to Burma in 1927 and responded to the name "Eric Blair" is the same person as the author of *Animal Farm* who responded to the name "George Orwell" just because the consciousness of the one can be extended backward to that of the other who conceives of himself as the first fellow and has over a period of decades.

Locke's influence is detectable in Orwell's fiction too. In *A Clergyman's Daughter*, after Dorothy loses her memory and wakes up in London, she indulges in some philosophical reflection:

> It was only now, after becoming aware of most of the things about her, that she became aware of herself. Hitherto she had been as it were a pair of eyes with a receptive but purely impersonal brain behind them. But now, with a curious little shock, she discovered her separate and unique existence; she could feel herself existing;

[43] Shelley Weinberg, *Consciousness in Locke* (Oxford: Oxford University Press, 2016), p. 153.
[44] Locke, *An Essay Concerning Human Understanding*, p. 144.

it was as though something within her were exclaiming "I am I!"
Also, in some way she knew that this "I" had existed and been
the same from remote periods in the past, though it was a past of
which she had no remembrance. (III: 86)

The Cartesian exclamation "I am I!" isn't much of a starting point
for Dorothy who has no "remembrance . . . not the dimmest notion
of who she was" (III: 86). A bit later, she wonders:

Was this the life to which she had been bred—this life of wan-
dering empty-bellied all day and shivering at night under drip-
ping trees? Had it been like this even in the blank past? Where
had she come from? Who was she? No answer came, and they
were on the road at dawn. (III: 106)

On Locke's conception, whoever woke up in London is not iden-
tical to Dorothy just because that person is not psychologically
continuous with Dorothy: their consciousness cannot be extended
backward to any past action or thought that reaches the identity of
Dorothy, at least not until Dorothy's memories come flooding back.

More Than Memories

While personal identity, for Locke, involves a person who considers
themself as the same thinking thing in different times and places,
neither Locke nor anyone else thinks that it requires two people to
have exactly the same memories to be the same person over time
since, as Orwell explains, "one's memories of any period must necessarily weaken as one moves away from it" and "One is constantly
learning new facts, and old ones have to drop out to make way for
them" (XIX: 359). And since the semantic borders of "consciousness" are fuzzy, it is far from clear why personal identity should consist only in continuity of memory. Whatever Locke says, a broadly

Lockean conception of personal identity locates personal identity in continuity of various psychological states, including but not limited to a person's values, such that a radical change to a person's psychological states is sufficient to disrupt psychological continuity and personal identity. This Lockean thesis is evident in *A Clergyman's Daughter* as well. The person who woke up in London suspects that "she was no longer the same person that she had been an hour ago" once she begins to recall what she had forgotten, adding that "Within her and without, everything was changed. It was as though a bubble in her brain had burst, setting free thoughts, feelings, fears of which she had forgotten the existence" (III: 126). She, the person, changes when lost thoughts are recalled, including various feelings and fears in addition to her memories.

Orwell also invokes considerations about personal identity in *Keep the Aspidistra Flying*, when Gordon, having come into a bit of money, mumbles to himself:

> It was queer how different you felt with all that money in your pocket. Not opulent, merely, but reassured, revivified, reborn. He felt a different person from what he had been yesterday. He *was* a different person. (IV: 171)

Could Gordon *literally* be a different person? A Lockean conception can allow that he was. If Gordon-with-money lacks the serious opposition to money and bourgeois culture that was so central to the character of Gordon-without-money, the two might be so psychologically discontinuous that they are not well regarded as the same person and Gordon can be understood literally. If we do not take Gordon literally—if we deny that he was a different person—that is presumably because we don't think that Gordon-with-money has changed all that much.

Orwell is not always consistent in his reflections on personal identity. In *The Lion and the Unicorn*, he asked, "what have you in common with the child of five whose photograph your mother keeps on the mantelpiece?" answering "Nothing, except that you happen to be the same person" (XII: 393). His answer is puzzling: if you have nothing in common with the child in the photograph, then you are entirely psychologically discontinuous with that child and a Lockean conception cannot explain the supposed identity. This line aside, Orwell is plausibly read as a Lockean who locates survival and personal identity in psychological continuity, broadly understood. It is this sympathy, paired with Orwell's Humean sympathies, that explains why he found the major problem of his time so vexing and the humanist's dilemma so difficult to solve.

On the Intractability of the Major Problem

In "Can Socialists Be Happy?," a 1943 column published in *Tribune* (and written under still another pseudonym, "John Freeman"), Orwell revealed the surprising objective of socialism. Somewhat dispiritingly, he explained that "the real objective of Socialism is not happiness," but something more abstract:

> The real objective of Socialism is human brotherhood. This is widely felt to be the case, though it is not usually said, or not said loudly enough. Men use up their lives in heart-breaking political struggles, or get themselves killed in civil wars, or tortured in the secret prisons of the Gestapo, not in order to establish some central-heated, air-conditioned, strip-lighted Paradise, but because they want a world in which human beings love one another instead of swindling and murdering one another. (XVI: 42–43)

Again, Orwell thought that there was a solution to the major problem of his time, that Marxism—again, democratic Socialism— could play the role previously played by belief in personal immortality and check our darker impulses. Still, he thought, potential converts to socialism *"will have to be persuaded and by methods*

that imply an understanding of his viewpoint" (V: 197); not just
any methods of persuasion will do, and some are bound to frustrate the cause and prove an obstacle to securing feelings of human
brotherhood and thus to cracking the humanist's dilemma. In this
section, I explain why the major problem seemed so intractable
to Orwell: its intractability is a function of the all but unavoidable
difficulties plaguing attempts to realize the objectives of socialism.

Windows, Class Sentiments, and Other Obstacles

In "Why I Write," Orwell famously declared that "Good prose is like
a window pane" (XVIII: 320), but in *The Road to Wigan Pier*, after
noting that class differences make "real intimacy impossible," he
laments that:

> Whichever way you turn this curse of class-difference confronts
> you like a wall of stone. Or rather it is not so much like a stone
> wall as the plate-glass pane of an aquarium; it is so easy to pretend
> that it isn't there, and so impossible to get through. (V: 145)

However clear, windows *literally obstruct* direct interaction with
and perception of what is on their other side and can seduce us into
forgetting this, a fact that should be remembered when reflecting
on Orwell's celebrated reference to clear windowpanes. For now,
I note the analogy: clear windows and class differences are both
easily ignored even as they obstruct. What of it?

The English class system was of great concern to Orwell. In
Homage to Catalonia, he recorded his thrill to find himself in an
environment where "The ordinary class division of society had
disappeared to an extent that is almost unthinkable in the money-
tainted air of England" (VI: 83)—that is, "the most class-ridden
country under the sun" (XII: 400). But while English class-division
is widespread so are patriotic sentiments and "Patriotism is usually

stronger than class-hatred" (XII: 398). Orwell repeatedly appealed to patriotism "out of a desire to found something stable, a basis for political morality, a myth—a substitute, in short, for religion."[45] By appealing to the sentiments already possessed by the English, Orwell thought, Socialists could popularize socialism *and* develop the human brotherhood he thought was constitutive of socialism's real objective: no need to introduce new sentiments, the pervasive English ones will work just fine. He hoped to work English patriotism against class animosity, to use some sensibilities to counteract others, and thereby popularize democratic Socialism and solve the major problem.

It is admittedly not clear how appealing to English patriotism will help secure human brotherhood generally. Orwell lamented that "the working class in England and in France have absolutely no feeling of solidarity with the coloured working class" (XI: 260), yet remained optimistic that "if you alter 'England' to whatever you prefer, you can see that it expresses one of the main motives of human conduct. . . . A very slight increase of consciousness, and their sense of loyalty could be transferred to humanity itself" (XII: 126). But at least two more problems await Orwell's strategy to solve the major problem. First, if English patriotism can be exploited by Socialists, it can be exploited by more nefarious agents too, including Fascists who Orwell thought had more successfully appealed to patriotic sentiments (V: 199). Second, even if patriotism is usually stronger than class-hatred, it might not be stronger than other sentiments constitutive of class identity. Orwell knew full well just how much of an obstacle some sentiments constitutive of class identity could be. One lesson from *The Road to Wigan Pier* is that "Political conversion . . . does not give a man the cultural attributes of another class, nor does any glib intellectual acceptance

---

[45] David L. Kubal, *Outside the Whale: George Orwell's Art and Politics* (Notre Dame: University of Notre Dame Press, 1972), p. 33.

of the desirability of a classless society."[46] Here again, his own case is suggestive.

In *The Road to Wigan Pier*, Orwell identified as bourgeois albeit a "down at heel" member (V: 43) born into "the lower-upper-middle class" (V: 113). He also explained that he found "it is almost impossible for me to think of myself as anything but a member of the bourgeoisie" (V: 209), an assessment worth taking literally. Chapter VIII documents the habits, traditions, attitudes, and feelings that yield "the chasmic, impassable quality of class distinctions" (V: 120), including the prejudice about the working class taught to him at a young age that "*The lower classes smell*" (V: 119). Orwell acknowledged that popularizing socialism requires abandoning such bourgeois sentiments that constituted "an impassable barrier" and explained in the very next paragraph that "you cannot have an affection for a man whose breath stinks—habitually stinks, I mean" (V: 119). But he also insisted that cooperation between classes "will not happen if their social prejudices"—that is, those of the bourgeoisie—"which in some of them are at least as strong as any economic consideration, are needlessly irritated" (V: 212). Orwell often sounds skeptical that this is possible: altering his "bourgeois identity" was "beyond my power" (V: 213), he thought. And in reply to his own question "is it ever possible to be really intimate with the working class?," Orwell explained, "I do not think it is possible" (V: 106), and some readers take him seriously.[47]

It is not at all clear why altering sentiments constitutive of class identity is impossible even if we lack rational control over them.

---

[46] Woodcock, *The Crystal Society*, p. 161.

[47] "So he became a thinking socialist and against 'class,' but like intellectual socialists in general he did not really mean it, *could not really mean it*, because to be against 'class' and all that was to be against oneself, and that was not possible, not honestly possible anyway": Robert Colls, *George Orwell: English Rebel* (Oxford: Oxford University Press, 2013), p. 193; he was "acutely conscious of his own unalterably different class identity": Zwerdling, *Orwell and the Left*, p. 119.

The real problem, I submit, is not that altering is impossible, but that it would come at a cost that Orwell and his fellow bourgeoise were unwilling to pay.

Breaking Persons and Class Breaking

Again, popularizing democratic Socialism called for appealing to sentiments already possessed by the English middle-class, just the sort of thing a sentimentalist would say. So why was Orwell so skeptical of success? He explained in this salient passage:

> For to get outside the class-racket I have got to suppress not merely my private snobbishness, but most of my other tastes and prejudices as well. I have got to alter myself so completely that at the end *I should hardly be recognizable as the same person.* What is involved is not merely the amelioration of working-class conditions, nor an avoidance of the more stupid forms of snobbery, but a complete abandonment of the upper-class and middle-class attitude to life. (V: 150, emphasis added)

Orwell is clear that almost everything that would interest a Lockean for purposes of assessing personal identity over time has its origins in his bourgeois sentiments: "nearly everything I think and do is a result of class-distinctions," including "All my notions—notions of good and evil, of pleasant and unpleasant, of funny and serious, of ugly and beautiful" (V: 149). Those sentiments are constitutive of his class identity, constitutive of who he is, and, apparently, beyond his power to alter: in response to those who would bully him about his bourgeois identity, Orwell explained that "you are telling me either that I am inherently useless or that I ought to alter myself in some way that is beyond my power," adding "I cannot proletarianise my accent or certain of my tastes and beliefs, and I would not if I could" (V: 213). And there lies the problem.

It cannot be understated how often Orwell links talk of revising bourgeois sentiments with talk of death, a point that deserves emphasis: he noted that "the manners and traditions learned by each class in childhood are not only very different but—and this is the essential point—generally persist from birth to death" (V: 208); he explained that "our proletarian brothers . . . are not asking for our greetings, they are asking us to commit suicide"; he insisted that "it is fatal to pretend to drop" one's snobbishness "before you are really ready to do so" (V: 156); he was at pains to clarify that "The fact that has got to be faced is that to abolish class-distinctions *means abolishing a part of yourself*" (V: 149, emphasis added). If he was being hyperbolic, he was hyperbolic repeatedly. But, on a Lockean conception of personal identity, he should probably be taken seriously. If his self-conception and values are all closely tied to bourgeois sentiments then a serious change to those sentiments should disrupt the psychological continuity Lockeans think is necessary for personal identity over time. So understood, dramatic changes to bourgeois values really would result in the death of a person and the birth of an altogether new one possessed of a very different consciousness.

We can now understand why Orwell thought that the supposed decay of belief in personal immortality was the major problem of his time and why he found it so intractable: it is because his sympathies with different aspects of British philosophy are in serious tension. On the one hand, we can solve the major problem of his day only if we seriously revise bourgeois sentiments. That is the upshot of his Humean moral psychology. But seriously revising bourgeois sentiments precludes the psychological continuity necessary for personal identity over time. That is the upshot of his Lockean conception of personal identity. So, solving the major problem of his day looks possible only if Orwell and his fellow bourgeoise are able and willing to change in deeply profound ways, *to become altogether different people*. One can perhaps understand if they were neither able nor willing: in a very real sense, Orwell thought, they were being asked to fall on their swords.

The Major Problem's Major Problem

Is all this too dramatic? Probably. If radical changes to a person's values can be fatal to personal identity, no sensible Lockean thinks that psychological continuity is disrupted if only *some* of a person's values change; it surely does persist if enough of a person's *other* values are retained. While Orwell suggested that *all* his normative notions are bourgeois, he surely overstated things: his commitment to democratic Socialism wasn't bourgeois, nor was his humanism discussed in Chapter 2, his commitment to common decency discussed in Chapter 5, his egalitarianism discussed in Chapter 6, and still more. Perhaps the self-conception of some of the bourgeoisie is exhausted by their normative notions constitutive of their class identity, but Orwell is not one of them and neither are most of us.

Why does Orwell blow things out of proportion here? Probably because he knew, as Michael Walzer suggests, "It is never a good idea for the left to set itself in stark opposition to the values of ordinary people."[48] Keep in mind that the editor of *The Road to Wigan Pier* chided him for being "a frightful snob" who struggled with "the compulsion to conform to the mental habits of his class" (V: 221). Perhaps Orwell issued some self-effacement to disarm readers suspicious of him. Perhaps he thought that the Eton-educated members of the lower-upper-middle class should show they can take a joke; that would be the sort of strategy that an advocate of ES

[48] Michael Walzer, "George Orwell's England," in *George Orwell*, edited by Graham Holderness, Bryan Loughrey, and Nahem Yousaf (New York: St. Martin's Press, 1988), p. 188.

might commend. If we don't have rational control over our desires and sentiments, including trust, we cannot will them into existence. Our self-conceptions often generate feelings of partisanship and hostility that do not cohere well with those feelings Orwell thought crucial to our survival. But what is needed is not heroic self-sacrifice but better propaganda that plays upon shared sentiments. Recall that, in "Why I Write," Orwell explained that "I have been forced into becoming a sort of pamphleteer (XVIII: 319). Since Orwell felt compelled to popularize socialism to solve the major problem of his time, then, given that the cultivation of the needed sentiments is largely not a rational process, it is no surprise that he felt that he needed to become one. Orwell's conscription into service as a pamphleteer flowed from his commitment to solving the major problem of his time but also from his Humean moral psychology.

Conclusion

Disagreement among the left about how best to organize has not vanished. We are told that "mobilization around non-class issues does not reinforce the causal force of class as a determinant of individual behavior,"[49] and some contemporary socialists call for abandoning identity politics and recommitting to principles of Marxism and the class struggle,[50] a call that asks some to alter their political sympathies in ways at odds with their self-identity: someone whose self-conception is most informed by their sexual orientation or race may struggle to prioritize their class identity while keeping a sense of who they are, just as someone whose self-conception is most informed by their class identity may

[49] Adam Przeworski, *Capitalism and Social Democracy* (Cambridge: Cambridge University Press, 1986), p. 106.

[50] See, for example, the 2019 statement from Class Unity, a caucus within the Democratic Socialists of America: https://classunity.org/. Note that the first asserted shared principle states: "Class politics, not identity politics."

struggle to sympathize with those who would prioritize differently. These are not exactly the matters that concerned Orwell, but they do suggest that the major problem of his time still wants for solving, that those desires and sentiments that motivate us cannot easily be revised in ways that lack consequences for our personal identities even if revising them is necessary to bring about justice. The major problem of Orwell's time is our problem too.

Hope is not lost. Some psychologists who research normative disagreement purport to have identified the psychological and neurobiological origins of our persistent tribal disagreements and have expressed hope that common ground can be found.[51] Some organizations have offered concrete proposals to restore civility in politics along with "the ability to disagree productively with others, respecting their sincerity and decency."[52] The call for returning decency to politics is notable given Orwell's interest in it. I worry that while it is of fundamental importance to Orwell, decency, as he understands it, is simply not up for the task that he assigns it. I explain why in Chapter 5.

[51] See, for example, Jonathan Haidt, *The Righteous Mind: Why Good People Are Divided by Politics and Religion* (New York: Vintage, 2012).
[52] https://www.civilpolitics.org/.

5

Orwellian Decency

It is easy to get the sense that ethics isn't that complicated for Orwell, no more so when we are told that "Morally speaking, the world for Orwell seemed like a reasonably simple place" demanding only that "People should be treated decently and should have the opportunity to live a decent life."[1] Decency is clearly a central concept in Orwell's ethics. He affirmed in *Homage to Catalonia* that "if you had asked me what I was fighting *for*" that "I should have answered: 'Common decency'" (VI: 188). And if combat left him "with memories that are mostly evil,"[2] he emerged "with not less but more belief in the decency of human beings" (VI: 186); he affirmed more than once that human nature is "fairly decent" (XVI: 297; XVIII: 62). In *The Road to Wigan Pier*, he repeatedly tied the concept of decency to democratic Socialism, explaining that "the only possible course for any decent person . . . is to work for the establishment of Socialism" (V: 204), that "Socialism is compatible with common decency" (V: 214), and that "Socialism means justice and common decency" (V: 164–165). The centrality of decency to Orwell's ethics has often been noticed by his readers. "Decency," the term, is "Orwell's highest praise,"[3] a "key Orwell phrase,"[4] a "significant Orwellian

---

[1] Craig L. Carr, *Orwell, Politics, and Power* (New York: Continuum Books, 2010), p. 18.

[2] However prone Orwell was to using "decency" frequently, he was about as prone as using "evil": see Richard Rees, *George Orwell: Fugitive from the Camp of Victory* (Carbondale: Southern Illinois University Press, 1962), p. 33. That said, I am inclined to read Orwell as something of an evil-skeptic. See my "Orwell's Evil-Scepticism," *George Orwell Studies*, Vol. 4, No. 2 (2020), pp. 64–77.

[3] Robert A. Lee, *Orwell's Fiction* (Notre Dame: Notre Dame University Press, 1969), p. 64.

[4] D. J. Taylor, *Orwell: A Life* (New York: Henry Holt and Company, 2003), p. 212.

George Orwell. Peter Brian Barry, Oxford University Press. © Oxford University Press 2023.
DOI: 10.1093/oso/9780197627402.003.0005

word,"[5] one of the "key words . . . in Orwell's writing,[6] a "key word in Orwell's ethical code,"[7] his favorite word,[8] his favorite phrase,[9] one that he "frequently employs . . . as a positive value-judgment,"[10] and "probably the best word to describe Orwell's ideal."[11] Decency is "fundamental to Orwell's moral view,"[12] a "specific recurring theme of his work,"[13] a "characteristic"[14] and a "intense concern"[15] that "characterizes all his writings,"[16] "a key feature of his secular morality"[17] and "the central morality on which we should focus in Orwell's writings."[18] His belief in decency is "foundational,"[19] and "his whole philosophy of life was built out of his unshakable belief" in it.[20] Decency is "a prerequisite for all other values"[21] and "the

---

[5] Alan Sandison, *The Last Man in Europe: An Essay on George Orwell* (New York: Harper and Row, 1974), p. 96.

[6] Stephen Ingle, *Orwell Reconsidered* (New York, Routledge, 2020), p. 112.

[7] William Stenihoff, *George Orwell and the Origins of 1984* (Ann Arbor: University of Michigan Press), p. 36.

[8] John Atkins, *George Orwell: A Literary and Biographical Study* (New York: Frederick Ungar, 1954), p. 23; Robert Colls, *George Orwell: English Rebel* (Oxford: Oxford University Press, 2013), p. 67.

[9] Valerie Myers, *George Orwell* (New York: St. Martin's Press, 1991), p. 3; Sant Singh Bal, *George Orwell: The Ethical Imagination* (New Delhi: Arnold-Heinemann, 1981), p. 24.

[10] David Ramsay Steele, *Orwell Your Orwell: A Worldview on the Slab* (London: Bloomsbury, 2020), p. 14.

[11] George Kateb, "The Road to 1984," *Political Science Quarterly*, Vol. 81, No. 4 (1966), p. 571.

[12] Kristian Williams, *Between the Bullet and the Lie: Essays on Orwell* (Chico, CA: AK Press, 2017), p. 77.

[13] Bernard Crick, *Orwell: A Life* (Boston: Little, Brown, 1980), p. xvii.

[14] Peter Marks, *George Orwell the Essayist: Literature, Politics, and the Making of Periodical Culture* (New York: Continuum, 2011), p. 19.

[15] Jeffrey Meyers, *Orwell: Life and Art* (Champaign: University of Illinois Press, 2010), p. 90.

[16] Sant Singh Bal, *George Orwell: The Ethical Imagination* (New Delhi: Arnold-Heinemann, 1981), p. 24

[17] Gordon Bowker, *Inside George Orwell: A Biography* (London: Palgrave Macmillan, 2003), p. 179.

[18] Harold K. Bush Jr., "Beating Back the Monsters: George Orwell and the Morality of Fiction," *Christianity and Literature*, Vol. 42, No. 2 (Winter 1993), p. 340.

[19] Anthony Stewart, *Orwell, Doubleness and Decency* (London: Routledge, 2003), p. 32.

[20] Christopher Hollis, *A Study of George Orwell: The Man and His Works* (Delaware: Racehorse Publishing, 2017), p. 203.

[21] David Dwan, *Liberty, Equality, and Humbug* (Oxford: Oxford University Press, 2018), p. 20.

"common element in all George Orwell's writing."[22] It was an "important . . . concept for Orwell,"[23] an "extraordinarily important" one[24] that "his work is dedicated to defining,"[25] "his secular faith."[26]

The importance of decency to Orwell might elude those familiar only with *Animal Farm* and *Nineteen Eighty-Four*: 'decency', the word, is absent in the former and limited in the latter to a passing reference to an old man's "decent dark suit" (IX: 34). Yet decency is present even in these works: Old Major's speech to the animals includes the rhetorical question "Is it because this land of ours is so poor that it cannot afford a decent life to those who dwell on it?" (VIII: 3) and Orwell's proposed preface to *Animal Farm* refers to decency twice (VIII: 101 and 108). Those who knew him well insisted that even in the last months of his life, "Orwell believed in the old Liberal principles of the value of truth and ordinary decency" and that "these principles demanded a democratic socialist structure of society" (XIX: 136). His concern for decency seemingly never wavered.

Still, some commentators complain that Orwell used the term "disingenuously,"[27] "uncritically"[28] and that "never analyzes the concept or even defines the word."[29] We are told that decency is an "ultimately indefinable moral standard,"[30] "extremely unhelpful,"[31] and "too vague to mean much."[32] Oddly, Orwell might endorse

[22] Atkins, *George Orwell: A Literary and Biographical Study*, p. 1.

[23] Peter Davison, *George Orwell: A Literary Life* (New York: St. Martin's Press, 1996), p. 81.

[24] George Woodcock, *The Crystal Spirit: A Study of George Orwell* (New York: Shocken, 1984), 49.

[25] David Wykes, *A Preface to Orwell* (New York: Longman, 1987), p. 49.

[26] John Rodden, *The Politics of Literary Reputation: The Making and Claiming of "St. George" Orwell* (Oxford: Oxford University Press, 1989), p. 364.

[27] Sandison, *The Last Man in Europe*, p. 97.

[28] Beatrix Campbell, *Wigan Pier Revisited: Poverty and Politics in the Eighties* (London: Virago Press, 1984), p. 220.

[29] Williams, *Between the Bullet and the Lie*, p. 77.

[30] Alan Sandison, *The Last Man in Europe: An Essay on George Orwell* (New York: Barnes and Noble Books, 1974), p. 96.

[31] Atkins, *George Orwell: A Literary and Biographical Study*, p. 21.

[32] Dorian Lynskey, *The Ministry of Truth: The Biography of George Orwell's "1984"* (New York: Doubleday, 2019), p. xvii.

these critiques, say, when he complains that Charles Dickens's moral criticism amounts to "an enormous platitude: If men would behave decently the world would be decent" (XII: 23), which is not necessarily a bad thing: "we live in a world of platitudes" (XIII: 160), apparently. And Orwell clearly thought that Dickens was onto something: " 'Behave decently,' " he thought, "is not necessarily so shallow as it sounds" (XII: 54).[33]

In this chapter, I do not dispute that decency is important and pervasive in Orwell's thought, but I worry that getting clearer about what Orwellian decency is reveals that it cannot do the job he wants it to do: Orwellian decency, whatever it is, is *not* a moral virtue. In what follows, I first reflect on the concept of decency. Then, I try to unify Orwell's various remarks to articulate a conception of Orwellian decency that reveals what it is for persons and actions to be decent. Finally, I explain why Orwellian decency is not a moral virtue.

Decency, the Very Thing

In Camus's *The Plague*, the noble Dr. Bernard Rieux explains that "there's no question of heroism in all this. It's a matter of common decency. That's an idea which may make some people smile, but the only means of fighting a plague is—common decency." When asked "What do you mean by 'common decency'?," Rieux answers, "I don't know what it means for other people. But in my case I know that it consists in doing my job."[34] While disagreement about what decency *is* should be expected, agreement at least at an abstract level remains possible. In this section, I consider the very concept of decency; I articulate Orwell's preferred conception of it later.

[33] See Robert Colls, *George Orwell: English Rebel* (Oxford: Oxford University Press, 2013), p. 164.

[34] Albert Camus, *The Plague* (New York: Vintage Books, 1975), p. 163.

The Concept of Decency

I have already distinguished the concept of decency and a conception of it. What's the difference? Early in *A Theory of Justice*, John Rawls explains that:

> Men disagree about which principles should define the basic terms of their association. Yet we may still say, despite this disagreement, that they each have a conception of justice. That is, they understand the need for, and are prepared to affirm, a characteristic set of principles for assigning basic rights and duties and for determining what they take to be the proper distribution of the burdens and benefits of social cooperation. Thus it seems natural to think of the concept of justice as distinct from the various conceptions of justice and as being specified by the role which these different ... conceptions have in common.[35]

I follow Rawls in supposing that concepts and conceptions are distinguished at their level of abstraction, that conceptions are more detailed and particularized, and that serious disagreement at the level of a conception is consistent with agreement at the level of a concept. At the level of a concept, we should expect "agreement ... around discrete ideas that are uncontroversially employed in all interpretations," while at the level of a conception "the controversy latent in this abstraction is identified and taken up."[36] Pervasive disagreements about what decency *is* are tolerable at the level of conceptions and do not rule out the possibility of agreement at some abstract level, ensuring that we are all talking about the same thing when we talk about decency.

[35] John Rawls, *A Theory of Justice* (Cambridge, MA: Harvard University Press, 1999), p. 5.
[36] Ronald Dworkin, *Law's Empire* (Cambridge, MA: Harvard University Press, 1986), pp. 70–71.

I begin by listing some ideas about decency that are uncontroversially employed in all interpretations. First, note that while "decent" can be used to evaluate any number of things—meals, cups of tea, health, weather, society, and more—its "core meaning" demands that the thing in question is "*adequate* or *minimally* acceptable as good."[37] "Decency" and "decent" are terms of praise but *faint* praise: to speak, as Orwell does, of decent food (I: 209), decent tailors (V: 115), decent clothes (VI: 142), and decent weather (XIX: 123) is not to suggest that these are great examples of such things, only that they are "a cut above the shamefully inadequate."[38] So, that which is not even decent, not even adequate or minimally good, must be pretty poor. For example, when Gordon gives up on decency in *Keep the Aspidistra Flying*, he speaks not of hitting bottom but going underground:

Before, he had fought against the money-code, and yet he had clung to his wretched remnant of decency. But now it was precisely from decency that he wanted to escape. He wanted to go down, deep down, into some world where decency no longer mattered; to cut the strings of his self-respect, to submerge himself—to *sink*, as Rosemary had said. It was all bound up in his mind with the thought of being *under ground*. He liked to think about the lost people, the under-ground people: tramps, beggars, criminals, prostitutes. It is a good world that they inhabit, down there in their frowzy kips and spikes. He liked to think that beneath the world of money there is that great sluttish underworld where failure and success have no meaning; a sort of kingdom of ghosts where all are equal. (IV: 227)

[37] Cheshire Calhoun, "Common Decency," in *Setting the Moral Compass: Essays by Women Philosophers*, edited by Cheshire Calhoun (Oxford: Oxford University Press, 2004), p. 130. Calhoun offers one of the few extended discussions of decency, the concept, and I follow her discussion closely.
[38] Ibid.

When Ravelston tries to convince him to find a decent place, Gordon explains "But I don't want a decent place. I want an indecent place. This one, for instance" (IV: 237), referencing the squalor that is his boarding room.

Philosophers have largely endorsed this core idea about decency. For example, Rawls understands a "decent" society as a nonliberal one that secures human rights for all its members, imposes *bona fide* moral duties and obligations on all persons within its territory, and is administered by legal officials guided by a common good idea of justice.[39] But the merely decent society does "not treat its members equally" and fails to "treat its own members . . . justly as free and equal citizens."[40] As such, decent societies merit some praise, but not as much as their liberal counterparts.[41] Avishai Margalit understands a just society, as one whose institutions do not act in ways that give citizens sound reasons to consider themselves humiliated.[42] But a society that refrains from humiliating its subjects may fall well short of other standards of political morality. Susan Wolf explains that "the goal of a theory of duty is to set minimal standards of moral decency," to "tell people who wish to be decent that they must *at least* do this much."[43] But accepting

[39] John Rawls, *The Law of Peoples* (Cambridge, MA: Harvard University Press, 2002), pp. 64–66.

[40] Ibid, p. 83.

[41] One gets the sense that Rawls doesn't quite want to affirm this comparative conclusion:

> If it should be asked whether liberal societies are, morally speaking, better than decent hierarchical and other decent societies, and therefore whether the world would be a better place if all societies were required to be liberal, those holding a liberal view might think that the answer would be yes. But this answer overlooks the great importance of maintaining mutual respect between peoples and of each people maintaining its self-respect, not lapsing into contempt for the other, on one side, and bitterness and resentment, on the other. (Ibid., p. 122)

[42] Avishai Margalit, *The Decent Society*, translated by Naomi Goldblum (Cambridge, MA: Harvard University Press, 1996), pp. 10–11. Margalit supposes that a decent society is best illustrated by Orwell's socialism (5–6).

[43] Susan Wolf, "Above and below the Line of Duty," *Philosophical Topics*, Vol. 14 (1986), pp. 139–140.

such standards is consistent with being unwilling to do much more than that.

A second thought: particular conceptions of decency vary according to local norms, customs, traditions, and other social parameters since "forms of . . . decency emerge only from within a social practice of morality"[44] and it is "Local conventions [that] supply the substantive content."[45] What counts as a decent tip varies given local custom, just as what counts as obscene is a function of contemporary community standards.[46] What is not up for debate is that decency is adequacy or minimal goodness even if what counts as decent varies according to local standards.

A final thought: decency implies minimal goodness, but not necessarily minimal *moral* goodness. Note that the OED entry for "Decency" lists "Appropriateness or fitness to the circumstances or requirements of the case; fitness, seemliness, propriety." Appropriateness and fittingness will vary as requirements vary, including nonmoral requirements: a decent wall is decent if it supports a structure, but the walls of a concentration camp are not morally good because they are decent walls.[47] If 'decent' and 'decency' connote faint praise they are not necessarily terms of moral praise, and that should be reflected in our understanding of the concept of decency.

The above thoughts help to articulate what decency is if only at a fairly abstract level. We might also wonder what it is to *be* decent, to

[44] Calhoun, "Common Decency," p. 134.

[45] Ibid., p. 138.

[46] At least, this is the case in American Constitutional law. In *Miller v. California*, the Supreme Court of the United States ruled that to determine that material is obscene, a trier of fact must determine whether the average person, applying contemporary community standards, would find that the work, taken as a whole, appeals to the prurient interest; depicts or describes, in a patently offensive way, sexual conduct specifically defined by the applicable state law; and lacks serious literary, artistic, political, or scientific value.

[47] Orwell observed that "The first thing that we demand of a wall is that it shall stand up. If it stands up it is a good wall. . . . And yet even the best wall in the world deserves to be pulled down if it surrounds a concentration camp" (XVI: 238).

be a decent person or action, for example. In the next section, I try
to explain while still operating at a fairly abstract level.

Decent People and Decent Actions

We might say *of* someone that they are decent, acted decently, and
so forth. Orwell did: he thought Valenti, a French waiter, "was a decent sort" (I: 66) in virtue of finding some occasion to treat Orwell
as an equal, that his hosts in England's North, the Searles, had "more
natural decency" (X: 421) than most, that the police constable who
aided Henry Miller during an unfortunate incident in England was
"The only person who showed a spark of decency in the whole af-
fair" (XVIII: 117–118), and so forth. So what is it for a person to be
decent? What is it for their actions to be decent?

Reflecting on Ebenezer Scrooge, a man lacking even decency,
suggests some important lessons. Importantly, Scrooge does what
morality minimally requires of him given that there is no one he
clearly *wrongs*: he violates no one's rights when he refuses to pay
employees who choose not to work on Christmas Day, declines his
nephew's invitation to a holiday celebration, demands his debtors
pay on time, and refrains from giving to charity. If Scrooge remains
*in*decent while fulfilling his minimal moral duties, then doing what
morality minimally requires cannot be the whole of decency; a decent person must have some tendency to go beyond her minimal
moral duties absent any requirement to do so.[48] She must have
some tendency to perform acts that are "not motivationally taxing"
and cost her "very little," whose moral value tends to be "obvious
and unambiguous," and are "not open to standard excuses" since
they are minimally taxing and costly.[49] A decent person must be a

---

[48] Calhoun, "Common Decency," pp. 128–130.
[49] Ibid., p. 137.

"minimally decent Samaritan," someone prone to helping others in need but not at great cost to himself.[50]

We can now say something about the concept of the decent person and decent action. Decent actions are those actions that are obviously and unambiguously of moral value, but not open to standard excuses since they are minimally motivationally taxing and costly. Their omission, unless justified by a nonstandard excuse, will make reactive attitudes like resentment and shame appropriate. They include familiar pleasantries, mercies, kindnesses, and favors. Being decent involves a propensity to perform decent actions, although a *merely* decent person who tends to perform decent actions lacks a tendency to perform other morally valuable actions, presumably because they are too taxing or costly. But a bit more should be said about the (merely) decent person. First, while the (merely) decent person is motivated to perform decent actions, they are not so strongly motivated that they are rightly regarded as exceptionally courageous or heroic lest they merit more praise than a minimally good or adequate person deserves. Second, decent personhood is not merely a matter of motivation: decent persons must also tend to feel something like shame or embarrassment when they fail to act decently. Someone who consistently shrugs off her failure to do what is decent is too weirdly like Scrooge, who lacks compunction in response to his indecency to count as even minimally good. Decent personhood thus involves both motivational and affective tendencies.

Conceptions of decent personhood and action will vary at the margins, but all should employ the criteria articulated above. Orwell says enough about each such that it is possible to articulate a conception of Orwellian decency that identifies what makes a person decent. I try to articulate this conception below.

---

[50] Judith Jarvis Thomson, "A Defense of Abortion," *Philosophy and Public Affairs*, Vol. 1, No. 1 (1971), p. 62.

Orwellian Decency

Again, decent people have some tendency to perform decent actions—acts that are obviously and unambiguously of moral value, but minimally motivationally taxing and costly and not open to standard excuses—and to feel something like shame when they don't. In this section, I identify what else Orwell understood to be necessary to be decent, but I first complain about a common though misleading characterization of Orwellian decency.

What Orwellian Decency Is Not

Orwellian decency is often thought to have origins in Christian thought and morality, that decency is Orwell's "religionless Christianity,"[51] that it is the "essence of the Christian morality, stripped of its superstitious and ascetic qualities,"[52] and "Christian morality minus the dogma."[53] We are told that he "emphasizes what might be called the basic Judeo-Christian civic virtues of decency and justice"[54] and that, for Orwell, "the traditional Judeo-Christian moral values could be equated with decency."[55] But the supposed relationship between Orwellian decency and Christianity is not affirmed by Orwell himself, although he is partially to blame for the confusion.

In *A Clergyman's Daughter*, Dorothy opines that "all that happens in church, however absurd and cowardly its supposed purpose may be, there is something—it is hard to define, but something of decency, of spiritual comeliness—that is not easily found in the

[51] Peter Davison, *George Orwell: A Literary Life* (London: Palgrave, 1996), p. 65.
[52] Williams, *Between the Bullet and the Lie*, p. 78.
[53] Bowker, *Inside George Orwell*, p. 421.
[54] Stephen Ingle, *George Orwell: A Political Life* (Manchester: Manchester University Press, 1993), p. 54.
[55] Ibid., p. 111.

world outside" (III: 249). In *Coming Up for Air*, George Bowling speaks of "a decent God-fearing shopkeeper's daughter and a decent God-fearing shopkeeper's wife" (VII: 111) along with "decent God-fearing women who cook Yorkshire puddings and apple dumplings (VI: 112). And in his review of Charlie Chaplin's "The Great Dictator," Orwell praises "the common man" who "everywhere, under the surface . . . sticks obstinately to the beliefs that he derives from the Christian culture" (XII: 315). No wonder some readers find their own religious convictions in Orwell.[56]

Yet in a hostile book review, Orwell declares explicitly that "it will not do to suggest . . . that a decent society can only be founded on Christian principles," adding, "Are we to say that a decent society cannot be established in Asia?" (XVI: 106). In a letter to Humphry House, he explains that "the vast majority of people believe in" common decency "without the need to tie it up with any transcendental belief" (XII: 140). At times, he suggests that decency and religiosity pair badly in the work of his contemporaries: Graham Greene's work, for example, yields "the fairly sinister suggestion that all ordinary human decency is of no value and that any one sin is no worse than any other sin" (XIX: 405) and the "essential theme" of Evelyn Waugh's *Brideshead Revisited* "is the collision between ordinary decent behavior and the Catholic concept of good and evil" (XIX: 417). None of this suggests that religiosity has much to do with being a decent person. So what did Orwell think made someone decent?

All Kinds of Decency

Orwell, a philosophical outsider, is never as precise as a professional philosopher might like, but there are some trends in his discussion

---

[56] Christopher Hollis intimates that much of what Orwell says "is only tenable if a man has a destiny beyond this world": Hollis, *A Study of George Orwell*, p. 40.

of decency that are suggestive. I identify some such trends and try to unify them into a coherent conception.

Decency and Cleanliness

In "Looking Back on the Spanish War," Orwell explained that "the central issue of the war was the attempt of people like this to win the decent life which they knew to be their birthright" (XIII: 509) and wondered whether they will "be allowed to live the decent, fully human life which is now technically achievable" (XIII: 510). What does a decent, fully human life require? Orwell explains that "the indispensable minimum without which human life cannot be lived at all" includes "Enough to eat, freedom from the haunting terror of unemployment, the knowledge that your children will get a fair chance, a bath once a day, clean linen reasonably often, a roof that doesn't leak, and short enough working hours to leave you with a little energy when the day is done (XIII: 509). Food and shelter are obvious requisites of a minimally good life consistent with the objective list theory of well-being I attribute to him in Chapter 2. Daily baths and clean linen might seem less obvious candidates, but, for Orwell, "Decency means cleanliness, in the most literal sense,"[57] and he prizes it repeatedly. The link between cleanliness and decency is especially obvious in *The Road to Wigan Pier*, where he explained that "even in the middle of them [that is, Northern industrial districts] there is still room for patches of cleanness and decency" (V: 16) but lamented that "Some people hardly seem to realize that such things as decent houses exist and look on bugs and leaking roofs as acts of God" (V: 47). He recorded "a great variation in the houses I visited. . . . Some were as decent as one could possibly expect in the circumstances, some were so appalling that I have no hope of describing them accurately" (V: 54) and that "with, say, six children in a three-roomed house it is quite impossible to keep

---

[57] Martin Green, "British Decency," *Kenyon Review*, Vol. 21, No. 4 (1959), p. 518.

anything decent" (V: 55). And, oddly, he insisted that "When all is said and done, the most important thing is that people shall live in decent houses and not in pigsties" (V: 67).

Why is living in decent homes *the* most important thing? And what does cleanliness have to do with being decent? Evildoers do not become morally better people having washed up. The connection is suggested by Orwell's observation that clean homes promise "A place where the children can breathe clean air" (V: 67) and "start life with better chances" (V: 65), one that implies more than the obvious fact that children raised in clean homes will grow up healthier. He often noted a connection between cleanliness and social status, most infamously when he recalled being taught as a bourgeois youth the "four frightful words . . . *The lower classes smell*," which he thought contained "the real secret of class distinctions in the West" (V: 119). Similarly, in *Keep the Aspidistra Flying*, he had Gordon note the social consequences of indecency:

> Don't you see that a man's whole personality is bound up with his income? His personality *is* his income. How can you be attractive to a girl when you've got no money? You can't wear decent clothes, you can't take her out to dinner or to the theatre or away for weekends, you can't carry a cheery, interesting atmosphere about with you. And it's rot to say that kind of thing doesn't matter. It does. (IV: 104–105)

Importantly, Gordon does not only bemoan how others treated him given he is moth-eaten; he also has little regard for *himself*. Writing about his own experience "Dressed in a tramp's clothes," Orwell recalled that "it is very difficult, at any rate for the first day, not to feel that you are genuinely degraded" (I: 130). Yet "with a smart-looking house," people will "improve in self-respect and cleanliness" (V: 65).

It is now easier to explain why cleanliness is relevant to Orwellian decency and why he sought "to create a world in which every man's right to self-respect would be jealously preserved."[58] Orwell was not alone in thinking that there is a connection between self-respect and justice. The British left commonly objected to economic inequality on the grounds that it fostered unacceptable hierarchies of social status that undermined both social solidarity and self-respect.[59] But Rawls explained why the left should care about self-respect in the first place. Rawls famously counted self-respect as "perhaps the most important primary good" since "Without it nothing may seem worth doing, or if some things have value for us, we lack the will to strive for them."[60] If nothing seems worth doing, then someone lacking self-respect will have little motivation to do even what is minimally morally good, and will therefore lack what is needed to be merely decent. So, if cleanliness helps secure self-respect, then cleanliness is instrumentally morally valuable and relevant to decent personhood. Orwell's obsession with cleanliness is not a remnant of bourgeois morality but reflects his recognition that even mere decency is unlikely without self-respect.

Decency as Common Decency

Orwell often speaks, not of decency, but *common* decency, the decency of common people. He praised Charles Dickens for his ability to "express in a comic, simplified and therefore memorable form the native decency of the common man" (XII: 55) and Charlie Chaplain for his ability to highlight "the ineradicable belief in decency that exists in the heart of ordinary people" (XII: 315). He expressed his frustration that "The mass of the people never get the chance to bring their innate decency into the control of affairs" (XI: 163). In a book review of *The Freedom of the Streets*, he identified Jack Common's voice as "the authentic voice of the

---

[58] Woodcock, *The Crystal Spirit*, p. 29.
[59] Ben Jackson, *Equality and the British Left: A Study in Political Thought, 1900–1964* (Manchester: Manchester University Pres, 2007), p. 25.
[60] Rawls, *A Theory of Justice*, p. 386.

ordinary man, the man who might infuse a new decency into the control of affairs if only he could get there" (XI: 163). By contrast, the elites in control lacked what the common people have, especially "the modern intelligentsia" who cannot "see that human society must be based on common decency" (XII: 141) and those "cranks, doctrinaires, parlour Bolsheviks" who made socialism unpalatable and ought be replaced "by better brains and more common decency" (V: 204–205).

Is there anything to be said about common decency besides the fact that it is, well, common? Orwell seems to regard it as a fraud when he references the "illusion . . . of the Western conception of honesty and common decency" (XII: 381), although it gets a better hearing in *Keep the Aspidistra Flying*:

> Our civilization is founded on greed and fear, but in the lives of common men the greed and fear are mysteriously transmuted into something nobler. The lower-middle-class people in there, behind their lace curtains, with their children and their scraps of furniture and their aspidistras—they lived by the money-code, sure enough, and yet they contrived to keep their decency. The money-code as they interpreted it was not merely cynical and hoggish. They had their standards, their inviolable points of honour. They "kept themselves respectable"—kept the aspidistra flying. (IV: 267)

The common people are praised faintly here: whatever their flaws, at least they kept themselves respectable. But common decency, insofar as it involves having standards and points of honor, is also of moral value: a capacity to keep one's standards suggests a degree of self-mastery necessary to be autonomous and an apt candidate for even faint praise. And if common decency is, again, common then there is some hope that the mass of people are capable of Orwellian decency, a somewhat optimistic assessment of things that Orwell shares.

Decency as Privation

In a vindictive moment, Orwell explained that "it is not easy to crash your way into the literary intelligentsia if you happen to be a decent human being" (V: 152), presumably because Orwellian decency precludes the flaws of the Oxbridge clique. Often, he suggested that decency has a *privative* aspect, that Orwellian decency demands the *absence* of certain character flaws.

Some of Orwell's talk of decency is not to be understood literally. In *Down and Out in Paris and London*, Boris, Orwell's white Russian compatriot, complains that "the Jew with whom he lived" lacks "the decency to be ashamed of it" (I: 34)—that is, being Jewish. Bozo, one of the memorable vagabonds Orwell tramped with, "considered himself in a class above the ordinary run of beggars, who, he said, were an abject lot, without even the decency to be ungrateful" (I: 168). In *The Road to Wigan Pier*, he recalled the ostentatious upper-class thought that " 'They don't *want* to work, that's all it is!' which you heard at every decent tea-table five years ago" (V: 80). In "Such, Such Were the Joys," he recalled Flip, his tormentor at St. Cyprian's, asking "I don't think it's awfully decent of you to behave like this, is it?" (XIX: 364). But his most obvious ironic uses of 'decency' are on display in *Burmese Days*. The dislikable love interest, Elizabeth, is of the mind that "decent people—people who shot grouse, went to Ascot, yachted at Cowes—were not brainy" and "didn't go in for this nonsense of writing books and fooling with paintbrushes; and all these Highbrow ideas—Socialism and all that" (II: 96). She thinks that to "turn deliberately away from all that was good and decent"—say, by living as an unemployed artist—is "shameful, degrading, evil" (II: 96). The detestable Ellis chides Flory for failing to rise to the defense of Ellis's racist proposal to keep the Burmese out of their private club: "My God," Ellis complains, "I should have thought in a case like this, when it's a question of keeping those black, stinking swine out of the only place where we can enjoy ourselves, you'd have the decency to back me up" (II: 21).

If Orwell was ironic in these instances, we have a template for constructing his conception of decent personhood: that which is commended by the ironic use of "decency" is inconsistent with Orwellian decency. So, if decency as Boris and Ellis understand it demands contempt for others because of their religion or race or ethnicity, Orwellian decency opposes it. If decency as Bozo understands it demands ingratitude and thanklessness in reaction to generosity, Orwellian decency precludes those sentiments. If decency as Elizabeth understands it is prim and snobbish, Orwellian decency excludes privilege, hostility, and materialism. And so forth.

Orwell's praise for decent people often makes the privative aspect of decency clear. He applauded an American journalist for having "an essentially decent cast of mind," and added that "he does not sink to the hypocrisy of pretending that any country which can be bought or bullied into the British orbit instantly becomes a democracy" (XI: 359). Bertrand Russell has "an essentially decent intellect" partly because he was "so consistently impervious to the fashionable bunk of the moment" (XI: 312), unlike Soviet sympathizers who altered their convictions when needed: "Don't imagine that for years on end you can make yourself the boot-licking propagandist of the Soviet regime, or any other regime, and then suddenly return to mental decency," he warned, adding the nasty "Once a whore, always a whore" (XVI: 365). Decent people will at least lack ordinary vices like hypocrisy and dishonesty, and Orwellian decency precludes them.

Orwellian decency also precludes the power fetish. Orwell regarded Dickens as a decent man partly because "he sees the stupidity of violence . . . he belongs to a cautious urban class which does not deal in socks on the jaw, even in theory" (XII: 43). Other real-life persons are praised for abandoning "the Machiavellianism practiced by politicians and defended by intellectuals" (XV: 202), and for seeing decency and "power politics" as opposed to one another (XV: 213). The "moral code of the English boys' papers" that so interested Orwell too "is a decent one" insofar as "Crime and dishonesty are never held up to admiration, [and] there is none of the cynicism and corruption of the American gangster story" (XII: 70). In *Coming Up for Air*, Bowling identifies "the decent people" with "the people who *don't* want to go round smashing faces in with spanners" (VII: 168). Orwellian decency and the power fetish are also clearly opposed when he explained that "Either power politics must yield to common decency, or the world must go spiraling down into a nightmare of which we can already catch some glimpses" (XV: 213).

Orwellian decency precludes many serious character flaws, but it does not follow that decent people must be just, gracious, kind, or otherwise possessed of especially valuable moral virtues, which seems right if decency demands no more than minimal goodness. Still, we have some idea of what Orwellian decency is by understanding what it is *not*.

Orwellian Decency, All Told

Orwellian decency requires certain valuable character traits and precludes others. It involves self-respect and self-mastery which will tend to ensure that the decent person will have some tendency to stick to their convictions and act decently. It ensures that the decent person lacks tribal hostilities based on religion, ethnicity, race, and nationality and familiar vices like snobbishness and hypocrisy, among others. Above all, Orwellian decency is inconsistent with admiration of gratuitous violence and other vulgar displays of power such that even merely decent people will be less prone to suffering from extreme moral vices, like cruelty and malice.[61] Orwellian decency is not an unattractive condition of character and goes some way to articulating what a minimally good person is like.

---

[61] For discussion of extreme vice, see my *Evil and Moral Psychology* (New York: Routledge, 2013), pp. 59–61.

But that is its weakness: since Orwellian decency only illuminates what a minimally good person is like, it is not a moral ideal worthy of widespread admiration nor the sort of thing that one should try to construct a moral theory out of. It also falls well short of a moral virtue. I explain why in the next section.

An Assault on Orwellian Decency

Orwell knew that "the sense of decency" varied as a function of time and people (X: 118), country and age (X: 389). He was especially interested in English decency, affirming that "England is the only European country where internal politics are conducted in a more or less humane and decent manner" (XVI: 222) and that "Tolerance and decency are deeply rooted in England" (VIII: 106). Jeffrey Meyers suggests that Orwellian decency involves a "synthesis of the traditional English virtues"[62] and equates "the distillation of English virtues" with "the concept of decency."[63] Other commentators regard Orwell as interested in working-class life because "They are the last repository of that indeterminate but solid virtue, decency,"[64] and that "Orwell located his virtues of decency and 'comeliness' in the era in which . . . he grew up in"[65]. My complaint is not with understanding Orwellian decency as *English* virtue, but with understanding it as English *virtue*. 'Decency' may be a term of praise, but Orwellian decency is simply not a moral virtue and, for a series of reasons, I am deeply suspicious that it can play the sort of foundational role in Orwell's ethics that he and others seem to attribute to it.

[62] Meyers, *Orwell: Life and Art*, p. 90.
[63] Ibid., p. 100.
[64] Edward M. Thomas, *Orwell* (London: Oliver and Boyd, 1965), p. 57.
[65] Averil Gardner, *George Orwell* (New York: Twayne Publishers, 1995), p. 13

Problem #1: Decency Lacks Aspects of Moral Virtue

Again, decency amounts to adequacy, to minimal goodness, and not much more. On a familiar Aristotelian account, virtue is a kind of *excellence* and moral virtues are excellences of character, character traits that make their possessor morally admirable and praiseworthy. Orwellian decency is therefore wrongly classified as an excellence and thus lacks aspects of moral virtue. Why all this should be so requires some explanation.

There is undoubtedly a connection between moral virtue and right action, but the moral virtues are not merely dispositions to act in certain constitutive ways. Generosity is not merely a matter of giving to those in need when the chance arises; an opportunistic miser can do *that*. The generous person also tends to give to those in need with feelings of joy while believing that the poor are deserving of help, unlike the miser who gives with contempt and believes that the poor are scum. Virtues, as I understand them, are complicated multitrack dispositions that dispose their agents to perform certain actions in certain circumstances with constitutive beliefs and feelings, and so forth.

Orwellian decency is less clearly a multitrack dispositional state—at least, it is less clearly the right sort of multitrack dispositional state. I have allowed that Orwellian decency involves a disposition to do what is morally required and a tendency to feel something like shame when failing to do so, but it does not follow that it demands any tendency to act with constitutive beliefs or feelings. Someone prone to acting decently—say, to giving up their seat on the bus—may do so hesitantly or with cool emotional regard, knowing that this is the sort of thing she is expected to do. And while a decent person may feel shame or regret if she doesn't give up her seat, it doesn't follow she feels anything if she does. It is in any case hard to see how the merely decent could enjoy the rich emotional life that the virtuous know well: someone who felt much affection for her fellow human beings and greatly pained at their suffering would also surely be disposed to do much, much more than the minimum and thus would be wildly undescribed as being simply decent.

Orwellian decency lacks other aspects of moral virtue too. Some character traits are best regarded as natural virtues, the kind of character traits we have by luck and not as a result of any effort on our part. Just as some people are naturally inclined to be strong and fast and smart, some people are naturally inclined to be helpful and brave and caring. But, again, on an Aristotelian account, moral virtues require practice and habituation to become moral virtues; no one is simply born generous or brave or just. Orwell sometimes talks as if Orwellian decency is more akin to a natural virtue, say, when he allows that "human beings are by nature fairly decent" (XVI: 297) and that "human nature is fairly decent to start with" (XVIII: 62). If Orwellian decency is natural to human beings, then it differs from moral virtue in another relevant respect.

For various reasons, Orwellian decency lacks certain aspects of moral virtue and is thus not well regarded as one. There are more problems.

Problem #2: Decency Is Consistent with Serious Moral Flaws

Moral virtue is incompatible with serious moral flaws. Orwellian decency is compatible with them. So, Orwellian decency is not moral virtue. Why think that Orwellian decency is compatible with serious moral flaws? Orwell says as much.

Orwell praised the Catalan working class in *Homage to Catalonia* and recalled being "struck by their essential decency; above all, their straightforwardness and generosity" (VI: 10), a case in which decency and moral virtue—namely, generosity—are in harmony. But too often, Orwell described some persons as decent and flawed. Some of these flaws he noted were trivial: he explained that

Jonathan Swift "couldn't see what the simplest person sees, that life is worth living and human beings, even if they're dirty and ridiculous, are mostly decent" (XIV: 161), noted that public schools were still "turning out the brave, stupid, fairly decent mediocrities who are still their typical products today" (XII: 261), and allowed that there are people who are "decent, but their minds have stopped" (VII: 168), suggesting that various intellectual deficiencies are compatible with decency. But he also suggested that decency is consistent with more serious moral flaws. For example, in a "Notes on the Way" column, Orwell recalled a clumsy coolie receiving a terrific kick from a police sergeant and noted the "ordinary, decent, middling people . . . watching the scene with no emotion whatever except a mild approval" (XII: 121). Their decency did not preclude racially inspired *schadenfreude*. *Keep the Aspidistra Flying* suggests that decency is consistent with a deficiency of compassion if it is "quite impossible to explain to any rich person, even to anyone so decent as Ravelston, the essential bloodiness of poverty" (IV: 101). Apparently, someone can be *evil* and decent, given a passage in *The English People* in which Orwell referenced a caricature of "The hanging judge, that evil old man in scarlet robe and horsehair wig . . . a symbol of the strange mixture of reality and illusion, democracy and privilege, humbug and decency" (XII: 397).[66]

The best reason to think that Orwellian decency is consistent with serious moral flaws is that Orwell clearly thought that decent people can be exploited by seriously unjust causes. Why fascists attract the loyalty of ordinary people is a pressing question,[67] and Orwell was worried that the decent might be charmed: he

[66] Muggeridge's diary includes a 12 January 1950 entry recording Orwell being "quite convinced that judges like Lord Goddard want to keep hanging because they derive erotic satisfaction from it." See *Orwell Remembered*, edited by Audrey Coppard and Bernard Crick (New York: Ariel Facts on File, 1984), p. 269.

[67] For a philosopher's take on such matters, see Jason Stanley, *How Fascism Works: The Politics of Us and Them* (New York: Random House, 2018). Stanley's suggestion that fascists "rewrite the population's shared understanding of reality" (xvi) and take for granted that "Reasoning does not attract, emotion does" (55) are Orwellian themes.

explained that it is "the most urgent need of the next few years is to capture those normal decent ones before Fascism plays its trump card" (V: 202) and that "Fascism has a great appeal for certain simple and decent people who genuinely want to see justice done to the working class and do not grasp that they are being used as tools by the big capitalists" (XI: 61). Some potential Fascists "dread the prospect of a world of free and equal human beings," but others are simply "people with something to lose" (XIII: 509), including the otherwise decent. And while it is dangerous to understand moral virtue in mythological terms, the genuinely morally virtuous person should have sufficient courage, justice, empathy, and practical wisdom to ensure that she will not be so easily charmed. Those who are prone to exploitation by seriously unjust causes must have some vulnerability that moral virtue tends to preclude. Since the decent are prone to be exploited by them, we have another reason to doubt that Orwellian decency is a moral virtue.

Problem #3: Decency Standards Are Not Moral Standards

Some thoughtful virtue ethicists have made it clear that deontologists are not the only ethicists who can conceive of morality in terms of rules: a morally virtuous person will tend to obey rules that call for her to do what is just and honest and refrain from doing what is unjust and brash, for example.[68] Moral virtue, so understood, involves compliance with adamantly moral standards. Orwellian decency may demand compliance with *some* standards but not necessarily with *moral* standards, another reason to doubt that Orwellian decency is a moral virtue.

---

[68] Rosalind Hursthouse, *On Virtue Ethics* (Oxford: Oxford University Press, 1999), pp. 36–39.

Again, Orwell praises the common people who contrive to keep their decency and "had their standards, their inviolable points of honour." But are those *moral* standards? Often, the standards he appeals to when he praises someone for their decency are dubiously regarded as moral ones. For example, in *Down and Out in Paris and London*, Orwell explains that he will not approach his gentleman friend for money since "it seemed hardly decent to do so yet" (I: 128) having just returned to England. In *Burmese Days*, we are told that while "Everyone was perishing [for a drink] . . . it seemed hardly decent to go down to the Club for drinks immediately after the funeral" (II: 250). In these passages, decency involves compliance with norms governing what is polite or mannerly or otherwise socially expected but not clearly with substantive moral norms. In "Raffles and Miss Blandish," Orwell pointed out that Raffles, the gentleman thief, and his partner-in-crime, Bunny, "are gentlemen, and such standards as they do have are not to be violated" adding that, for them, "Certain things are 'not done'" (XVI: 348). But he also explained that Raffles and Bunny "have no real ethical code," only "certain rules of behaviour which they observe semi-instinctively" (XVI: 348). If the Raffles stories "belong to a time when people had standards," he thought that "they happened to be foolish standards" and that "The line that they draw between good and evil is as senseless as a Polynesian taboo" (XVI: 349). The standards that Raffles embraces—do not abuse hospitality, be chivalrous in sportsmanship, and so forth—are better understood as amoral standards reflective of class position and status, not moral standards.

Orwell had a bit of fun with taboos that specify that certain things "are not done," suggesting that he knew that supposed standards need not be taken all that seriously. In *Keep the Aspidistra Flying*, Gordon fiercely rejects Rosemary's offer to pay for dinner on the grounds that "one can't do that sort of thing. It isn't done" (IV: 131). Rosemary's reply that "You'll be saying it's 'not cricket' in another moment" and "Are we living in the reign of

Queen Victoria?" are supposed to highlight just how silly Gordon is being as he clings to his standards. In "Freedom of the Press," Orwell explained that:

> At any given moment there is an orthodoxy, a body of ideas which it is assumed that all right-thinking people will accept without question. It is not exactly forbidden to say this, that or the other, but it is "not done" to say it, just as in mid-Victorian times it was "not done" to mention trousers in the presence of a lady. Anyone who challenges the prevailing orthodoxy finds himself silenced with surprising effectiveness. A genuinely un-fashionable opinion is almost never given a fair hearing, either in the popular press or in the highbrow periodicals. (VIII: 100)

It is hard to read this passage without coming away with the conclusion that we should not suppose that a standard has ethical content just because it has popular currency. But then it is simply unclear why decency, insofar as it involves having standards, is evidence of moral virtue which demands more.

Some of the standards Orwell recorded as relevant to decency are not simply silly or amoral, but clearly unjust. In a much-discussed passage from *The Road to Wigan Pier*, Orwell expressed his preference for patriarchal working-class standards governing the home:

> In a working-class home . . . you breathe a warm, decent, deeply human atmosphere which it is not so easy to find elsewhere. . . .
> I have often been struck by the peculiar easy completeness, the perfect symmetry as it were, of a working-class interior at its best. Especially on winter evenings after tea, when the fire glows in the open range and dances mirrored in the steel fender, when Father, in shirt-sleeves, sits in the rocking chair at one side of the fire reading the racing finals, and Mother sits on the other with her sewing, and the children are happy with a pennorth of mint

humbugs, and the dog lolls roasting himself on the rag mat—it is a good place to be in, provided that you can be not only in it but sufficiently *of* it to be taken for granted. (V: 108)

In response, Beatrix Campbell rightly criticizes Orwell's "sentimental fallacies about the perfect symmetry of family life"[69] and Daphne Patai suggests that Orwell fetishizes "this patriarchal image" that "allows him to create a myth" of symmetry while ignoring domestic inequality.[70] Orwellian decency is apparently consistent with standards that are not just amoral but ethically dubious.

A final point. I allowed above that keeping one's standards suggests a kind of self-mastery that we often think is valuable. But keeping one's standards merely for the sake of keeping them is foolish. When Gordon is deliberating about continuing his war on the money-god, he observes that "He ought to stand firm. He had made war on money—he ought to stick it out. After all, hitherto he *had* stuck it out, after a fashion" (IV: 258), a fallacious bit of reasoning about sunk costs. While self-mastery is a condition of character worth pursuing, it is a condition of character distinct from virtue. Intuitively, some cases of *inverse akrasia*—that is, cases in which a person acts rightly in virtue of failing to do what they had mistakenly concluded was the right thing to do, all things considered—can reflect a good character or at least a better character than if one maintained self-control and acted badly.[71] If Orwellian decency demands keeping silly or amoral or unjust standards while moral virtue demands abandoning them, we have yet another reason to doubt that Orwellian decency is moral virtue.

[69] Beatrix Campbell, *Wigan Pier Revisited: Poverty and Politics in the 80s* (London: Virago Press, 1984), p. 93.

[70] Daphne Patai, *The Orwell Mystique: A Study in Male Ideology* (Amherst: University of Massachusetts Press, 1984), p. 78.

[71] Nomy Arpaly, *Unprincipled Virtue: An Enquiry into Human Agency* (Oxford: Oxford University Press, 2002).

So What Is Orwellian Decency?

Having said something about the very concept of decency and Orwell's favored conception of it, I conclude that Orwellian decency is not a moral virtue. So what *is* it?

I suggest that Orwellian decency is best understood as a character trait like loyalty. On its face, loyalty seems to be a good thing: we would like our children to be loyal people, we typically respect loyal people because of their loyalty, it can motivate us to do good, and so forth. Yet loyalty is dubiously regarded as a moral virtue since it can conflict with other paramount moral virtues, like justice: loyalty in the service of the wrong cause has little moral value, and misplaced loyalty is evidence of serious vice, say, in the case of those Soviet apologists that Orwell scrapped with who would be better if they were less loyal. That said, loyalty metered by other virtues, moral and intellectual, is a good thing and truly reflects a condition of character we hope our children develop. We want them to be loyal but loyal to the right people and causes, having thought hard about what that might mean, and lacking the convictions of a fanatic.[72] Decency is like loyalty in these respects. We want our children to be decent but not merely so: we want them to be decent *and* to have good politics, good convictions, and good moral sense. Their decency needs to be augmented by moral virtue if it is going to reliably lead to good conduct and just results. A fully virtuous person will be decent, just as she will be loyal, but she is underdescribed as being simply either, and both her decency and loyalty will be grounded in her moral virtue: just as a morally virtuous person is loyal because she has and exercises moral virtues like friendship and care, so the morally virtuous person will be decent because she has and exercises moral virtues like magnanimity (which ensures her self-respect), justice (which ensures that she

---

[72] For discussion, see Simon Keller, *The Limits of Loyalty* (Cambridge: Cambridge University Press, 2007), esp. Chap. 7.

will lack tribal hostilities), and courage (which ensures that she has and keeps to her standards). Still, neither loyalty nor Orwellian decency is per se morally valuable, only if they are derived from moral virtues that are.

Conclusion

In my first book, I closed with the plea offered by Kurt Vonnegut:

> I have had some experiences with love, or I think I have, anyway, although the ones I have liked best could easily be described as "common decency." I treated somebody well for a little while, or maybe even for a tremendously long time, and that person treated me well in turn. Love need not have had anything to do with it. . . . Please—a little less love, and a little more common decency.[73]

As a consequence of reflecting on Orwell, I have come to wonder about the wisdom of Vonnegut's plea. In this chapter, I have reflected on decency itself and tried to articulate Orwell's conception of it. I have also explicated his favored conception of decent personhood, what I call "Orwellian decency." But my purpose has been not simply to explicate Orwellian decency but to criticize it and for several reasons I doubt that Orwellian decency is well understood as a moral virtue. Accordingly, I have real doubts that decency can do the job that Orwell wanted it to do. To the extent that decency is supposed to play a central role in Orwell's ethics, Orwell's ethics might seem imperiled. For example, note that some of his readers have suggested that "He knew, as the democratic socialist must know, that the good society must have its foundation

[73] Kurt Vonnegut, *Slapstick, or, Lonesome No More!* (New York: Dial Press, 2010), p. 3. For my use of Vonnegut's plea, see Peter Brian Barry, *Evil and Moral Psychology* (New York: Routledge, 2013), p. 158.

in a commitment to decency among its members."[74] Others equate Orwell's democratic Socialism with his conception of "common decency."[75] If that's right, then Orwell's favored democratic Socialism too is in big trouble. And if his ethics bottoms out in aphorisms like "People should be treated decently and have the opportunity to live a decent life," Orwell's ethics would be perilously shallow, which is probably a good reason to doubt that Orwellian decency constitutes the nerve of Orwell's ethics.

Still, if Orwellian decency does not constitute the nerve of Orwell's ethics, his talk of decency might tell us what is. In what initially seems like a throwaway line, Orwell affirms that "Either we all live in a decent world, or nobody does" (XV: 33). I call this a throwaway line as it seems dubious: why, exactly, can't some people live in a decent world while others don't? Why does decency for some require decency for all? Perhaps what Orwell is after here is not decency, or at least not decency for its own sake. Ian Slater rightly observes that Orwell's "Calls for . . . 'decency,' for all their vagueness, do signify an intent to improve the quality of life, to move away from inequality wherein privilege takes precedence over ability."[76] Insofar as equality is relational, we cannot speak of equality in isolation of other persons. Perhaps Orwell thinks that we either all live in a decent world or none of us do because he thinks that decency is tied up with equality in some interesting sense and inseparable from it. Perhaps a world lacking in Orwellian decency must be in virtue of that fact an unjust one and unjust because inegalitarian.

Those interested in locating the nerve of Orwell's ethics should not ignore what he says about common decency, but they would do better to look to his egalitarianism, his commitment to equality, to find it. In Chapter 6 I discuss Orwell's egalitarianism, and

---

[74] Norman Dennis and A. H. Halsey, *English Ethical Socialism: Thomas More to R. H. Tawney* (Oxford: Clarendon Press, 1988), p. 121.

[75] Stephen Ingle, *Orwell Reconsidered* (New York: Routledge, 2020), p. 125 and 140.

[76] Ian Slater, *Orwell: The Road to Airstrip One* (New York: W. W. Norton & Company, 1985), p. 87.

in Chapter 8 I contend that his egalitarianism is central to and explains his interest in democratic Socialism. Noting that Orwell is an egalitarian is not exactly an original insight, and many of his readers rightly regard him as one. Still, it is remarkable how little about has been said about what Orwell's egalitarianism *is* especially given how much philosophers have had to say about egalitarianism. Understanding Orwell and his egalitarianism requires some philosophy. I turn to these topics in the next chapter.

6

Orwell's Egalitarianism

Echoing Marx, Orwell explained that "the Western world has been haunted by the idea of freedom and equality" (XII: 55).[1] Orwell was haunted by these ideas too: *Homage to Catalonia* "presents a picture of what a truly egalitarian society might be like,"[2] but equality is also one of the "key concepts" of *Animal Farm*,[3] and *Nineteen Eighty-Four*'s curious appendix notes that "The concept of political equality no longer existed" (IX: 323) during the Party's reign. Bernard Crick rightly identifies egalitarianism as one of the "recurrent themes" in Orwell's work,[4] while other commentators note his egalitarian style of writing,[5] egalitarian linguistic views,[6] the egalitarian spirit that powered his moral angst,[7] his egalitarian instincts,[8] the egalitarianism that informs so much of his work,[9] and his literary taste which grew out of his egalitarianism.[10] Arguably,

[1] Also, when he closes *The Road to Wigan Pier* with "We have nothing to lose but our aitches" (V: 215).

[2] G. Wesley McCullough, *George Orwell: A Reader's Approach* (London: Athena Press, 2002), p. 84. A similar passage opens Stuart White, *Equality* (Malden, MA: Polity, 2007), pp. 1–2.

[3] David Dwan, "Introduction," in George Orwell, *Animal Farm* (Oxford: Oxford University Press, 2021), p. xxiv.

[4] Bernard Crick, *George Orwell: A Life* (Boston: Little, Brown, 1980), p. xvii.

[5] Richard I. Smyer, *Animal Farm: Pastoralism and Politics* (Boston: Twayne, 1988), p. 8.

[6] Whitney French Bolton, *The Language of 1984: Orwell's English and Ours* (Knoxville: University of Tennessee Press, 1984), p. 96.

[7] Craig L. Carr, *Orwell, Politics, and Power* (New York: Continuum, 2010), p. 20.

[8] Christopher Hitchens, *Orwell's Victory* (London: Penguin, 2002), p. 98; Ruth Ann Lief, *Homage to Catalonia: The Prophetic Vision of George Orwell* (Columbus: Ohio University Press, 1969), p. 28.

[9] Alex Woloch, *Or Orwell* (Cambridge: Harvard University Press, 2016), p. 56.

[10] Alex Zwerdling, *Orwell and the Left* (New Haven, CT: Yale University Press, 1974), p. 189.

George Orwell. Peter Brian Barry, Oxford University Press. © Oxford University Press 2023.
DOI: 10.1093/oso/9780197627402.003.0006

"Few writers made a better case for the nobility of equality as an ideal."[11]

While Orwell's egalitarianism is widely acknowledged, some surprisingly basic questions have gone unanswered and largely unasked. True, "Egalitarians believe in equality," but "From there, it gets complicated."[12] For example, egalitarians disagree about the "currency" of egalitarian justice, the dimension or respect in which people should be made more equal.[13] When asked "Equality of what?," some egalitarians might demand equality of wealth or welfare, but philosophers have more typically appealed to resources,[14] opportunity for welfare,[15] access to advantage,[16] capabilities,[17] and still more. How would Orwell answer the question? What should be justly distributed? Who are the proper recipients of those distributions? In what circumstances, if any, can unequal distributions be justified? Does he even conceive of equality in distributive terms? In short, if Orwell is an egalitarian, what *kind* of egalitarian is he?

An explosion of philosophical research into egalitarianism[18] ensures that philosophy can help us to better understand this aspect of Orwell's thought. In this chapter, I first distinguish two especially influential conceptions of egalitarianism: *luck egalitarianism* and *relational egalitarianism*. I then consider some textual

[11] David Dwan, *Liberty, Equality, and Humbug* (Oxford: Oxford University Press, 2018), p. 71.

[12] Peter Stone, "In the Shadow of Rawls: Egalitarianism Today," *Ethical Theory and Moral Practice*, Vol. 25 (2022), p. 157.

[13] Gerald A. Cohen, "On the Currency of Egalitarian Justice," *Ethics*, Vol. 99, No. 4 (1989), p. 906.

[14] Ronald Dworkin, *Sovereign Justice* (Cambridge, MA: Harvard University Press, 2000).

[15] Richard Areneson, "Equality and Equal Opportunity for Welfare," *Philosophical Studies*, Vol. 56, No. 1 (1989), pp. 77–93.

[16] Cohen, "On the Currency of Egalitarian Justice," pp. 906–944.

[17] Amartya Sen, "Equality of What?," in *Tanner Lectures on Human Values*, edited by S. McMurrin (Cambridge: Cambridge University Press, 1980), pp. 197–220.

[18] For a helpful summary of the now 50-plus years of egalitarian thought prompted by the publication of John Rawls's influential *A Theory of Justice*, see Katrina Forrester, *In the Shadow of Justice* (Princeton: Princeton University Press, 2019).

evidence suggesting that Orwell is well understood as a luck egalitarian, and some reasons to question whether he is well understood as one. I then make the case that he is best understood as a relational egalitarian.

Two Kinds of Egalitarianism

Two conceptions of egalitarianism have come to dominate contemporary egalitarian scholarship. According to *luck egalitarianism*, roughly, inequality is bad or unjust when it reflects differences in factors that are beyond the control of the worse off, but perhaps not if it doesn't. According to *relational egalitarianism*, roughly, inequality is bad or unjust when it tends to make it the case that persons do not relate to one another as equals, but perhaps not if allows people to enjoy the same fundamental status, rank, or power. These are rival conceptions, since the former conceives of justice primarily in distributive terms while the latter does not. I summarize each below.

About Luck Egalitarianism

True, "*In its simplest form*, luck egalitarianism asserts that inequalities are just if and only if they are not due to luck,"[19] but the typical luck egalitarian holds that only *some kinds* of bad luck merit compensation. The following works better as an initial statement of luck egalitarianism's commitments:

The concern of distributive justice is to compensate individuals for misfortune. Some people are blessed with good luck, some

---

[19] George Sher, *Equality for Inegalitarians* (Cambridge: Cambridge University Press, 2014), p. 1, emphasis added.

are cursed with bad luck, and it is the responsibility of society—
all of us regarded collectively—to alter the distribution of goods
and evils that arises from the jumble of lotteries that constitutes
human life as we know it. . . . Distributive justice stipulates that
the lucky should transfer some or all of their gains due to luck to
the unlucky.[20]

Much then depends on what it is to be unlucky in a way that calls
for compensation. Ronald Dworkin influentially contrasts *option
luck* and *brute luck* here:

Option luck is a matter of how deliberate and calculated gambles
turn out—whether someone gains or loses through accepting an
isolated risk he or she should have anticipated and might have
declined. Brute luck is a matter of how risks fall out that are not
in that sense deliberate gambles. If I buy a stock on the exchange
that rises, then my option luck is good. If I am hit by a falling me-
teorite whose course could not have been predicted, then my luck
is brute. . . . If someone develops cancer in the course of a normal
life, and there is no particular decision to which we can point as
a gamble risking the disease, then we will say that he has suffered
brute bad luck. But if he smoked cigarettes heavily then we may
prefer to say that he took an unsuccessful gamble.[21]

The distinction that Dworkin gestures at here is a tricky one but
the idea is that bad option luck should be identified, not with the
negative consequence of choices that persons make,[22] but with the
negative consequences of *voluntary* choices.[23] Brute bad luck, by

[20] Richard Areneson, "Rawls, Responsibility, and Distributive Justice," in *Justice,
Political Liberalism, and Utilitarianism: Themes from Harsanyi,* edited by Maurice Salles
and John A. Weymark (Cambridge: Cambridge University Press, 2008), p. 80.

[21] Ronald Dworkin, "What Is Equality? Part 2: Equality of Resources," *Philosophy and
Public Affairs,* Vol. 10, No. 4 (1981), p. 293.

[22] Sher, *Equality for Inegalitarians,* p. 9.

[23] Samuel Scheffler, "What Is Egalitarianism?," in his *Equality and Tradition: Questions
of Value in Moral and Political Theory* (Oxford: Oxford University Press, 2010), p. 176.

contrast, is involuntary disadvantage for which the sufferer cannot be held responsible,[24] has no control over,[25] suffers through no fault of their own,[26] or reflects nothing other than their comparative exercise of responsibility.[27] With Dworkin's distinction in place, the luck egalitarian insists upon two theses: first, that inequality is unjust only if it reflects the differential effects of brute bad luck, and second, that justice demands that the differential effects of brute bad luck should be neutralized through compensation.[28] Luck egalitarianism thus demands fairly substantial and widespread compensation for the unlucky if natural talents, creativity, intelligence, skills, and abilities are widely distributed and mostly the consequence of brute luck: some persons will enjoy good brute luck insofar as they are born with favorable genetics or upbringing, many others will suffer brute bad luck insofar as they get undesirable distributions of such things. It will be hard for the luck egalitarian to resist the conclusion that unjust inequalities abound if even seemingly voluntary choices and actions result from those unfortunate distributions.

Just *why* luck egalitarians should tolerate inequalities that emerge from bad option luck is an interesting question; perhaps respect for autonomy demands both that we tolerate what results from responsible agency and correct for that which frustrates it. If so, then the suggestion that "the primary egalitarian impulse is to extinguish the influence on distribution of both exploitation and brute luck"[29] makes good sense for the luck egalitarian: exploitation, like brute bad luck, is an enemy of autonomy. But respect for autonomy also suggests a very different conception of egalitarianism, one that does not conceive of justice primarily in distributive terms.

---

[24] Cohen, "On the Currency of Egalitarian Justice," p. 908.

[25] White, *Equality*, p. 78.

[26] Larry S. Temkin, *Inequality* (New York: Oxford University Press, 1993), p. 13.

[27] Kasper Lippert-Rasmussen, *Relational Egalitarianism: Living as Equals* (Cambridge: Cambridge University Press, 2018), p. 3.

[28] Iwao Hirose, *Egalitarianism* (New York: Routledge, 2015), p. 45.

[29] Cohen, "On the Currency of Egalitarian Justice," p. 908.

About Relational Egalitarianism

In her own influential discussion, Elizabeth Anderson suggests that while luck egalitarianism has come to dominate egalitarian thought, it has "lost sight of the distinctively political aims of egalitarianism."[30] According to her preferred conception:

> The proper negative aim of egalitarian justice is not to eliminate the impact of brute luck from human affairs, but to end oppression, which by definition is socially imposed. Its proper positive aim is not to ensure that everyone gets what they morally deserve, but to create a community in which people stand in relations of equality to others.[31]

Anderson sees a tight connection between the demands of relational egalitarianism and democracy, a particularly important constituent of a society in which people relate to one another as social equals rather than as inferiors and superiors.[32]

Relational egalitarians tend to be critical of luck egalitarianism insofar as they tend to see our basic commitment to equality as calling for nondomination rather than the equal distribution of some currency; they "are fundamentally concerned with the relationships within which goods are distributed, not only with the distribution of goods themselves."[33] Relational egalitarians may condemn a distribution as unjust but only because it tends to disrupt equal social relations. A large body of research suggests strong associations between high economic inequality and high levels of distrust, crime, and lower average levels of health,[34] all of which

[30] Elizabeth Anderson, "What Is the Point of Equality?," *Ethics*, Vol. 109, No. 2 (January 1999), p. 288.
[31] Ibid., pp. 288–289.
[32] Niko Koldony, "Rule over None II: Social Equality and the Justification of Democracy," *Philosophy and Public Affairs*, Vol. 42, No. 4 (2014), pp. 287–336.
[33] Anderson, "What Is the Point of Equality?," p. 314.
[34] White, *Equality*, p. 158.

are obstacles to effectively accessing the social conditions of one's freedom. So if relational egalitarians think that economic inequality is unjust they need not claim that it is unjust per se, only if and because it yields unequal social relations.

If luck egalitarians must answer the question "Equality of what?," relational egalitarians must answer the question "Equals along what dimensions?" Relating to one another as equals might involve treating each other's interests as equally constraining, giving equal epistemic weight to the testimony of others, acknowledging the equal moral standing of other persons, abandoning aesthetic norms about appearance as morally insignificant, or letting empirical matters be settled solely by the relevant evidence.[35] It is worth keeping in mind just how dynamic social relations can be, that there may be no one social relation relevant to relating as equals. Still, the goal of the relational egalitarian is the elimination of barriers to egalitarian social relations and only tangentially to distributions of goods and resources.

Two Interpretations of Orwell's Egalitarianism

Orwell sometimes expressed sympathy with both egalitarian conceptions, and there are textual reasons to attribute each to him. In this chapter, I consider two different interpretations, each of which implies that Orwell was sympathetic with one or the other conception. On the *luck interpretation*, Orwell is best understood as a luck egalitarian. On the *relational interpretation*, he is best understood as a relational egalitarian. I consider the case for each below.

---

[35] Lippert-Rasmussen, *Relational Egalitarianism*, pp. 63–70.

On the Luck Interpretation

The best argument for the luck interpretation begins by noting how often Orwell talks like a luck egalitarian. In this section, I consider various occasions that he does.

Bad Luck in Paris and London

In his first book, *Down and Out in Paris and London*, the topic of luck is recurrent. Boris, Orwell's white Russian companion, frequently notes the radical contingency in life: "*Ah, mais, mon ami, the ups and downs of life!*," he tells Orwell, adding, "You never know when a stroke of luck is coming" (I: 21–22). Boris reassures Orwell that "The luck always changes" (I: 28) and notes when it changes for the better (I: 30; I: 40; I: 52; I: 104). Orwell records that "the better-class beggars do have runs of luck, when they earn a living wage for weeks at a time" (I: 171), that Parisian waiters mostly "die poor" although some "have long runs of luck occasionally" (I: 76), and that the *plongeur* "Except by a lucky chance . . . has no escape from this life, save into prison" (I: 117). Bad luck is endemic to being down and out since "Mean disasters [that] happen and rob you of your food . . . are part of the process of being hard up" (I: 14) but it is Orwell's discussion of tramps that most clearly supplies evidence for the luck interpretation.

Having ascribed to the English "a strong sense of the sinfulness of poverty" that precludes "deliberately turning parasite" he adds:

> Indeed, if one remembers that a tramp is only an Englishman out of work, forced by law to live as a vagabond, then the tramp monster vanishes. I am not saying, of course, that most tramps are ideal characters; I am only saying that they are ordinary human beings, and that if they are worse off than other people it is the result and not the cause of their way of life. (I: 205)

Tramps, Orwell thinks, are not generally responsible for their miserable state: a tramp tramps "not because he likes it, but for the same reason as a car keeps to the left: because there happens to be a law compelling him to do so" (I: 204). Similarly, in *The Road to Wigan Pier*, Orwell explained that "a fair proportion" of the tramps he encountered "were decent young miners and cotton-workers gazing at their destiny with the same sort of dumb amazement as an animal in a trap" (V: 79). He concluded that "the 'Serve them damned well right' attitude normally taken towards tramps is no fairer than it would be towards cripples or invalids" (I: 205). So, if justice demands compensating cripples and invalids for their brute bad luck, it demands compensating tramps for theirs, since both are the victims of brute bad luck.

Orwell's recollection of Bozo, one of his most memorable tramping companions, also lends support to the luck interpretation. Orwell recorded Bozo's thought that "Being a beggar . . . was not his fault" and that he "refused either to have any compunction about it or to let it trouble him" (I: 168). Bozo assured Orwell that "If you've got any education, it don't matter to you if you're on the road for the rest of your life" and that:

> If you set yourself to it, you can live the same life, rich or poor. You can still keep on with your books and your ideas. You just got to say to yourself, "I'm a free man in *here*" '—he tapped his forehead—and you're all right. (I: 167)

Perhaps Bozo is not suffering, but Orwell knew that Bozo's sound psychological condition was not universally shared among tramps, and he regarded forcing an ignorant man to tramp all day with nothing to do as akin to chaining a dog in a barrel, another "silly piece of cruelty" (I: 200). The typical tramp is thus doubly imperiled by brute bad luck: they are not to be blamed for being tramps, nor for their inability to cope with their fallen state. Orwell concluded that tramps should be compensated—but more on this later—which seems like the conclusion of a luck egalitarian and evidence for the luck interpretation.

Orwell did not suppose that all down and outs are victims of brute bad luck. Speaking of one Henri, he wrote that "Bad luck seemed to have turned him half-witted in a single day" (I: 4). Henri fell in love with a chronically unfaithful woman, stabbed her for her infidelity, went to prison, returned to her intent on marriage, went on a drinking binge after her continued infidelity, returned to jail, and upon his release could only find work in the Parisian sewers. Henri's plight is partly the consequence of brute bad luck—most of us don't choose who we fall in love with—but returning to her, stabbing her, and going on a bender might seem more like risky gambles than bad breaks. Orwell did not say that poor Henri should be left to rot, but neither did he rise to Henri's defense. Orwell's ambivalence about compensating Henri also suggests sympathy with the luck interpretation supposing that it is unclear whether Henri's plight is (too much) the product of bad option luck.

Orwell's discussion of unlucky down and outs supports the luck interpretation, but he hints at more. Above, Bozo noted his education, another resource that tramps typically lack. Orwell knew that education was a resource typically distributed unequally via "accidents of birth," and his critique of English education is still more evidence for the luck interpretation.

A Mere Accident of Birth

In "Boys' Weeklies," Orwell explained that "in England education is mainly a matter of status" (XII: 62) which he found objectionable. In *The Road to Wigan Pier*, he called for "a certain uniformity of education" (V: 175) and in *The Lion and the Unicorn* for "Reform of the educational system along democratic lines" (XII: 422), adding that "our talk of 'defending democracy' is nonsense" so long as it is "a mere accident of birth that decides whether a gifted child shall or shall not get the education it deserves" (XII: 424). (The phrase, "accident of birth," was used in John Stuart Mill's *Autobiography*, a book that Orwell asked Francis Westrope to send to Marrakech in 1939 (XI: 319) and was among Orwell's books at the time of his death in 1950 (XX: 294).[36]) He would return to this theme in a manifesto revised in dialogue with Arthur Koestler and Bertrand Russell, where Orwell identified four "main functions of the State," the first of which is "To guarantee the newborn citizen his equality of chance."[37] Whatever else educational reform demanded, Orwell thought it demanded the "abolition of all hereditary privilege" (XII: 410), the sort of accident of birth that afforded some lucky few with special advantages for no moral reason at all.

Orwell's distaste for affording those of gentle birth the privileges of high-quality education is evidence for the luck interpretation, but his apparent sympathy with meritocracy needs to be addressed. He calls for "abolishing the autonomy of the public schools and the older universities" but also for "flooding them with State-aided pupils chosen simply on the grounds of ability" (XII: 424),[38] a recommendation that should strike the luck egalitarian as misplaced. Only the children of Lake Wobegon are all above average, so if eligibility for placement in desirable schools is determined by assessing

[36] Mill explained that he and Harriet looked forward to a time when "the division of the produce of labour, instead of depending, as in so great a degree it now does, on the accident of birth, will be made by concert on an acknowledged principle of justice." See John Stuart Mill, *Autobiography and Literary Essays* from *Collected Works of John Stuart Mill*, Vol. 1, edited by John M. Robson and Jack Stillinger (New York: Routledge, 1981), p. 239. And in *Chapters on Socialism*, he explained, "No longer enslaved or made dependent by force of law, the great majority are so by force of poverty; they are still chained to a place, to an occupation, and to conformity with the will of an employer and debarred by the accident of birth both from the enjoyments, and from the mental and moral advantages, which others inherit without exertion and independently of desert." See John Stuart Mill, *On Liberty and Other Writings*, edited by Stefan Collini (Cambridge: Cambridge University Press, 2007), p. 227.

[37] As quoted in David Smith, *George Orwell Illustrated* (Chicago: Haymarket Books, 2018), p. 232.

[38] Some Orwellians follow Orwell into this trap, praising him for his commitment to "an egalitarian future" and social democrats who supplied "affordable higher education for everyone with talent": Dennis Glover, *Orwell's Australia: From Cold War to Culture Wars* (Melbourne: Scribe Publications, 2003), pp. 2–3.

ability, only a subset of children will get access. And children's abilities are also largely accidents of birth: some will be born with native talents and faculties, some will not; some will be born into wealthy families capable of providing valuable resources and support, many will go without. It is frankly hard to see how an appeal to option luck could justify inequitable distributions of educational resources with respect to children.[39]

Still, if Orwell's call to reform English education does not fully draw out the consequences of luck egalitarianism, his proposal is nonetheless some evidence for the luck interpretation and, paired with what Orwell says about tramps, we have good reason to find it plausible. Still, I have come to think that the luck interpretation is mistaken. I explain why in the next section.

Against the Luck Interpretation

If some textual evidence supports the luck interpretation, still more speaks against it. Interestingly, on several occasions, Orwell's work illustrates objections to luck egalitarianism raised by contemporary critics.

Option Luck and Moralism

The compatibility of free will and moral responsibility with determinism has been debated largely in terms of retributive justice, not distributive justice,[40] but there are exceptions. Samuel Scheffler finds luck egalitarianism dubious because he thinks that the crucial distinction between brute and option luck must "tacitly . . .

---

[39] Shlomi Segall, *Equality and Opportunity* (Oxford: Oxford University Press, 2013), p. 148.

[40] Saul Smilansky, *Free Will and Illusion* (Oxford: Oxford University Press, 2000), p. 108.

depend on a form of metaphysical libertarianism" about free will that he rejects.[41] I am uncertain luck egalitarians must depend on metaphysically loaded views about free will to make the crucial distinction, although getting it right may leave us "up to our necks in the free will problem."[42] But, more plausibly, Scheffler complains that luck egalitarianism can foster an unattractive moralism, one that entails that persons forfeit all claims to assistance having made foolish choices, risky gambles, or whatever.[43] Orwell, for his part, illustrated why the luck egalitarian should worry about this objection.

Early in his tramping, Orwell worried that his Etonian accent would give him away (I: 130). At a spike outside of Lower Binfield, the feared Tramp Major heard his schoolboy accent, leading to the following exchange:

"Then you are a gentleman?"

"I suppose so."

He gave me another long look. "Well, that's bloody bad luck, guv'nor," he said; "bloody bad luck that is." And thereafter he treated me with unfair favouritism, and even with a kind of defence. He did not search me, and in the bathroom he actually gave me a clean towel to myself—an unheard-of luxury. So powerful is the word "gentleman" in an old soldier's ear. (I: 197)

Orwell, who was "much luckier than the others," was also awarded a plum job in the workhouse where he feasted as other tramps were

[41] Samuel Scheffler, "What Is Egalitarianism?," in his *Equality and Tradition: Questions of Value in Moral and Political Theory* (Oxford: Oxford University Press, 2010), p. 187–188.

[42] Cohen, "On the Currency of Egalitarian Justice," p. 934.

[43] Samuel Scheffler, "Choice, Circumstance, and the Value of Equality," in his *Equality and Tradition: Questions of Value in Moral and Political Theory* (Oxford: Oxford University Press, 2010), pp. 222–223. See also Anderson, "What Is the Point of Equality?," pp. 295–302. Anderson concludes this section with an appeal to "Big Brother" (302). See also Thomas M. Scanlon, *Why Does Inequality Matter?* (Oxford: Oxford University Press, 2020), p. 39.

denied the abundant leftover food, a result he thought "unfair" (I: 198). Paddy, a fellow tramp, assured Orwell that this was for the best: "These here tramps are too lazy to work, that's all that's wrong with them," he explained, adding "They're scum, just scum" (I: 200–201). Orwell's plight was assumed to be the product of brute bad luck, while his fellow tramps were taken to be responsible for their bad option luck and denied good will accordingly.

Luck egalitarians will reject this nasty moralism and the inequitable treatment of Orwell and his fellow tramps; at least, nothing commits them to endorsing it. But how to guarantee that luck egalitarianism won't result in such nasty moralism when put into practice? The Tramp Major's moralism is the result of class prejudice, leading him to show concern only for a fallen gentleman. Orwell, who "refused to distinguish between the deserving and the undeserving poor" and thought that "If someone had fallen on especially hard times, he or she deserved help *as of right*"[44] also knew the role that class prejudice could and did play in moral judgments and would surely be suspicious of implementing an egalitarianism that depended on making a distinction that was so likely going to be infected by class prejudice. The right move, surely, is to correct for class prejudices in the first place, the gambit of a relational egalitarian. Orwell's apparent skepticism about implementing the luck egalitarian's crucial distinction is at least some evidence against the luck interpretation.

Meanness and the Means Test

In *The Road to Wigan Pier*, Orwell complained about the Means Test instituted with the Unemployment Insurance Act of 1934 under which unemployment benefits were supervised by an

---

[44] Philip Bounds, *Orwell & Marxism: The Political and Cultural Thinking of George Orwell* (London: I. B. Tauris, 2009), p. 33.

Unemployment Assistance Board tasked with collecting information about family wealth and income. Orwell opposed the Means Test, partly given its propensity to break up families, its "most cruel and evil effect" (V: 73), but also because of another evil it generated, one identified by Jonathan Wolff in his criticism of luck egalitarianism.

Luck egalitarians, Wolff thinks, nicely articulate one "idea" that is part of egalitarianism's ethos: fairness, the demand that no one should be advantaged or disadvantaged by arbitrary factors.[45] But, Wolff worries, the equally important idea of respect may be "compromised" were luck egalitarianism put into practice.[46] Failures of respect, Wolff thinks, include failures of common courtesy, trust, and demands for people to demean themselves.[47] Orwell's discussion of the Means Test illustrates what such failures look like and why luck egalitarians will not easily prevent them.

To determine that someone has been disadvantaged by brute bad luck, Wolff thinks, "We would have to know how much of an individual's fortune was a result of his or her choices and how much a result of unchosen circumstances."[48] That means collecting data, asking questions, and investigating people's private lives which will invariably humiliate subjects even when done with the best of intentions, as Orwell illustrates when he recalled a man denied relief because he supposedly had a job carting firewood who was forced to explain the firewood was his furniture and he was shooting the moon (V: 72). It will likely also manifest discourtesy as Orwell recounted when he recalled "the disgusting public wrangle about the minimum weekly sum on which a human being could keep alive" (V: 87), a wrangle that is probably unavoidable when determining the baseline for eligibility for public assistance. But

[45] Jonathan Wolff, "Fairness, Respect, and the Egalitarian Ethos," *Philosophy and Public Affairs*, Vol. 27, No. 2 (1998), p. 106.
[46] Ibid., p. 103.
[47] Ibid. pp. 108–109.
[48] Ibid., p. 110.

Orwell is especially useful in illustrating how implementing luck egalitarianism can result in failures of trust. Administering the Means Test, Orwell explained, "brings into existence an army of spies and informers" (XII: 98) and "much spying and tale-bearing, when, for instances, somebody is taking in a lodger, in which case a deduction would be made from his benefit if it were known" (X: 543). Indeed, the only time Orwell wasn't visited with warmth and kindness in working-class homes was when he was confused "for a Means Test nark" (V: 68).[49]

If Wolff hypothesizes that implementation of luck egalitarianism will violate the egalitarian value of respect, Orwell supplied good reason to think Wolff is right.

The Problem of the Pigs

The pigs of *Animal Farm* famously transformed the seventh commandment into the inegalitarian "ALL ANIMALS ARE EQUAL BUT SOME ANIMALS ARE MORE EQUAL THAN OTHERS" (VIII: 90), but they also help to illustrate a stubborn challenge to luck egalitarianism: the problem of *expensive tastes*.[50]

Arguably, luck egalitarianism entails that persons whose tastes are such that only very expensive commodities or experiences can make them as well off as otherwise similarly situated persons with

[49] Sydney Smith recalls that he and his friends "became suspicious immediately" when Orwell began quizzing them about their employment; see *Orwell Remembered*, edited by Audrey Coppard and Bernard Crick (London: Ariel Books, 1984), p. 137.

[50] For discussion, see Ronald Dworkin, "What Is Equality? Part 1: Equality of Welfare," *Philosophy and Public Affairs*, Vol. 10, No. 3 (1981), p. 228, and *Sovereign Virtue* (Cambridge, MA: Harvard University Press, 2000), pp. 48–59. See also Cohen, "On the Currency of Egalitarian Justice," p. 923. For a slight revision, see Cohen, "Expensive Taste Rides Again," in his *On the Currency of Egalitarian Justice and Other Essays in Political Philosophy*, edited by Michael Otsuka (Princeton: Princeton University Press, 2011)," pp. 87–89.

cheap tastes must be compensated in the name of equality given their bad luck to have developed or acquired expensive tastes. And if luck egalitarianism demands subsidizing expensive tastes in the name of justice, surely the worse for it. One might try to soften the blow and claim that luck egalitarianism does not demand compensation for expensive tastes that were deliberately formed or cultivated, only those that result or persist from brute bad luck,[51] unless of course persons could not have helped forming or cultivating them.[52] I do not say that the problem of expensive tastes cannot be solved, only that it would be evidence against the luck interpretation if Orwell wound up illustrating the problem.

For his part, Orwell explained that the "turning-point of the story" (XVIII: 507) in *Animal Farm* occurred when the milk and apples go missing, which "The animals had assumed as a matter of course . . . would be shared out equally (VIII: 22). Orwell emphasized this moment in the script for a 1947 BBC radio broadcast of *Animal Farm*, adding the following lines:

259. Clover: . . . Do you think that is quite fair?
260. Molly: What, keep the apples for themselves?
261. Muriel: Aren't we to have any?
262. Cow: I thought they were going to be shared out equally. (VIII: 153)[53]

[51] Ronald Dworkin, *Sovereign Virtue* (Cambridge, MA: Harvard University Press, 2000), pp. 48–59.
[52] Cohen, "On the Currency of Egalitarian Justice," p. 923. For a slight revision, see Cohen, "Expensive Taste Rides Again," in his *On the Currency of Egalitarian Justice and Other Essays in Political Philosophy*, edited by Michael Otsuka (Princeton: Princeton University Press, 2011)," pp. 87–89.
[53] These lines were ultimately struck and not delivered as part of the performance. A review of scripts housed in the George Orwell Archive at University College London reveals that later adaptions also tended to leave Orwell's additions out. Still, in the 1957 radio version of Orwell's adaptation, revised by Rayner Heppenstall, Molly asks, "But really do you think that's quite fair, Benjamin?," and he responds "(quietly) No." In the 1964 stage adaptation by Nelson Bond (first delivered in 1961), the narrator simply announces, "The animals had assumed these would be shared equally," no dialogue.

We learn that the milk was mixed into the pigs' mash and that they hoarded the apples for themselves.[54] Squealer, on behalf of the pigs, rationalizes this inequitable distribution:

"Comrades!" he cried. "You do not imagine, I hope, that we pigs are doing this in a spirit of selfishness and privilege? Many of us actually dislike milk and apples. I dislike them myself. Our sole object in taking these things is to preserve our health. Milk and apples (this has been proved by Science, comrades) contain substances absolutely necessary to the well-being of a pig. We pigs are brainworkers. The whole management and organisation of this farm depend on us. Day and night we are watching over your welfare. It is for *your* sake that we drink that milk and eat those apples." (VIII: 23)

Squealer's rationalization is bogus, though some readers seem sympathetic,[55] but suppose that the pigs were constituted such that nothing but milk and apples makes them happy. The luck egalitarian would seem committed to agreeing with Squealer that the pigs *should* get an inegalitarian distribution of milk and apples since, because of brute bad luck, they suffer with expensive tastes, unlike Boxer, who is happy with hay and barley. The luck egalitarian would then be committed to concluding that justice *demands* that the pigs be allowed to hoard milk and apples, an absurd result.

Again, the luck egalitarian undoubtedly has responses, but that *Animal Farm* seems to illustrate the problem of expensive tastes is evidence against the luck interpretation.

[54] That "All the pigs were in full agreement on this point, even Snowball and Napoleon" (VIII: 23) should quell any thought that Snowball is a hero betrayed in *Animal Farm*. See George Woodcock, *Orwell's Message: 1984 and the Present* (British Columbia: Harbour Publishing, 1984), p. 106.

[55] T. S. Eliot noted that "your pigs are far more intelligent than the other animals, and therefore the best qualified to run the farm" (XVI: 283).

What to Do for Tramps?

Perhaps the best reason to be suspicious of the luck interpretation arises from Orwell's proposed remedy of the evils suffered by tramps, especially three "especial evils" (I: 205): hunger and a dearth of good food; "perpetual celibacy" and "being entirely cut off from contact with women" (I: 205), which humiliates and damages self-respect (I: 207); and "enforced idleness" (I: 207). Orwell commended providing tramps with assistance, suggesting that they be given work that is beneficial and productive along with resources, like workhouses or kitchen gardens, to do so (I: 208), which seems like compensation for their brute bad luck. But if that was Orwell's goal why take such a roundabout strategy? Why not simply put them on the dole? Similarly, in *The Road to Wigan Pier*, he proposed that unemployed men be given a patch of land and free tools (V: 78). Why not simply extend them generous unemployment benefits?

The answer to such questions, I think, is that such mechanisms of compensation might solve some of the evils suffered by tramps and the unemployed, but not all of them and not the most important ones. Public assistance and unemployment benefits might tend to relieve the first evil Orwell identifies but not the second and third: they neither rehabilitate anyone's damaged self-respect, nor give them anything to do. Note that Orwell's expressed goal is to allow tramps a chance at "living a settled life" and to "take a respectable place in society" (I: 209). That Orwell thinks that the self-respect of men is tied up with having a job and sex with women suggests that he endorsed a conception of masculinity that some will cringe at, but that shouldn't distract from the current point: Orwell's aim is not simply to compensate tramps for their brute bad luck which could be accomplished by putting them on the dole. Instead, he hoped to remove those conditions that enable their domination and make them unable to look their fellows in the eye without feeling fear or deference.[56] He favored, not compensation, but giving tramps the means to live on terms of equality with others. So while Orwell's proposed solutions for tramps looks like evidence for the luck interpretation it is actually evidence against it and for the luck interpretation.

In sum, I do not deny that Orwell sometimes sounded like a luck egalitarian, but that he so often talks like a critic is a serious challenge to the luck interpretation. A different interpretation is called for.

On the Relational Interpretation

The best argument for the relational interpretation begins by noting how often Orwell talks like a relational egalitarian. For example, he commended Bertrand Russell's suggestion that democracy requires only "approximate economic equality" (XI: 313) and explained that socialism only demands "approximate equality of income" (XII: 410), adding that "It is no use at this stage of the world's history to suggest that all human beings should have *exactly* equal incomes" (XII: 423). While he denied that justice demanded equality of distributions, he did think that there were limits: he proposed that "there is no reason why ten to one should not be the maximum normal variation" of income and that "within those limits some sense of equality is possible" (XII: 424), although he sometimes suggested that the maximum variation is five to one (XVI: 27). But what is not negotiable is that economic inequality must not upset "close and friendly relations" (XVI: 27). In Chapter 8, I will make the case that Orwell's democratic Socialism flows from his ethical commitments, including his egalitarianism,

---

[56] This is Pettit's "eyeball test" for determining what level of freedom people must enjoy to count as having access to justice, democracy, and sovereignty. See Philip Pettit, *Just Freedom: A Moral Compass for a Complex World* (New York: W. W. Norton, 2014).

but it is not right to say that "his primary motivation for becoming a socialist" was his belief that "income inequality was an inherent feature of capitalism."[57] His concern was clearly with social relations and not income inequality per se.

Below, I note other places in which Orwell's concerns are those of the relational egalitarian, with ending oppression and creating a community in which people stand in equal relations to one another. My argument for the relational interpretation is that Orwell's concerns so often map onto those of self-identified relational egalitarians. At the close of this section, I consider an objection to understanding Orwell as an egalitarian of special interest to the relational egalitarian.

Spanish Bombs

While Orwell retained "the most evil memories of Spain" (VI: 178), *Homage to Catalonia* also recalled breathing "the air of equality" (VI: 83, 210), a more favorable memory. If "Hatred of hierarchy is the animating passion of his social criticism,"[58] *Homage to Catalonia* nicely illustrates what the absence of hierarchy looks like in practice.

Here, Anderson explains how social hierarchies can preclude persons from living together as equals:

Consider three types or dimensions of social hierarchy: of authority, esteem, and standing. In a hierarchy of authority, occupants of higher rank get to order subordinates around. They exercise arbitrary and unaccountable power over

[57] Jennifer Roback, "The Economic Thought of George Orwell," *American Economic Review*, Vol. 75, No. 2 (May 1985), p. 127.

[58] Michael Walzer, "George Orwell's England," in *George Orwell*, edited by Graham Holderness, Bryan Loughrey, and Nahem Yousaf (New York: St. Martin's Press, 1988), p. 193.

their inferiors. In a hierarchy of esteem, occupants of higher rank despise those of inferior rank and extract tokens of deferential honor from them, such as bowing, scraping, and other rituals of self-abasement that inferiors display in recognition of the other's superiority. In a hierarchy of standing, the interests of those of higher rank *count* in the eyes of others, whereas the interests of inferiors do not; others are free to neglect them, and, in extreme cases, to trample upon them with impunity.[59]

Orwell's recollection of Spain illustrates the *absence* of these three dimensions. Throughout *Homage to Catalonia*, he emphasized the absence of hierarchies of authority in the Spanish resistance. He explained that "The essential point of the system was social equality between officers and men" and that "each militia was a democracy and not a hierarchy" where it was understood that "when you gave an order you gave it as comrade to comrade and not as superior to inferior" (VI: 26). To solicit compliance, one appealed to class-loyalty and comradeship, not "the discipline of a bourgeois conscript army" (VI: 27). If a militia member disliked an order he would step out of the ranks and argue fiercely with the officer who issued it (VI: 7). Orwell knew that traditional military types would doubt success here, but he insisted that it worked.[60] And if hierarchies of authority can be purged from the military, they can be purged anywhere.

Hierarchies of esteem were also noticeably absent in Spain. Within Orwell's militia, there were "no titles, no badges, no heel-clicking and saluting" (VI: 26), "no privilege and no boot-licking" (VI: 84). "A revolutionary army," Orwell explained in his "Wartime Diary," that he "would *start* by abolishing saluting" (XII: 196).

---

[59] Elizabeth Anderson, *Private Government: How Employers Rule Our Lives (and Why We Don't Talk about It)* (Princeton: Princeton University Press, 2017), pp. 3–4.

[60] Although in "Looking Back on the Spanish War," he suggested that "the relationship of officer and man has to be the relationship of superior and inferior" (XIII: 498).

Tokens of veneration were also absent in Spain, at least when Orwell first arrived in Barcelona:

> Waiters and shop-walkers looked you in the face and treated you as an equal. Servile and even ceremonial forms of speech had temporarily disappeared. Nobody said "*Señor*" or "*Don*" or even "*Usted*"; everyone called everyone else "*Comrade*" and "*Thou*," and said "*Salud!*" instead of "*Buenos dias.*" Tipping was forbidden by law; almost my first experience was receiving a lecture from a hotel manager for trying to tip a lift-boy. (VI: 3)

The following passage is especially useful to connect Orwell's understanding of equality with the absence of hierarchies of esteem and the widespread existence of alternative sentiments:

> Up here in Aragon one was among tens of thousands of people, mainly though not entirely of working-class origin, all living at the same level and mingling on terms of equality. In theory it was perfect equality, and even in practice it was not far from it. . . . Many of the normal motives of civilized life—snobbishness, money-grubbing, fear of the boss, etc.—had simply ceased to exist. The ordinary class-division of society had disappeared to an extent that is almost unthinkable in the money-tainted air of England; there was no one there except the peasants and ourselves, and no one owned anyone else as his master. (VI: 83)

Orwell's animus for tokens of veneration predated and outlasted his time in Spain: he "resented passionately the indignity of . . . servile action that was demanded of him" when he was expected to touch his cap when an Etonian master passed by[61] and his first contribution after leaving *Tribune* was going to argue that Labour's first tasks

[61] See Christopher Hollis, *A Study of George Orwell: The Man and His Works* (Delaware: Racehorse Publishing, 2017), p. 17.

included abolishing all titles.[62] Equality demanded nothing less than the abolition of hierarchies of authority, esteem, and standing.

During his last weeks in Barcelona, Orwell detected "a. peculiar evil feeling in the air," one that emerged from "an atmosphere of suspicion, fear, uncertainty, and veiled hatred" (VI: 148). He recalled "the horrible atmosphere of political suspicion and hatred" (VI: 153) and "lies and rumours circulating everywhere" (VI: 177), explaining that "You seemed to spend all you time holding whispered conversations in corners of cafes and wondering whether that person at the next table was a police spy" (VI: 148). The "equalitarian spirit of the first few months of the revolution" (VI: 198) was destroyed just when persons no longer felt trust or affection, sentiments that enable us to live together as equals. The Spanish egalitarianism that Orwell prized withered just when equitable social relations did, a point he made as clear as he could.

On Status Inequality

Egalitarians might find inequality objectionable per se or because of its consequences. One objectionable consequence of inequality, when paired with prevailing evaluative errors, is that it generates *status inequality*, a chronic but imposed inability to enter desirable social relationships.[63] Poverty is well regarded as objectionable because it generates social inequality[64] and Orwell helped to illustrate how the poor are rendered unable to enter desirable social

---

[62] Tosco Fyvel, "The Years at *Tribune*," in *The World of George Orwell*, edited by Miriam Gross (New York: Simon and Schuster, 1971), p. 115.

[63] Note that this concern is not exclusive to the egalitarian left. F. A. Hayek, insofar as he thought that capitalist societies depend on a sense of independence and fundamental equality, should also be concerned if capitalism tends to produce status inequality. For discussion, see Daniel Halliday and John Thrasher, *The Ethics of Capitalism: An Introduction* (Oxford: Oxford University Press, 2020), p. 51.

[64] Scanlon, *Why Does Inequality Matter*, p. 31.

relationships given the ways that they are thought to dress, live, and consume.

Orwell often pointed out how the dress of the poor had undesirable consequences. In "Such, Such Were the Joys," he recalled that poorer boys at school "were humiliated over clothes and petty possessions" (XIX: 363). Gordon's rant in *Keep the Aspidistra Flying* expresses the frustration that some down and outs must have felt:

> Don't you see that a man's whole personality is bound up with his income? His personality *is* his income. How can you be attractive to a girl when you've got no money? You can't wear decent clothes, you can't take her out to dinner or to the theatre or away for week-ends, you can't carry a cheery, interesting atmosphere about with you. And it's rot to say that kind of thing doesn't matter. It does. (IV: 104–105)

For his part, Orwell recorded feeling "genuinely degraded" upon first dressing in a tramp's clothes: covered "in a patina of filth," he felt shame that one might feel during one's first night in prison (I: 130). Poverty plus prevailing beliefs about how the poor live— Orwell recorded popular middle-class beliefs that the poor are content to live in slums (V: 15) and indecent housing (V: 58), disinclined to work (V: 80), and marry on the dole (V: 81)—can also generate undesirable consequences. The food and diet of the poor is also a source of shame, apparently: "Curse it, what can one do on bread and potatoes?," Boris wonders in *Down and Out in Paris and London*, adding "It is fatal to look hungry" and "It makes people want to kick you" (I: 49). Orwell speculated that "perhaps the really important thing about the unemployed . . . is the diet they are living on" (V: 85), one he thinks "appalling" (V: 88). Orwell documented the tendency of the poor to waste money on unhealthy food, an understandable trend since tasty but unhealthy food fills "the need of half-starved people for cheap palliatives" (V: 83). But the popular belief that the poor don't know how to budget their money is a humiliating one that makes desirable social relations more difficult.

Note that status inequality is not going to be resolved simply by compensating the unlucky poor. While Orwell praised "the mass-production of cheap smart clothes since the war" that allow a young man to "buy himself a suit which, for a little while and at a little distance, looks as though it had been tailored in Savile Row" (V: 81) and suggested that "the post-war manufacture of cheap clothes . . . toned down the surface differences between class and class" (V: 123), he knew that snobs have a way of sniffing out knockoffs and jealously guarded the conventions governing how their class was to dress: a bourgeois Socialist "still leaves his bottom waistcoat button undone" (V: 127), for example, revealing his class status in a way that an imitator could not anticipate. Further, beliefs about the habits of the poor might be stubborn: Orwell detected the smell of a "synthetic soup" and immediately concluded that the person cooking it was poor—"People who drink Bouillon Zip are starving, or near it" (I: 24), he explained. If the egalitarian Orwell could not shed such evaluative errors—might someone just enjoy synthetic bouillon?—supplementing the wealth of the poor need not get them status equality.

Class, Castes, and Subcastes

Caste is by its nature relational: "There is never caste," the Dalit leader Ambedkar said, "Only castes."[65] A caste is *not* simply a group of people with some characteristic in common that affects their lives and constitutes an important part of their identity.[66] Rather, it involves social arrangements in which some persons are

---

[65] Bhimrao Ambedkar, *Castes in India: Their Mechanism, Genesis, and Development* (Columbia, SC: LM Publishers, 2020), p. 47.
[66] Cf. David Edmonds, *Caste Wars: A Philosophy of Discrimination* (London: Routledge, 2006), p. 123.

treated as *inferior*.[67] Arguably, caste is consistent with fairly equal distributions of resources, supposing that unlucky lower castes are compensated, and might even be consistent with equality of opportunity.[68] But it is clearly inconsistent with living together as equals. So, hatred of caste is especially indicative of sympathy with relational egalitarianism. Orwell hated it. One of Orwell's readers suggests that since Orwell "could not take the class/caste system at face value" we ought to conclude that "his moral conscience was fundamentally egalitarian."[69] Fair enough, but it would be more precise to infer from Orwell's hatred of caste that his conscience was fundamentally that of a *relational* egalitarian.

Orwell sometimes conflated class and caste, regarding himself as "sufficiently typical of my class, or rather sub-caste" (V: 113). He also recalled "three castes in the school" including one composed of "underlings . . . the sons of clergyman, Indian civil servants, struggling widows and the like" (XIX: 363), and he disparaged the English "shadowy caste-system" (V: 114) that ensures that "nearly everyone's destiny is fixed for him at birth . . . mixing only with his own sub-caste and cut off from all the rest by dense walls of prejudice" (XII: 142). Talk of caste is pervasive in *Down and Out in Paris and London*, where he described "the elaborate caste system existing in a hotel" (I: 69): *Plongeurs*, like Orwell, were repeatedly treated in inegalitarian ways without consequence, as when he was forced to shave his iconic moustache since "waiters in good hotels do not wear moustaches, and to show their superiority they decree that *plongeurs* shall not wear them either" (I: 69). He explained that "it is an etiquette in hotel life that between hours everyone is equal" (I: 63), but even the decent Valenti, who "treated me almost as an equal when we were alone . . . had to speak roughly when there was

[67] Scanlon, *Why Does Inequality Matter?*, p. 5. See also Isabel Wilkerson, *Caste: The Origins of Our Discontents* (New York: Random House, 2020), pp. 141 and 160.
[68] Brian Barry, *Theories of Justice*, Vol. 1 (Berkeley: University of California Press, 1989), p. 224n.
[69] Craig L. Carr, *Orwell, Politics, and Power* (New York: Continuum, 2010), p. 20.

anyone else present, for it does not do for a waiter to be friendly with *plongeurs*" (I: 66). Egalitarians should not be indifferent to social relations in the workplace: if the goal of relational egalitarianism is to dismantle social hierarchy generally, then the workplace too should be targeted for reform.[70]

It will be helpful for my argument in Chapter 8 to note presently that Orwell's hatred of caste also led him to prefer democratic Socialism to nondemocratic versions: "The real issue," he thought, "is between democratic Socialism and some form of rationalized caste-society (XII: 123) since "Everywhere the world movement seems to be in the direction of centralised economies . . . which are not democratically organized and which tend to establish a caste system" (XVI: 190). Later I will argue that Orwell's egalitarianism led him to socialism but also to embrace democratic Socialism in particular. His hatred of caste crossed ideological lines.

On Orwell's Sexism

As I noted in Chapter 1, Orwell has been dogged by charges that complicate a study of his ethics: he has been accused of homophobia, anti-Semitism, cruelty, disloyalty, and still more. Presently, I consider the charge of sexism, partly because the case for regarding him as sexist is comparatively stronger than the case for some other charges and because it is especially problematic for the relational interpretation.

Evidence of Orwell's sexism is easily found. In letters to Brenda Salkeld, Orwell mockingly thanked her for meeting him "in spite of my hideous prejudice against your sex" (X: 268) and chided a lunch companion who was "a bit of a feminist" for raising the possibility that a woman could throw a stone, construct a syllogism, and

---

[70] Elizabeth Anderson, *Private Government: How Employers Rule Our Lives (and Why We Don't Talk about It)* (Princeton: Princeton University Press, 2017).

keep a secret if she were brought up as a man (X: 344). In an unpublished essay, he endorsed the view that intelligent women are rare like albinos and that intelligent, pretty women are rarer still like left-handed albinos (XIX: 349). He identified the job of *plongeur* as "the sort of job that would always be done by women if women were strong enough" (I: 76–77). In Chapter 5 I noted the passage from *The Road to Wigan Pier* where he praises the "perfect symmetry" of the patriarchal working-class home (V: 108), but not the shot he takes at "birth-controllers" who would upset this idyllic scene (V: 109) nor the fact that he seems oblivious to the significance of and contributions by working-class women.[71] Note too that some of Orwell's friends thought him misogynistic, even "very misogynist."[72] Confusion about the semantics of "misogyny"[73] might lead some readers to remark, in the same text, that Orwell stands accused of misogyny and "rightly so," but also that he "was distinctly un-misogynistic," and that "Orwell's attitude to women is far more complex."[74] Still, it is difficult to resist concluding that he too often resembles "one of those male socialists who were opposed to every oppression, except that of women."[75]

Orwell's sexism is disappointing, but how should it inform our understanding of his egalitarianism? According to Daphne Patai, if we assess Orwell by the very standards that "he himself proclaimed: honesty, decency, egalitarianism, justice . . . he must be found wanting," an assessment that "gives many of his moral claims

[71] For a brief but devastating summary of his ignorance, see Selina Hall, "Introduction," in George Orwell, *The Road to Wigan Pier* (Oxford: Oxford University Press, 2021), pp. xxv–xxvii.

[72] As quoted in Bowker, *Inside George Orwell*, p. 128.

[73] For discussion, see Kate Manne, *Down Girl: The Logic of Misogyny* (Oxford: Oxford University Press, 2018), esp. pp. 31–54.

[74] Richard Lance Keeble, *George Orwell, the Secret State, and the Making of "Nineteen Eighty-Four"* (Suffolk: Abramis, 2020), pp. 58, 60, and 104.

[75] John Newsinger, *Hope Lies in the Proles: George Orwell and the Left* (London: Pluto Press, 2018), p. 154. Orwell was hardly alone: "class inequality in Britain was certainly the Left's dominant concern in this period, sometimes to the exclusion of any other form of injustice": Ben Jackson, *Equality and the British Left: A Study in Political Thought, 1900–1964* (Manchester: Manchester University Press, 2007), p. 5.

a peculiarly hollow sound."[76] And while Patai finds in *Burmese Days* "an incipient morality . . . of true egalitarianism," it is one that "Orwell never allows . . . to mature into a rejection of all forms of domination, all instances of using others as a means to one's own ends."[77] Beatrix Campbell similarly concludes that "Liberty, justice and patriotism are key words in his litany of moral virtue . . . not democracy and egalitarianism."[78]

I take for granted that sexist attitudes do not reconcile well with a relational egalitarianism that prides living together as equals, but that is sort of the point: if Orwell's sexism disappoints us, it is surely *because* he is otherwise well regarded as a relational egalitarian. We expect better from him *because* he is responsive to moral reasons for abandoning other morally dubious beliefs and practices of his day, evidence that he was capable of eschewing patriarchal beliefs and practices and affirming the dignity and standing of women. He seems to understand that treatment that has a disparate impact along gender lines is unjust, having noted that, in Spain, "only male quails were caught, which struck me as unfair" (VI: 80). That his sexism disappoints us is, oddly, evidence of his relational egalitarianism, albeit the relational egalitarianism of an egalitarian who failed to see and live up to the implications of his view. Similarly, while Orwell was so often an advocate for the working class, he could easily be read as being patronizing and condescending: his suggestion in "Looking Back on the Spanish War" that "The struggle of the working class is like the growth of a plant"—a plant, that is, which "blind and stupid" though "knows enough to keep pushing upwards towards the light" (XIII: 506)—is not the only backhanded compliment he serves up. So often in Orwell, "eloquent statements of the right of all people to be treated equally, as human beings, are haunted by the suspicion that some human beings are more human

---

[76] Patai, *The Orwell Mystique*, p. 20.
[77] Ibid., p. 51.
[78] Beatrix Campbell, *Wigan Pier Revisited: Poverty and Politics in the 80s* (London: Virago Press, 1984), p. 219.

than others."[79] But if Orwell couldn't ever quite overcome his own class biases and hostilities, as noted in Chapter 4, his failures are disappointing and surprising just because he was so often the advocate of an egalitarianism that demanded nothing less than correcting them.

Conclusion

I have argued that Orwell's egalitarianism is best understood as relational egalitarianism. While he has much to say about luck, the balance of his corpus supports the relational interpretation.

While Orwell thought that equality was morally valuable, he did not think that it was the only thing that was morally valuable: he complained of H. G. Wells that "the only evil he cares to imagine is inequality (V: 188), a complaint that makes sense only if other things matter too. Allowing that equality is not all that matters morally helps the egalitarian escape the familiar leveling-down problem[80] that Orwell references inchoately. In *The Road to Wigan Pier*, he imagines an upper-class person who objects to becoming more like the working class, asking, "Why must we level *down*? Why not level *up*?" (V: 151). Orwell did sometimes think that equality demanded leveling down: speaking of the luxury laws in England during wartime, he thought that "since certain luxuries . . . obviously can't be distributed to everybody, then it is better that nobody should have them" (XVI: 102). But egalitarians, like Orwell, should be just as happy with bringing everyone up the level of the bourgeoisie as they would if everyone were brought down to the level of tramps only if they thought that equality was all that mattered. The best response to the leveling-down problem is, I think, to insist that while

---

[79] Douglas Kerr, *Orwell and Empire* (Oxford: Oxford University Press, 2022), p. 26.
[80] Derek Parfit, "Equality or Priority?," in *The Ideal of Equality*, edited by Matthew Clayton and Andrew Williams (Basingstoke, UK: Palgrave Macmillan), pp. 98–99.

188 GEORGE ORWELL: THE ETHICS OF EQUALITY

equality matters it is not all that matters and if leveling up is better that is because leveling up secures something else besides equality that also matters.[81] Orwell was a value pluralist in this respect: he too thought equality mattered but that other things mattered too.

What else did Orwell think mattered? Liberty clearly mattered to Orwell, which raises some interesting questions about the compatibility of liberty and equality and foreshadows a concern of Chapter 7, where I consider Orwell's status as a left-libertarian.

[81] As Larry Temkin says, "do I *really* think that there is some respect in which a world where only some are blind is worse than one where all are? Yes. Does this mean I think it would be better if we blinded everyone? No. Equality is not all that matters. But it matters some." See Temkin, "Equality, Priority, and the Levelling Down Objection," in *The Ideal of Equality*, p. 155.

7

George Orwell and Left-Libertarianism

If Orwell was sometimes frustrated by various figures on the left, he nonetheless declared that "I belong to the Left and must work inside it" (XVII: 385). He supported leftist politics in England even in his final days: in July of 1949, mere months before he died, he clarified that *Nineteen Eighty-Four* "is *not* an attack on socialism, or on the British Labor party," and that he was "a supporter" (XX: 135) if not a member of the latter.[1] Some are convinced that if he lived a bit longer he would have become a conservative,[2] but such unfalsifiable speculation is contradicted by his own self-assessment: Orwell belonged to the left.

Among his biographers, Bernard Crick thought Orwell "was both an egalitarian and a libertarian."[3] Among his readers, Diana Trilling thought that *Nineteen Eighty-Four* can be easily read "as the work of . . . an old-fashioned libertarian."[4] Among those who knew him well, Richard Rees spoke of Orwell's "libertarian radicalism,"[5] while George Woodcock thought of Orwell as "a socialist trying to

---

[1] Orwell's declarations were printed in *Life* and the *New York Times*, which accounts for the Americanized spelling.

[2] Norman Podhoretz, "If Orwell Were Alive Today," *Quadrant*, Vol. 10, No. 27 (October 1983), pp. 48–53.

[3] Bernard Crick, *Orwell: A Life* (Boston: Little, Brown and Company, 1980), p. 278.

[4] Diana Trilling, in *George Orwell: The Critical Heritage*, edited by Jeffrey Meyers (Boston: Routledge & Kegan Paul, 1975), p. 261. Originally published in *Nation*, 25 June 1949, pp. 716–717.

[5] Richard Rees, *George Orwell: Fugitive from the Camp of Victory* (Carbondale: Southern Illinois University Press, 1961), p. 25.

George Orwell. Peter Brian Barry, Oxford University Press. © Oxford University Press 2023.
DOI: 10.1093/oso/9780197627402.003.0007

preserve libertarian values,"[6] that he "remained a libertarian socialist to the end of his life,"[7] and that he was "an independent socialist with libertarian tendencies."[8] After the publication of *Animal
Farm*, Fenner Brockway recalled Orwell being "emphatic that he
remained a libertarian socialist" and understood him as defending
"a libertarian form of socialism,"[9] an interpretation that more
than a few of Orwell's readers have also taken up.[10] Christopher
Hitchens was not alone in finding Orwell to be "a libertarian before
the word gained currency."[11] A 1948 letter to Malcolm Muggeridge
revealed that Orwell thought that "The real division is not between
conservatives and revolutionaries but between authoritarians and
libertarians."[12] Focus on the division that interested Orwell: he was

[6] George Woodcock, "Utopias in Negative," in *"Nineteen Eighty-Four" to 1984: A
Companion to Orwell's Classic Novel* (New York: Carroll and Graf Publishers, Inc., 1984),
p. 120.

[7] Ibid., p. 75.

[8] George Woodcock, "George Orwell" 19th Century Liberal," in *George Orwell: The
Critical Heritage*, edited by Jeffrey Meyers (Boston: Routledge & Kegan Paul, 1975),
p. 236. Originally published in *Politics*, December 1946, 384–388.

[9] As quoted in *The Orwell Tapes*, edited by Stephen Wadhams (Toronto: Locarno
Press, 2017), pp. 184–185.

[10] "For the last decade of his life, Orwell was a free-thinking but hardly atypical Labour
libertarian leftist": Paul Anderson, "In Defence of Bernard Crick," in *George Orwell
Now!*, edited by Richard Lance Keeble (New York: Peter Lang, 2015), p. 86; "he believed
until the end of his life that a totalitarian future could still be averted by the concerted
action of libertarian socialists": Philip Bounds, *Orwell and Marxism: The Political and
Cultural Thinking of George Orwell* (New York: I. B. Tauris, 2009), p. 27; "He was a libertarian, but showed no interest in weighing up the two types of liberty": Robert Colls,
George Orwell: English Rebel (Oxford: Oxford University Press, 2013), p. 143; "He was
also a libertarian, but of a specifically democratic Socialist kind": Crick, *George Orwell: A
Life*, p. 278; "George Orwell was more or less a libertarian socialist": Eric Laursen, *The
Duty to Stand Aside: "Nineteen Eighty-Four" and the Wartime Quarrel of George Orwell
and Alex Comfort* (Chico, CA: AK Press, 2018), p. 3; "He belonged to the *libertarian*
socialist, rather than the collectivist socialist, tradition": Stuart Hall, "Conjuring
Leviathan: Orwell on the State," in *Inside the Myth—Orwell: Views from the Left*, edited
by Christopher Norris (London: Lawrence and Wishart, 1984), p. 218; "Orwell fought
for something entirely different—a planet of *libertarian socialism*" and "as a chorus of his
friends attests, Orwell's libertarianism was *socialist*": Smith, *George Orwell Illustrated*,
pp. 210 and 212; "he shared the feeling of most libertarian Socialists that we have no right
to plot the future which others may live": George Woodcock, *The Crystal Spirit: A Study
of George Orwell* (New York: Shocken, 1984), p. 285.

[11] Christopher Hitchens, *Orwell's Victory* (New York: Penguin, 2002), p. 75.

[12] "Letter to Malcolm Muggeridge, from 4 December 1948," in *The Lost Orwell*, edited
by Peter Davison (London: Timewell Press, 2006), p. 116.

no authoritarian. Should we not conclude therefore that he was a libertarian? What other side of the divide could he be on?

If Orwell was of the left and he was a libertarian, then via some principle of agglomeration, he would seem to be a left-libertarian. But I am skeptical that he is well-regarded as such, and in this chapter I explain why. I first consider Orwell's relationship with anarchism, a school of thought historically identified with left-libertarianism. Next, I identify the commitments of left-libertarianism, a task made easier given that some of its best advocates have identified them: left-libertarians suppose that all persons are self-owners, in a sense that needs to be explained, and that all persons are due some equal share of natural resources. I then consider whether Orwell shared those commitments. In the third section below, I note several of his positive proposals that are inconsistent with left-libertarianism's first commitment to self-ownership. In the fourth section, I suggest reason to be skeptical that he endorsed left-libertarianism's second commitment to an egalitarian distribution of natural resources. My conclusion is something of a deflationary one: if Orwell was a man of the left, it was not because he was a left-libertarian.

Orwell among the Anarchists

British historian David Goodway contends that, prior the rise of right-libertarianism, some anarchists understood "libertarian" and "anarchist" as synonymous[13] and that "left-libertarianism" is a "less emotive term" for "anarchism."[14] Similarly, Woodcock titled his historiography of anarchist thought *Anarchism: A History of Libertarian Ideas and Movements*. If all anarchists are

[13] David Goodway, *Anarchist Seeds beneath the Snow: Left-Libertarian Thought and British Writers from William Morris to Colin Ward* (Oakland, CA: PM Press, 2012), p. 154.
[14] Ibid., p. 1.

left-libertarians and Orwell was an anarchist, then he was a left-libertarian, an argument that promises to close this chapter just as it begins. For argument's sake, I do not question the universal premise of this argument and focus instead on Orwell's relationship with anarchists and anarchism. Orwell is not usually regarded as an anarchist by his readers and rightly so, but one reason to consider his status as an anarchist is that he called himself one, sort of.

In "Politics vs. Literature," Orwell called Jonathan Swift "a Tory anarchist" (XVIII: 425), and he called himself one in dialogue with others[15] well into the 1930s,[16] and some commentators have followed suit.[17] Woodcock warns that "it is unwise" to ignore the younger Orwell who called himself a Tory anarchist when considering the older Orwell who wrote *Nineteen Eighty-Four* and assures us that Orwell's "temperament . . . was both Tory and anarchist."[18] But Orwell's self-identification is minimally helpful without knowing what Tory anarchism *is*: it is, apparently, "not a 'philosophy' or a 'theory'" but "a stance or a posture against the prevailing norms of the age,"[19] which doesn't really distinguish Tory anarchists from contrarians generally.

Still, Orwell often said things that hint at more than mild sympathy with the anarchism of the Tory anarchist. Towards the end of his service in Burma, he had "worked out an anarchistic theory that all government is evil, that the punishment always does more harm than the crime and that people can be trusted to behave decently if only you will let them alone" (V: 137). In *Homage to Catalonia*, he favorably references the "ever-present Anarchist

[15] Rayner Heppenstall, *Four Absences* (London: Barrie and Rockcliff, 1960), p. 32.

[16] Gordon Bowker, *Inside George Orwell: A Biography* (New York: Palgrave Macmillan, 2003), p. 174; Crick, *Orwell: A Life*, p. 164.

[17] Orwell was "a sort of Bohemian tory-anarchist": Rees, *Fugitive from the Camp of Victory*, p. 44; "his anti-authoritarianism and anti-imperialism took a 'Tory anarchist' form": Crick, *Orwell: A Life*, p. 131.

[18] George Woodcock, *Orwell's Message: 1984 and the Present* (British Columbia: Harbour Publishing, 1984), pp. 126–127.

[19] Peter Wilkin, *The Strange Case of Tory Anarchism* (Oxfordshire: Libri Publishing, 2010), p. 13.

tinge" of the Spanish who "would make even the opening stages of Socialism tolerable if they had the chance" (VI: 84). He fought with the Spanish POUM—the Partido Obrero de Unificación Marxista, or the Workers' Party of Marxist Unification—but, as he explained in *Homage to Catalonia*, given his "purely personal preferences [he] would have liked to join the Anarchists" (VI: 96) and, as he explained in a letter to Jack Common, had he "understood the situation a bit better [he] should probably have joined the Anarchists" (XI: 93). He also seems to have run in anarchist circles for some time. Vernon Richards recalls that Orwell had been associated with anarchists on a number of issues since 1938 and that he was an active sponsor of the International Anti-Fascist Solidarity, an organization launched by the Spanish Anarchists and organized by Emma Goldman.[20] In 1946, Orwell was named as a forthcoming speaker to the London Anarchist Group, evidence of his "sympathy for and proximity to anarchism."[21] Also in 1946, he explained in "The Intellectual Revolt" that socialists and anarchists aimed at the same goal, namely, "The good society . . . in which human beings are equal and in which they co-operate with one another willingly and not because of fear or economic compulsion" (XVIII: 67). It might matter that Orwell described the Italian soldier that he memorialized in *Homage to Catalonia* as having "the kind of face you would expect in an Anarchist" (VI: 1). It might also matter that Orwell would leave his adopted son, Richard, in the care of Lilian Wolfe, a seventy-three-year-old veteran of the British anarchist movement who lived in an anarchist colony.[22]

Some of Orwell's commentators regard him as some kind of anarchist[23] or at least as having "a great deal of sympathy with the

[20] Vernon Richards, "Orwell the Humanist," in *George Orwell at Home (and among the Anarchists): Essays and Photographs* (London: Freedom Press, 1998), p. 13.

[21] Goodway, *Anarchist Seeds beneath the Snow*, p. 347.

[22] Crick, *Orwell: A Life*, p. 388.

[23] Orwell was "at heart . . . a simple-minded anarchist": Isaac Deutscher, *Heretics and Renegades: And Other Essays* (London: Jonathan Cape, 1969), pp. 47–48; he was "a kind of intellectual anarchist": Jon Kimchee, as quoted in Crick, *Orwell: A Life*, p. 163; Orwell's "socialism became anarchism": V. S. Pritchett, in *George Orwell: The Critical Heritage*,

anarchists."[24] But while he kept friendships with self-identified anarchists, he attacked their doctrine savagely.[25] If a younger Orwell thought that all government is evil, the older Orwell looked back on this view as "sentimental nonsense," adding that "I see now as I did not see then, that it is always necessary to protect peaceful people with violence" (V: 137), an odd thing for an anarchist to say.[26] Just as he suspected that holy rollers were infected with the power fetish, so he thought that "Creeds like pacifism and anarchism, which seem on the surface to imply a complete renunciation of power, rather encourage this habit of mind" (XIX: 66) and that there is a "totalitarian tendency . . . explicit in the anarchist or pacifist vision of Society" (XVIII: 424). Similarly, in "Politics vs. Literature," he hinted that an "anarchist outlook" might be "covering an authoritarian cast of mind" (XVIII: 426) and that there is a "totalitarian tendency . . . explicit in the anarchist or pacifist vision of Society" (XVIII: 424). But if Orwell had an actual argument against anarchism, it was hinted at in a book review where he takes a shot at Gandhi, contending that creeds like pacifism "have the advantage that they aim at the impossible and therefore demand very little" (XV: 215). Richards elaborates here:

edited by Jeffrey Meyers (London: Routledge and Kegan Paul, 1975), p. 294; he had "a kind of Bohemian Anarchist attitude": Richard Rees in Orwell Remembered, edited by Audrey Coppard and Bernard Crick (New York: Ariel Facts on File, 1984), p. 124; "Conservatism and socialism form the two poles of Orwell's political thought," they are held together by "the never wholly abandoned strain of anarchism" and that "Anarchism remained a restless piece of his mind right to the end": Woodcock, The Crystal Spirit, p. 234.

[24] Stephen Spender in Orwell Remembered, edited by Audrey Coppard and Bernard Crick (New York: Ariel Facts on File, 1984), p. 262.

[25] Woodcock explains that "to the end of his life, though he sometimes attacked anarchists on specific issues, he remained temperamentally very close to them": George Woodcock, Orwell's Message: 1984 and the Present (British Columbia: Harbour Publishing, 1984), p. 69.

[26] Alex Zwerdling suggests that Orwell came to treat his youthful anarchist sympathies as "childish wish-fulfillment": see Zwerdling, Orwell and the Left (New Haven: Yale University Press, 1974), p. 28.

The principal reason why Orwell was never an anarchist seems to me to be that he thought of himself as a "realist," and that it was useless to talk of social revolution when its realisation seemed so remote; we had to face the immediate problems. As a result, he found himself in the position of having continually to choose between the lesser and greater evils.[27]

To be sure, Orwell rejected realism as he understood it—in a 1944 AIP column, he suggested that "realism" normally means "dishonesty" (XVI: 124)—but Richards's explanation tracks Orwell's humanism discussed in Chapter 2: if anarchism can yield no practical guidance when moral dilemmas present themselves, then anarchism yields nothing good for human beings and thus is not good simpliciter.[28] Orwell is a "realist" not because he thinks that might makes right, but because he has little use for moral theories that cannot be profitably utilized by human beings. One commentator explained that one of Orwell's attractions for the left "is his immersion in the here and now," that he "wrote to the question of how to live in the possible world, not how to die in an impossible one."[29] I would have said that he is of interest because he advocated that which would help us live in the actual world, not a merely possible one, but I share the sentiment and it underlies his criticism of anarchism.

We can make Orwell *seem* like an anarchist if we are willing to slice the semantics of 'anarchist' thin. Goodway, at one point,

[27] Vernon Richards, "Orwell the Humanist," in *George Orwell at Home (and among the Anarchists)*, p. 9. In the same volume, we are told that Orwell's "acceptance of the lesser evil" reveals "very clearly the difference between Orwell's attitude . . . and the point of view of adopted by anarchist writers": see Colin Ward, "Orwell and Anarchism," in *George Orwell at Home (and among the Anarchists)*, p. 28.

[28] Richards allows that "in the event of a revolutionary situation presenting itself . . . Orwell would have been wholeheartedly with the anarchists, for, in such a situation, his *ethical* anarchism and his 'realism' would both find expression": see Richards, "Orwell the Humanist," p. 11.

[29] Philip Rieff, "George Orwell and the Post-Liberal Imagination," *Kenyon Review*, Vol. 16, No. 1 (Winter 1954), pp. 49–50.

suggests that "philosophic or philosophical anarchism is best understood as the standpoint that anarchism, that society without state or government, is the *ideal*, but that is not really practicable, at least not at the present."[30] By such a standard, Orwell is an anarchist but so are Hobbes, Rousseau, and Nozick. Better to conclude that Orwell's philosophical sympathies were not the product of any sympathy with anarchism because he was "critical of the unrealistic element in its theory."[31]

Left-Libertarianism in Theory

One route to concluding that Orwell was a left-libertarian is closed; others might be open. The most passable route goes through contemporary attempts to identify the commitments of left-libertarians and notes that those commitments are also Orwell's. While the tradition of democratic thought sometimes suggests a conflict between claims of liberty and equality,[32] Orwell, for his part, "denied fiercely that equality necessarily negates liberty"[33] and thought that "liberty without equality was meagre fare."[34] In a 1946 article published as part of a series for the *Manchester Evening News*, he acknowledged some "pessimists" who thought that "the attempt to establish liberty and equality always ends in the police state" (XVIII: 58), having previously noted that "Liberty, according to some, is incompatible with equality" (XVI: 217). But he held out

[30] Goodway, *Anarchist Seeds beneath the Snow*, p. 159.

[31] Zwerdling, *Orwell and the Left*, p. 29.

[32] John Rawls, *Justice as Fairness: A Restatement*, edited by Erin Kelly (Cambridge, MA: Harvard University Press, 2001), p. 2.

[33] Bernard Crick, *Orwell: A Life* (Boston: Little, Brown and Company, 1980), p. xiv. In response to a question from Crick suggesting that there might be an inherent contradiction between liberty and equality, David Astor, Orwell's editor at *The Observer*, explained that "I haven't seen anything in his writing which says that he felt that was an impossibility": see *Orwell Remembered*, edited by Audrey Coppard and Bernard Crick (London: Ariel Books, 1984), p. 192.

[34] Robert Colls, *George Orwell: English Rebel* (Oxford: Oxford University Press, 2013), p. 185.

hope that "In England, if anywhere it would be possible to abolish poverty without destroying liberty" (XVI: 222) suggesting some optimism about the compatibility of equality and liberty.

I emphasize Orwell's seeming optimism about the compatibility of liberty and equality because some left-libertarians have argued that any supposed conflict between liberty and equality is largely an illusion.[35] The commitments of left-libertarians generally are nicely captured here:

> Left-libertarian theories of justice hold that agents are full self-owners and that natural resources are owned in some egalitarian manner. Unlike most versions of egalitarianism, left-libertarianism endorses full self-ownership, and thus places specific limits on what others may do to one's person without one's permission. Unlike the more familiar right-libertarianism (which also endorses full self-ownership), it holds that natural resources—resources which are *not* the results of anyone's choices and which are necessary for any form of activity—may be privately appropriated only with the permission of, or with a significant payment to, the members of society.[36]

A familiar complaint directed at right-libertarians who only endorse a thesis concerning full self-ownership is that their conception of liberty is fatally flawed insofar as the right-libertarian must tolerate enormous gaps in wealth, resources, and opportunities in the name of preserving liberty, and, as some left-libertarians have asked, "What is liberty, when one class of men starve another?"[37]

[35] Michael Otsuka, *Libertarianism without Inequality* (Oxford: Clarendon Press, 2003), p. 12.
[36] Peter Vallentyne, "Introduction: Left-Libertarianism—A Primer," in *Left-Libertarianism and Its Critics: The Contemporary Debate*, edited by Peter Vallentyne and Hillel Steiner (New York: Palgrave, 2000), p. 1. See also Peter Vallentyne, "Left-Libertarianism and Liberty," in *Contemporary Debates in Political Philosophy*, edited by T. Christiano and J. Christman (Oxford: Blackwell Publishers, 2009), pp. 137–151.
[37] Jacques Roux, as quoted in George Woodcock, *Anarchism: A History of Libertarian Ideas and Movements* (New York: Meridian Books, 1962), p. 57.

By contrast, left-libertarians endorse two distinct theses: one about self-ownership, the other natural resources. It will help to spend time on each.

On Self-Ownership

If left-libertarianism turns partly on the thesis that persons are, at least initially, self-owners, much depends on what self-ownership entails. On an influential way of putting things, if persons are self-owners, then "each person possesses over himself, as a matter of moral right, all those rights that a slaveholder has over a complete chattel slave as a matter of legal right, and he is entitled, morally speaking, to dispose over himself in the way such a slaveholder is entitled, legally speaking, to dispose over his slave."[38] If the owner of a chattel slave can rent, sell, transfer, or destroy their property as a matter of legal right, then self-owners can similarly rent, sell, transfer, or destroy *themselves* as a matter of moral right. The right to self-ownership endows us with the same privileges, claims, powers, and immunities over ourselves, our persons and our bodies, that more familiar property rights endow us with as concerns our property.

Some disagreements among left-libertarians as concerns the right of self-ownership should be recorded. First, left-libertarians do not agree about how strong a right of self-ownership is. As noted above, some understand left-libertarianism as endorsing full self-ownership, but what does full ownership of a self amount to? Peter Vallentyne explains that "Full ownership of an entity consists in a full set" of various rights, including familiar Hohfeldian incidents (say, a liberty right to use the entity, a power to authorize its use by others, and a claim right that others not use it without

---

[38] G. A. Cohen, *Self-Ownership, Freedom and Equality* (Cambridge: Cambridge University Press, 1995), p. 68.

authorization), as well as rights to compensation, enforcement rights including rights of prior restraint and punishment, rights of transfer, immunities to nonconsensual loss of these rights, and more.[39] He also explains that "Full ownership is a logically strongest set of ownership rights that one can have over a thing that is compatible with others having the same kind of ownership rights over everything else in the world."[40] But, as Michael Otsuka contends, full self-ownership, so understood, would commit the libertarian to a kind of "moral fanaticism" that "rules out any seriously harmful incursions whatsoever on the bodies of innocents," even when those incursions are merely foreseen and not intended and even when they are the unforeseen result of activities reasonably thought to be minimally or not at all harmful. To avoid this charge, Otsuka commends understanding the right of self-ownership as less than full but strong enough to afford "A very stringent right of control over and use of one's mind and body that bars others from intentionally using one as a means" and "A very stringent right to all of the income that one can gain from one's mind and body (including one's labour)."[41]

In what follows I shall understand the right of self-ownership to afford persons stringent rather than full rights, partly because libertarians generally have resisted understanding rights in absolute terms,[42] but also because I am interested in understanding whether Orwell would assent to even this more modest way of conceiving of the right of self-ownership—that is, as very stringent but not full—to test his credentials as a left-libertarian. If he does not even recognize a very stringent right of self-ownership

---

[39] Peter Vallentyne, "Left-Libertarianism," in *The Oxford Handbook of Political Philosophy*, edited by David Estlund (Oxford: Oxford University Press, 2012), p. 154. See also Cohen, *Self-Ownership, Freedom and Equality*, p. 213.

[40] Ibid.

[41] Otsuka, *Libertarianism without Inequality*, pp. 13–15. See also Michael Otsuka, "Self-Ownership and Equality: A Lockean Reconciliation," *Philosophy and Public Affairs*, Vol. 27 (1998), pp. 66–67.

[42] Jason Brennan, *Libertarianism: What Everyone Needs to Know* (Oxford: Oxford University Press, 2012), pp. 40–41.

then he does not recognize a full right. But what is not negotiable for left-libertarian credentials is that the right of self-ownership is understood to be strong enough that, other things being equal, persons have a unique privilege to use their own mind and body, a claim against others to refrain from treating the person merely as a means and using force or threat of force to compel action or inaction, a unique power to waive or annul or transfer that right of self-ownership, and that the right be strong enough that it can only be justly invaded in fairly dire circumstances. This left-libertarian understanding of the right of self-ownership, as I understand it, tracks the threshold deontology I ascribed to Orwell in Chapter 2: rights of self-ownership must be respected, even when invading them would yield significant utility, except in those cases in which invading them is necessary to prevent consequences that are not merely bad but *horrendous* but not otherwise.

Second, left-libertarians do not always agree about the scope of the right of self-ownership. John Stuart Mill, defender of the "one very simple principle" that justifies interfering with liberty only to prevent harm to others, nonetheless approved of laws that would deny persons the power to transfer their right of self-ownership to another by selling themselves into slavery; at least, he thought that laws prohibiting voluntary slavery are not unjust.[43] Other left-libertarians infer that a right of self-ownership does afford self-owners the power to voluntarily sell themselves, or allow themselves to be sold, into slavery. Arguably, left-libertarians can only "self-contradictorily" affirm a right of self-ownership and deny that self-owners can sell themselves.[44]

To my knowledge, Orwell never considered the ethics of voluntary slavery, although I am inclined to think he would have opposed it, given his hatred of caste noted in Chapter 6: slave castes do

[43] John Stuart Mill, *On Liberty and Other Writings*, edited by Stefan Collini (Cambridge: Cambridge University Press, 2007), pp. 102–103.
[44] Hillel Steiner, *An Essay on Rights* (Blackwell: Cambridge, 1984), pp. 232–234.

not become lesser obstacles to relating to one another as equals if they are entered into voluntarily, and the most obvious reasons for choosing to enter a slave market involve desperate circumstances and prospects for exploitation. A concern for relational equality might lead the left-libertarian to conclude that while persons have a power to waive or annul their right of self-ownership, no one is empowered to take ownership of another person since doing so conflicts with egalitarian justice: my right to discard something need not afford you any right to pick it up,[45] especially if picking it up would harm others by disrupting valuable egalitarian social relations. Still, we already have some reason to worry about the prospect of dissolving conflicts between liberty and equality, although the second constitutive left-libertarian thesis is supposed to provide cause for optimism here. I consider it next.

On Ownership of Natural Resources

Left-libertarians are unique among libertarians in supposing that persons, in addition to being self-owners, are entitled to some share of natural resources that can be owned privately only with the consent of others or by compensating them for their loss. Reference to natural resources denotes those resources external to persons and does not include their minds and bodies. One might agree with Rousseau that the first instance of private property usurped what should have been freely accessible to all,[46] but left-libertarians have

---

[45] Vallentyne, "Introduction," p. 4.

[46] "The first man who, having enclosed a piece of ground, bethought himself of saying *This is mine*, and found people simple enough to believe him, was the real founder of civil society. From how many crimes, wars and murders, from how many horrors and misfortunes might not any one have saved mankind, by pulling up the stakes, or filling up the ditch, and crying to his fellows, 'Beware of listening to this impostor; you are undone if you once forget that the fruits of the earth belong to us all, and the earth itself to nobody'": see Jean-Jacques Rousseau, *A Discourse on Inequality* (New York: Penguin, 1984), p. 109. Judith Shklar suggests that "*1984* is decidedly the product of a Rousseauist imagination": see Judith N. Shklar, "*Nineteen Eighty-Four*: Should Political Theory Care?," *Political Theory*, Vol. 13, No. 1 (February 1985), p. 14.

tended to appeal, not to Rousseau, but to John Locke as the source of their second constitutive thesis.

Here, Locke famously affirms both a right of self-ownership and a restriction on taking natural resources out of common stock:

> Though the Earth, and all inferior Creatures be common to all Men, yet every Man has a *Property* in his own Person. This no Body has any Right to but himself. The *Labour* of his Body, and the *Work* of his Hands, we may say, are properly his. Whatsoever then he removes out of the State that Nature hath provided, and left it in, he hath mixed his *Labour* with, and joyned to it something that is his own, and thereby makes it his *Property*. It being by him removed from the common state Nature placed it in hath by this *labour* something annexed to it, that excludes the common right of other Men. For this *Labour* being the unquestionable Property of the Labourer, no Man but he can have a right to what that is once joyned to, *at least where there is enough, and as good left in common for others.*[47]

Different libertarians have understood Locke differently. Some have concluded that "each individual has a right to an equal share of the basis non-human means of production."[48] Others that we can acquire natural resources if and only if our acquisition places nobody else at a disadvantage.[49] Still others that we must leave enough for others to have an opportunity for well-being that is at least as good as the opportunity for well-being that one obtained in using or

---

[47] John Locke, *Two Treatises of Government*, edited by Peter Laslett (Cambridge: Cambridge University Press, 2005), pp. 287–288. Locke has other restrictions on the taking of unowned natural resources as well, that "As much as anyone can make use of to any advantage of life before it spoil; so much he may by his labour fix a Property in it. Whatever is beyond this, is more than his share, and belongs to others" (290).

[48] Hillel Steiner, "The Natural Right to the Means of Production," *Philosophical Quarterly*, Vol. 27 (1977), p. 49.

[49] Robert Nozick, *Anarchy, State, and Utopia* (New York: Basic Books, 1974), p. 178.

appropriating the natural resource.[50] But however Locke is understood, he is clear that self-owners are bound by *some* limits in justly acquiring natural resources and that self-owners are owed *some* share of natural resources as a matter of right. Left-libertarians are inclined to agree even if they disagree about the details.

For example, left-libertarians do not agree about how shares of natural resources are to be determined, allocated, or governed: some left-libertarians suppose that natural resources are jointly owned and no one may use or appropriate them without permissions from the collective; others suppose that persons can use jointly owned natural resources, consistent with terms of fair use decided upon collectively, but cannot claim any exclusive right to them; others allow that exclusive right can be asserted but exclusive owners thereby acquire enforceable obligations, including the obligation to compensate others in some manner.[51] But for purposes of evaluating Orwell's left-libertarian credentials, I will focus on a particularly influential take on the right to natural resources.

The nineteenth-century economist, Henry George, came close to affirming both constitutive theses of left-libertarianism when he suggested that "the exertion of labor in production *is the only title to exclusive possession*."[52] On the one hand, that he thinks that we can claim exclusive possession of the products of our labor tracks the left-libertarian thesis concerning self-ownership. On the other hand, that he thinks we can *only* claim exclusive possession of the products of our labor implies that no one can claim exclusive possession of natural resources, an implication that is at least consistent with the second left-libertarian thesis: everyone has a claim to some share of natural resources only if no one has

---

[50] Michael Otsuka, *Libertarianism without Inequality* (Oxford: Clarendon Press, 2003), pp. 24–29.

[51] See, for example, John Cunliffe, "Introduction: Left-Libertarianism—Historical Origins," in *The Origins of Left-Libertarianism: An Anthology of Historical Writings*, edited by Peter Vallentyne and Hillel Steiner (New York: Palgrave, 2000), pp. 1–19.

[52] Henry George, "The Injustice of Private Property in Land," in *The Origins of Left-Libertarianism*, p. 197.

exclusive claim to all them. Indeed, George appears to argue that our exclusive right to the products of our labor rules out exclusive claims to natural resources, land in particular, when he contends that "For as labor cannot produce without the use of land, the denial of the equal right to the use of land is necessarily the denial of the right of labor to its own produce."[53] Presumably, the idea is that since labor alone produces nothing, the right of self-ownership has no value unless self-owners also have a right to some stock of natural resources.[54] But the right of self-ownership does have value. So, self-owners must have some right to some stock of natural resources. Thus, George affirmed that "The equal right of all men to the use of land is as clear as their equal right to breathe the air—it is a right proclaimed by the fact of their existence,"[55] and he repeatedly suggests that exclusive claims to land are akin to slavery.[56]

Still, George does not reject exclusive claims to natural resources, and favored letting current landowners retain their land and personal property derived from it. "*It is not necessary to confiscate land,*" George argued, "*it is only necessary to confiscate rent*" and he offers "the simple yet sovereign remedy . . . *to appropriate rent by taxation.*"[57] This is the *only* tax liability that George commends—he calls for the abolishment of all other taxes[58]—either because he thinks them unjust or unnecessary. George allowed that persons may use and appropriate land, thereby laying exclusive claim to it, so long as they pay for its competitive value via taxation; having paid for the land's competitive value, they fully own it and any net benefits they generate. Their payments would go into a common fund that

[53] Ibid., p. 201.

[54] Otsuka's example of the person who weaves items of value from their own hair probably shows that self-owners do not need external natural resources to create artifacts of value: Otsuka, *Libertarianism without Inequality*, p. 17. But the rarity of such examples should be acknowledged.

[55] George, "The Injustice of Private Property in Land," p. 199.

[56] Ibid., pp. 203, 213, and 215.

[57] Ibid., p. 212.

[58] Ibid., p. 213.

GEORGE ORWELL AND LEFT-LIBERTARIANISM 205

would then be spent in ways that promote equality: he speaks of raising wages, increasing the earnings of capital, extirpating pauperism, abolishing poverty, supplying remunerative employment, affording free scope to human powers, lessening crime, elevating morals, taste, and intelligence, purifying government, and carrying civilization to nobler heights as a consequence of appropriating rent via taxation from landowners who would lay exclusive claims to land.[59] Realizing half of these objectives would go a long way to neutralizing inequalities, especially those inequalities that preclude relating to one another as equals. If his proposal works, if taxing exclusive claims to land can fund the elimination of relational inequalities, then the left-libertarian project of showing that liberty and inequality are not unavoidably in conflict has more than a chance of success.

Since George has become "the most popular exponent of 'left-libertarianism' both in his time and to later generations,"[60] his proposal concerning self-ownership and the taxation of land can serve as something of an acid test for left-libertarian credentials: sympathy with Georgist proposals is evidence of sympathy with left-libertarian's second thesis, antipathy towards them is evidence of antipathy to it.

From Theory to Practice

There is some reason to think that Orwell was sympathetic with the two constitutive theses of left-libertarianism. Crick thought that he shared Locke's views about land and labor[61] and Orwell's objectives, "that nobody should have the power to tell anybody else what to do or to think or to feel" and "That nobody should be

---

[59] Ibid., p. 212.
[60] Cunliffe, "Introduction," p. 17.
[61] Crick, *Orwell: A Life*, p. xvii.

poor,"[62] track each thesis. That said, there is also reason be skeptical that he endorsed one or both theses. In the next two sections, I explain why skepticism is appropriate.

Left-Libertarianism in Practice 1: Orwell and Self-Ownership

Orwell's corpus does sometimes suggest that persons have a right of self-ownership. Old Major's speech in *Animal Farm* includes admonitions that "the produce of our labour is stolen from us by human beings" and "get rid of Man and the produce of our labour would be our own" (VIII: 4–5), and while he documents other cruelties suffered by the animals, his principal complaint seems to be that the product of their labor, something they have a right to if they have a right of self-ownership, is taken from them. Indeed, compelled labor, slavery, is as blatant a violation of the right of self-ownership as there is. Yet Orwell often spoke in favor of practices and policies that are inconsistent with a stringent right to self-ownership. Iterating those practices and policies that he endorsed that are inconsistent with a stringent right of self-ownership should suffice to justify skepticism that he endorsed left-libertarianism's first constitutive thesis.

First, consider what Orwell said about state coercion. His "No, Not One" named "two facts which underlie the structure of modern society," including the fact that:

> Civilisation rests ultimately on coercion. What holds society together is not the policeman but the good will of common men, and yet that good will is powerless unless the policeman is there

---

[62] As quoted in Peter Lewis, *The Road to 1984* (New York: Harcourt Brace Jovanovich, Publishers, 1981), p. 16. Lewis regards this "as accurate a summary as it is possible to give" (16).

to back it up. Any government which refused to use violence in its own defence would cease almost immediately to exist, because it could be overthrown by any body of men, or even any individual, that was less scrupulous. Objectively, whoever is not on the side of the police is on the side of the criminal, and vice versa. (XIII: 40)

This argument affords the state a monopoly on coercive power that should trouble libertarians who allow that a state may use force for defensive purposes, but to defend the rights of *persons*. It is one thing to afford a minimal nightwatchman version of a state with such a monopoly to enable it to protect persons and quite another to afford it with such a monopoly to enable it to protect itself. Appeals to defense of the state can and have ballooned into absurd justifications for state interference into policing the most private and intimate aspects of our lives. Famously, Sir Patrick Devlin found the conclusion that a state can police conduct popularly regarded as immoral from the premise that such conduct is analogous to treason and sedition threatening to the continued existence of the state.[63] It is probably unfair to associate the view that Orwell articulated above with such bungled argumentation, but his appeal to the allegedly objective fact that those who are not on the side of the police are on the side of criminals invites such a response.

Second, Orwell's views about conscription are dubiously consistent with a stringent right of self-ownership. He regarded conscription, along with increased censorship, as "two inevitable evils of modern war" (XI: 333), and worried that "the discipline of a bourgeois conscript army is based ultimately on fear" in contrast to that of a voluntary army motivated by class loyalty (VI: 27), and that conscription might accentuate a labor shortage (XVIII: 482). Still, in "In Front of Your Nose," he explained that:

---

[63] Patrick Devlin, *The Enforcement of Morals* (Oxford: Oxford University Press, 1965), pp. 1–25.

For years before the war, nearly all enlightened people were in favour of standing up to Germany: the majority of them were also against having enough armaments to make such a stand effective. I know very well the arguments that are put forward in defence of this attitude; some of them are justified, but in the main they are simply forensic excuses. As late as 1939, the Labour Party voted against conscription, a step which probably played its part in bringing about the Russo-German pact and certainly had a disastrous effect on morale in France. Then came 1940, and we nearly perished for lack of a large, efficient army, which we could have had if we had introduced conscription at least three years earlier. (XVIII: 162)

Even if one thinks that a right of conscientious refusal is only a pro tanto right that can be overridden to prevent horrendous consequences, a position consistent with Orwell's threshold deontology, the case for conscription suggested in this passage is surely too weak to override such a right. Even if failing to institute conscription in the 1930s yielded a smaller army, lessened morale in France, and somehow helped bring about the Russo-German pact, none of this rises to the level of horrendous consequences even if being vanquished by Germany would (and of course that didn't happen). The problem is not that Orwell favors conscription in some circumstances but that he favors it in circumstances in which the right of self-ownership should make conscription wrongful.

Third, Orwell's views about targeting civilians in war, noted in Chapter 2, are dubiously consistent with a stringent right of self-ownership. Again, Orwell appears to think that civilian immunity is not absolute when he commended dropping bombs on mothers, smashing dwelling houses, and burning holes in children in lieu of enslavement by more ruthless persons (XI: 113). To be sure, targeting civilians as part of a campaign to break the will of an unjust enemy might end unjust aggression more quickly, but to use innocents in this manner is to treat them merely as a means and his breezy willingness to sacrifice them suggests that the right of self-ownership is not being given its due here.

Fourth, Orwell's commitment to a right of free expression is not as robust as one might expect. In "Freedom of the Press," he allowed that "when one demands liberty of speech and of the press, one is not demanding absolute liberty" and that "There always must be, or at any rate there always will be, some degree of censorship, so long as organized societies endure" (XVII: 257), another conclusion that a threshold deontologist can probably endorse. Here, Orwell seems on safe libertarian ground:

> If the intellectual liberty which without a doubt has been one of the distinguishing marks of western civilization means anything at all, it means that everyone shall have the right to say and to print what he believes to be the truth, provided only that it does not harm the rest of the community in some quite unmistakable way. (XVII: 257)

But compare Orwell's reasoning with this:

> The question in every case is whether the words used are used in such circumstances and are of such a nature as to create a clear and present danger that they will bring about the substantive evils. . . . It is a question of proximity and degree. When a nation is at war many things that might be said in time of peace are such a hindrance to its effort that their utterance will not be endured so long as men fight, and that no court could regard them as protected by any constitutional right.[64]

This quote is taken from the majority opinion written by Chief Justice Oliver Wendell Holmes in *Schenck v. United States*, where the Supreme Court of the United States upheld the convictions

---

[64] *Schenck v. United States*, 249 U.S. 47 (1919).

of Charles Schenck and Elizabeth Baer for obstructing the enlist-
ment service by passing out pamphlets contending that conscription was unconstitutional and urging the working class to resist the
draft. There are differences: Orwell speaks of harming a community while Holmes speaks of evils; Orwell would deny protection
to speech that harms a community in some quite unmistakable
way while Holmes denies protection to speech that creates a clear
and present danger. But Orwell and Holmes both fall short of the
more robust standards protecting free expression that the SCOTUS
would articulate in later cases.[65] If Holmes's opinion could not protect the free expression of political dissidents, Orwell's might fare
no better. And if Orwell too tolerates the criminalization of manifestly free expression, then it is far from clear that he could endorse
left-libertarianism's first constitutive thesis.

Fifth, Orwell's views about sexuality and reproductive rights
fall well short of what a stringent right of self-ownership demands.
Surely a self-owner has the right to decide for herself what will
happen to and in her body, especially as pertains to profoundly
personal and important decisions about having children. But there
is nothing in Orwell to suggest he agreed. He too often seems to
share Gordon's view in Keep The Aspidistra Flying that "This birth-
control business" is "just another way they've found out of bullying
us" (IV: 157) and objects to a socialism that would include "Free
abortion-clinics on all the corners" (IV: 97). In The Road to Wigan
Pier, he identified the belief that women should have access to birth
control among various "half-baked antinomian opinions" (V: 129)
and his worry that "there won't be so many children . . . if the birth-
controllers have their way" (V: 109) surely cannot justify overriding rights of bodily autonomy. No wonder Woodcock lamented
that Orwell's "most truly reactionary proposals" include "crushing

---

[65] For example, in Brandenburg v. Ohio 395 U.S. 444 (1969), the SCOTUS held that advocacy could be punished only "where such advocacy is directed to inciting or producing
imminent lawless action and is likely to incite or produce such action."

penal taxation of childless people and a more rigorous repression of abortion,"[66] policies that are surely inconsistent with a right of self-ownership.

Sixth, Orwell's views about the right to bear arms merit some comment. The right to bear arms—at least, the one referenced in the Second Amendment of the United States Constitution—has been understood in two ways: on the *Individual Right Model*, it protects the rights of individual persons to own and bear arms, say, for defense of self or home; on the *Collective Right Model*, it protects only the right of States to form a well-regulated militia or contemporary equivalent. The Individual Right Model is typically endorsed by libertarians.[67] But insofar as Orwell discusses a right to bear arms, he seems to favor the Collective Right Model. The capital letters in this passage from a 1941 article written for *The Evening Standard* are his:

> The totalitarian states can do great things, but there is one thing they cannot do: they cannot give the factory-worker a rifle and tell him to take it home and keep it in his bedroom. THAT RIFLE HANGING ON THE WALL OF THE WORKING-CLASS FLAT OR LABOURER'S COTTAGE, IS THE SYMBOL OF DEMOCRACY. IT IS OUR JOB TO SEE THAT IT STAYS THERE. (XII: 363)

Orwell thought that "rifles, muskets, longbows and hand grenades are inherently democratic weapons" (XVII: 319), since they are cheap and simple to use, but he clearly regarded that rifle hanging on the wall as an instrument of the Home Guard, a volunteer local defense organization purposed to defend England from invasion.

---

[66] Woodcock, *The Crystal Spirit*, p. 261.

[67] The 2022 platform of the Libertarian Party of the United States affirms that "the individual right recognized by the Second Amendment to keep and bear arms, and oppose the prosecution of individuals for exercising their rights of self-defense." See https://www.lp.org/platform/.

If Orwell commended arming his fellow Englishmen, his advocacy suggests sympathy with the Collective Right Model, not the Individual Right Model, a result that might seem inconsistent with a stringent right of self-ownership.[68]

There may be more reasons to be suspicious: I have not mentioned Orwell's democratic Socialism which will almost certainly demand redistributing wealth and resources in ways that will generate complaints of forced labor and theft. But we have enough grounds, I think, to be suspicious that Orwell endorsed a stringent right of self-ownership. And that means he probably did not endorse the first of left-libertarianism's constitutive theses. What about the second?

Left-Libertarianism in Practice 2: Orwell and Ownership of Natural Resources

Margaret Nelson, Orwell's laird in Jura, recalled that he thought that the whole of Jura should be divided into smallholdings, though she does not identify what he thought should be done with them.[69] A more general call for dividing up natural resources would better suit the left-libertarian, say, this passage from *The Road to Wigan Pier*, where Orwell appealed to a familiar metaphor:

The world is a raft sailing through space with, potentially, plenty of provisions for everybody; the idea that we must all cooperate and see to it that everyone does his fair share of the work and gets his fair share of the provisions seems so blatantly obvious that one

---

[68] I acknowledge that there are some libertarians who think that bearing or otherwise possessing arms threatens the rights of others or diminishes their liberty. For an argument to this effect, see https://www.theatlantic.com/ideas/archive/2022/06/second-amendment-gun-regulations/661208/. If such an argument is sound, it is difficult to see why a right of self-ownership would entail an individual right to bear arms.

[69] See *Orwell Remembered*, edited by Audrey Coppard and Bernard Crick (New York: Ariel Facts on File, 1984), p. 228.

would say that no one could possibly fail to accept it unless he had some corrupt motive for clinging to the present system." (V: 159)

The world-raft metaphor has been employed by philosophers[70] but also by George, who suggested that:

> We arrive and we depart, guests at a banquet continually spread, spectators and participants in an entertainment where there is room for all who come; passengers from station to station, *on an orb that whirls through space*—our rights to take and possess cannot be exclusive; they must be bounded everywhere by the equal right of others. Just as the passenger in a railroad car may spread himself and his baggage over as many seats as he pleases, until other passengers come in, so may a settler take and use as much land as he chooses, until it is needed by others ... when his right must be curtailed by the equal rights of the others.[71]

If George and Orwell understood the plight of humanity similarly, perhaps Orwell, like George, endorsed left-libertarianism's second thesis. He came close in moments.

Orwell's critique of a "Professor Sainsbury," also in *The Road to Wigan Pier*, notes Sainsbury's suggestion that "it is questionable whether strict justice demands it"—that is, that every human being ought to have the chance of earning at least a tolerable livelihood. Sainsbury also quickly dismissed "the insane doctrine that being born in a country give some right to the possession of the soil of that country," a doctrine he thought "hardly requires notice" (V: 125). Orwell gave Sainsbury credit for saying what a more timid person would only think—"Most people are a little shy of putting that kind of thing on paper ... It takes a lot of guts to be *openly*

---

[70] Onora O'Neill (neé Nell), "Lifeboat Earth," *Philosophy and Public Affairs*, Vol. 4, No. 3 (1975), pp. 273–292.

[71] Ibid., p. 202, emphasis mine.

such a skunk as that"—and dismissed Sainsbury as "a confessed reactionary" (V: 126). But while he clearly thinks little of his target, Orwell never quite affirms that persons do have a right to the possession of the soil of the country of their birth or that they have any positive right to some share of natural resources at just the moment made sense to do so. Orwell's critique of Sainsbury is a missed opportunity to endorse left-libertarian's second thesis.

A series of AIP columns are also suggestive without being dispositive. In a 5 August 1944 AIP column, Orwell lamented the return of wooden railings around various squares in London partly because he thought them ugly but also for reasons having to do with justice. The purpose of such railings, he thought, was to "to keep the populace out" and ensure that "the lawful denizens of the squares can make use of their treasured keys again, and the children of the poor can be kept out" (XVI: 318). He returned to the subject about two weeks later, responding to a reader who objected that his 5 August comments advocated theft of private property. Here is Orwell's response in full:

> If giving the land of England back to the people of England is theft, I am quite happy to call it theft. In his zeal to defend private property, my correspondent does not stop to consider how the so-called owners of the land got hold of it. They simply seized it by force, afterwards hiring lawyers to provide them with title deeds. In the case of the enclosure of the common lands, which was going on from about 1600 to 1850, the land-grabbers did not even have the excuse of being foreign conquerors; they were quite frankly taking the heritage of their own countrymen, upon no sort of pretext except that they had the power to do so. (XVI: 336)

He continued:

> Except for the few surviving commons, the high roads, the lands of the National Trust, a certain number of parks, and the

sea shore below high-tide mark, every square inch of England is "owned" by a few thousand families. These people are just about as useful as so many tapeworms. It is desirable that people should own their own dwelling-houses, and it is probably desirable that a farmer should own as much land as he can actually farm. But the ground-landlord in a town area has no function and no excuse for existence. He is merely a person who has found out a way of milking the public while giving nothing in return. He causes rents to be higher, he makes town planning more difficult, and he excludes children from green spaces: that is literally all that he does, except to draw his income. The removal of the railings in the squares was a first step against him. It was a very small step, and yet an appreciable one, as the present move to restore the railings shows. For three years or so the squares lay open, and their sacred turf was trodden by the feet of working-class children, a sight to make dividend-drawers gnash their false teeth. It that is theft, all I can say is, so much the better for theft. (XVI: 336)

Undoubtedly, Orwell thought that current holdings of land were not distributed justly, and that landowners did not do enough to advance the public good. But his replies do not amount to an endorsement of left-libertarianism's second thesis. If anything, they too mark a missed opportunity to affirm left-libertarianism's second thesis. Further, insofar as he offers a critique of the ground-landlords of his day, he offers two competing lines of thought, only one of which supported left-libertarianism.

On the one hand, Orwell suggested that the distribution of land in England was the product of manifest right violations: current landowners possessed their holdings only because they seized and laid exclusive claim to common lands, thereby depriving their countrymen of their heritage. Putting things as such, current holdings of natural resources were unjust because they were acquired unjustly, that is, in violation of the rights of past persons. On the other hand, Orwell suggested that current holdings of natural resources were unjust on consequentialist grounds: landowners were useless and serve no function, and it was desirable that people should own their homes and farms; ground-landlords made town planning more difficult and deprived children of valuable resources to their detriment while contributing nothing; and so forth. This second line of reasoning surely suggests that there is something amiss with the distribution of land, but not that it violated anyone's rights to natural resources. While what Orwell says here is certainly consistent with supposing that persons have a right to an equal share of natural resources, he again misses a chance to affirm that persons have such a right.

This is my general reading of Orwell with respect to ownership of natural resources: he is not unsympathetic to left-libertarianism's second thesis, but he never quite endorsed it. Perhaps this should not be a surprise given that, as I argued in Chapter 6, Orwell's egalitarianism is not best understood in distributive terms even if it is central to his ethical thought. In any case, the case for concluding that Orwell endorses left-libertarianism's second commitment is largely lacking.

Conclusion

This chapter is somewhat deflationary, since I argue that the case for thinking that Orwell is well-understood as a left-libertarian is underdetermined. None of this upsets various platitudes about Orwell—that he cared about liberty, that liberty is one of his core values—but if he is not well-regarded as a left-libertarian then some care should be taken in describing his commitment to liberty. Libertarians generally do not simply care about liberty or value it greatly, just as egalitarians do not simply care about equality or value it greatly; more plausibly, they understand liberty as being especially morally valuable, more morally valuable than other things that are also valuable, including equality. But then we are left with tricky questions: which did Orwell value more? If he could max-imize only one, which would he select? If forced to choose be-tween two evils, repression or inequality, which would he settle for? I think an argument can be mounted that while Orwell valued both equality and liberty, he valued equality more. On more than a few occasions in previous chapters, I have noted Orwell's self-identification as a democratic Socialist, although I have had little to say about his understanding of socialism, what he thought that a commitment to democratic socialism involved, and why it was preferable to other economic regimes. In Chapter 8, I suggest that insofar as Orwell made a case for democratic Socialism, that case most obviously appealed to the egalitarian consequences of implementing socialism rather than to implications for liberty and self-ownership. If his case for democratic Socialism, which Orwell himself thought was central to his ethical commitments, flows from his egalitarianism and not from a commitment to a stringent right of self-ownership, then we have some reason to think that Orwell valued equality more than liberty.

But how strong *is* Orwell's case for democratic Socialism? I do not dispute his self-identification, but his case for democratic Socialism is not as persuasive as one might hope. Indeed, I think Orwell's case for democratic Socialism is *incomplete* for reasons that I explain in Chapter 8.

8
Orwell's Incomplete Case for Socialism

That Orwell embraced socialism is not really in dispute, even if there is some question about just when he first embraced it without remainder. In *The Road to Wigan Pier*, he explained that "I loosely described myself as a Socialist" when he was seventeen or eighteen although he "had not much grasp of what Socialism meant and no notion that the working class were human beings" (V: 130–131). He also wrote that, in Burma, he had "no interest in socialism or any other economic theory" (V: 139).[1] Some of those who knew him before and during his trip to Wigan recall him having some socialist sympathies, some not.[2] What is not in dispute is that Orwell's road to Damascus went through Barcelona, that any embryonic socialist sympathies he may have had blossomed into a full-blown commitment after seeing what he understood to be socialism in action. "I have seen wonderful things & at last really believe in Socialism, which I never did before" (XI: 28), he wrote to Cyril Connolly. And in *Homage to Catalonia*, he explained that "In theory it was perfect equality, and even in practice it was not far from it" and that "that the prevailing mental atmosphere was that of Socialism" (VI: 83).

---

[1] Crick thinks Orwell exaggerated, that while "He may have not been a socialist . . . it was untrue that" he had no interest in socialism: see Bernard Crick, *Orwell: A Life* (Boston: Little, Brown, 1980), pp. 102 and 108.

[2] Mabel Fierz, occasional reviewer for *The Adelphi* who would have first met Orwell in the summer of 1930, suggested that "my recollection of him was he always was a socialist." Jerry Kennan, who met Orwell in Wigan, explained that "I wouldn't say by any means that he was a convinced socialist, although he was convinced that drastic changes was required." See *Orwell Remembered*, edited by Audrey Coppard and Bernard Crick (London: Ariel Books, 1984), pp. 96 and 133.

George Orwell. Peter Brian Barry, Oxford University Press. © Oxford University Press 2023.
DOI: 10.1093/oso/9780197627402.003.0008

That Orwell converted upon seeing socialism, Spanish-style, is also suggested in "Why I Write" where, again, he explained that "Every line of serious work that I have written since 1936 has been written, directly or indirectly, *against* totalitarianism and *for* democratic Socialism, as I understand it" (XVIII: 319), a fact minimized by some readers.[3] George Woodcock insisted that Orwell "only became politicized . . . after his experience in Spain, which showed him what he was—a democratic or libertarian socialist."[4]

Orwell's socialism informed his politics. He criticized the 1 percent before it was cool.[5] In a 1947 piece, he explained that "a Socialist United States of Europe seems to me the only worthwhile political objective today" (XIX: 164). He joined only one political party in his life, the Independent Labour Party, a "Left-wing, egalitarian . . . strange English mixture of secularized evangelism and non-Communist Marxism,"[6] because (the boldface is his) **"the I.L.P. is the only British party—at any rate the only one large enough to be worth considering—which aims at anything I should regard as Socialism"** (XI: 168). Some readers thought that *Animal Farm* and *Nineteen Eighty-Four* are evidence that Orwell abandoned socialism in his final years, but while *Animal Farm* tells of a revolution betrayed, it does not question that "The animals were happy as they had never conceived it possible to be" after they took

[3] The introduction to the 1956 Signet edition of *Animal Farm*, written by C. M. Woodhouse, conveniently if partially has Orwell explain that "Every line I have written since 1936 has been against totalitarianism . . .": as quoted in John Rodden, *Scenes from an Afterlife: The Legacy of George Orwell* (Wilmington, DE: ISI Books, 2003), pp. 211–212. The ellipses are Woodhouse's own and end there.

[4] George Woodcock, *Orwell's Message: 1984 and the Present* (British Columbia: Harbour Publishing, 1984), p. 89.

[5] In his "War-time Diary," Orwell responded to a "Lady Oxford," who noted that there was little entertaining in London since most people had to part with their cooks and lived in hotels, concluding, "Apparently nothing will ever teach these people that the other 99% of the population exist" (XII: 176).

[6] Bernard Crick, *Orwell: A Life* (Boston: Little, Brown and Company, 1980), p. 162. He later distanced himself from the ILP because, as he explained in a 1940 biographical sketch that "at the beginning of the present war . . . I considered that they were talking nonsense and proposing a line of policy that could only make things easier for Hitler" (XII: 148).

collective ownership of Manor Farm (VIII: 18), a fact minimized in the 1954 CIA-funded animated film.[7] And while we are reminded throughout *Nineteen Eighty-Four* that the Party endorsed INGSOC, English socialism, we are also told that it "rejects and vilifies every principle for which the Socialist movement originally stood, and it chooses to do this in the name of Socialism" (IX: 225). Orwell remained a socialist until his final days, a point many readers have insisted upon.[8]

I do not dispute that Orwell was a socialist, but I do regard his case for socialism as *incomplete*. The problem is not, I think, that Orwell had little to say about capitalism,[9] as Michael Walzer has suggested. Reasonable people can disagree about the semantics of 'little,' but I contend that Orwell did offer or at least hint at some familiar critiques of capitalism. Further, he does have arguments for democratic Socialism, including an argument that is parasitic on his critique of capitalism that must be sussed out. The problem is that Orwell's case, even if cogent, does not singularly justify democratic Socialism. I articulate what I call "the Rawlsian challenge,"

---

[7] See Daniel J. Jeab, *Orwell Subverted: The CIA and the Filming of Animal Farm* (University Park: The Pennsylvania State Press, 2007).

[8] "Orwell never wavered in his claim that he was a socialist": Robert Colls, *George Orwell: English Rebel* (Oxford: Oxford University Press, 2013), p. 174; "Orwell died professing the only political faith he ever had, namely, faith in equalitarian and democratic socialism": George Kateb, "The Road to 1984," *Political Science Quarterly*, Vol. 81, No. 4 (1966), p. 567; in a chapter titled "Fighting for Spain," Jeffrey Meyers writes, "For the rest of his life he cherished this vision of social equality and human dignity": Jeffrey Meyers, *Orwell: Wintry Conscience of a Generation* (New York: W. W. Norton & Co., 2000), p. 143; "Orwell remained a self-described 'democratic socialist' until his dying day" (12) and "never relinquished his socialist ideals": Rodden, *Scenes from an Afterlife*, pp. 12–13; "Orwell's lifelong commitment to socialism is not seriously in doubt": Elinor Taylor, "The Problem of Hope: Orwell's Workers," in *The Cambridge Companion to "Nineteen Eighty-Four"*, edited by Nathan Waddell (Cambridge: Cambridge University Press, 2020), p. 156; "There is no doubt that George Orwell saw himself, from the Spanish Civil War in 1937 to the end of his short life in 1950, as a committed democratic socialist": Woodcock, *Orwell's Message*, p. 124; "Orwell's socialism was not a phase, but a lifelong commitment": Alex Zwerdling, *Orwell and the Left* (New Haven, CT: Yale University Press, 1974), p. 62.

[9] Michael Walzer, "George Orwell's England," in *George Orwell*, edited by Graham Holderness, Bryan Loughrey, and Nahem Yousaf (New York: St. Martin's Press, 1988), p. 195.

an argument that suggests that any cogent reasons that Orwell identified tending to support democratic Socialism *also* tend to support the property-owning democracy, a nonsocialist alternative to capitalism. So, I conclude, his case for democratic Socialism is incomplete.

Orwell's Case for Democratic Socialism

Some of Orwell's readers are quick to dismiss his socialism as "misty and imprecise"[10] or regard him as having nothing but "an early gut attraction to a sort of folk Marxism."[11] But Orwell was part of a recognizable tradition of socialist thought and situating him in the tradition of English socialism will help to clarify his critique of capitalism.

An Unhappy Family

"[W]hat sort of family is it that has, say, both Joseph Stalin and George Orwell among its members?,"[12] one might ask. The answer is "socialism," although, like Orwell's England, it resembled a family with the wrong members in control (XII: 401).[13] In a 1938 letter, he explained that "I am not a Marxist" (XI: 256), as did Marx,[14] and

---

[10] George Woodcock, *Orwell's Message: 1984 and the Present* (British Columbia: Harbour Publishing, 1984), p. 124.

[11] Robert Colls, *George Orwell: English Rebel* (Oxford: Oxford University Press, 2013), p. 10.

[12] Anthony Wright, *Socialisms: Theory and Practices* (Oxford: Oxford University Press, 1987), p. vii.

[13] Raymond Williams weirdly explained that "If I had to say which [of Orwell's] writings have done the most damage it would be . . . the dreadful stuff from the beginning of the war about England as a family with the wrong members in charge": see Raymond Williams, *Politics and Letters: Interviews with New Left Review* (London: New Left Books, 1981), p. 391.

[14] Famously, Marx expressed his disagreement with some contemporaries by suggesting that if their politics represented Marxism, "*ce qu'il y a de certain c'est que moi,*

his 1940 review of Charlie Chaplin's *The Great Dictator* included the observation that "an education in Marxism and similar creeds consists largely in destroying your moral sense" (XII: 315), while in a 1944 book review he identified Marxists as "enemies of freedom of thought" (XVI: 297). I'm unsure what to do with the fact that George and Eileen had a dog named "Marx"[15] but *The Road to Wigan Pier* is peppered with abuse directed at Marxists, including the charge that the ordinary working man "is a truer Socialist than the orthodox Marxist, because he does remember, what the other so often forgets, that Socialism means justice and common decency" (V: 163). Orwell was not entirely hostile to Marx: he thought that "a crude version of his doctrine is believed in by millions and is in the consciousness of all of us" (XI: 105), and, as I noted in Chapter 4, after noting the need to "evolve a system of good and evil which is independent of heaven and hell" he allowed that "Marxism, indeed, does supply this, but it has never really been popularized" (XIV: 113). There is also a strong case to be made that his interest in English character, his interpretation of mass culture, and his essays on the relationship between politics and literature were influenced by some of his Marxist counterparts.[16] Still, not everyone in the family got along.

Orwell came to embrace socialism for avowedly ethical reasons, a point many readers have insisted upon.[17] The British socialist

---

je ne suis pas Marxiste" ("what is certain is that I myself am not a Marxist"). See https://www.marxists.org/archive/marx/works/1880/05/parti-ouvrier.htm.

   [15] In a letter to Norah Meyers, Eileen wrote that "We have a poodle puppy. We called him Marx to remind us that we never read Marx and now we have read a little and taken so strong a personal dislike to the man that we can't look the dog in the face when we speak to him": see *The Lost Orwell*, edited by Peter Davison (London: Timewell Press Limited, 2006), p. 72. That said, "Eileen liked to tease": Colls, *George Orwell: English Rebel*, p. 9.

   [16] See Philip Bounds, *Orwell & Marxism: The Political and Cultural Thinking of George Orwell* (London: I. B Tauris, 2009).

   [17] A. J. Ayer thought that Orwell understood socialism "primarily as an instrument of justice": In *Orwell Remembered*, edited by Audrey Coppard and Bernard Crick (London: Ariel Books, 1984), p. 211; "his socialism was always moral in character": William Steinhoff, *George Orwell and the Origins of 1984* (Ann Arbor: University of Michigan Press), p. 213; "Orwell saw socialism . . . as the social aspect of an

tradition to which Orwell belonged[18] "was 'unashamedly ethical' even when it was other things too" with a "message . . . that socialism was about values, and that to be a socialist was to make a moral choice and not merely to assert an economic interest or to recognize a historical necessity."[19] For their part, the Marxist left of Orwell's day regarded ethical socialism as politically impotent and theoretically misguided: it appealed to weak moral sentiments rather than the concrete struggle for power by the working class, and misunderstood the status of moral propositions, wrongly believing them to be independent of economic conditions while historical materialism had demonstrated otherwise. Since different classes conceived of justice differently as a result of their material circumstances, there was no general conception of justice or any other ethical concept that could be appealed to that would organize the working and middle classes.[20] No surprise so many Marxists responded with hostility to *The Road to Wigan Pier*, separate and apart from Orwell's missives: he was too reliant on moral exhortation, ignored the urgent reality of class conflict, and failed to see that emotional pleas could not unite persons who lived and thought too differently.[21]

Orwell would turn this Marxist critique on its head, as should be expected given the ethical concerns identified in previous chapters. First, he denied that ordinary persons will be motivated by appeals to economic interests and class struggles, beyond appeals to "better wages and shorter hours and nobody bossing you about"

---

all-embracing moral attitude": George Woodcock, *The Crystal Spirit: A Study of George Orwell* (New York: Shocken, 1984), p. 283.

[18] For an extended discussion of English socialism and Orwell's place in it, see Bernard Crick, "Orwell and English Socialism," in *George Orwell: A Reassessment*, edited by Peter Buitenhuis and Ira B. Nadel (New York: St. Martin's Press, 1988), pp. 3–19.

[19] Anthony Wright, "Introduction," in *British Socialism: Socialist Thought from the 1880s to 1960s*, edited by Anthony Wright (London: Longman, 1983), p. 27.

[20] Ben Jackson, *Equality and the British Left: A Study in Progressive Thought, 1900–64* (Manchester: Manchester University Press, 2007), pp. 96–97.

[21] Ibid., p. 98.

(V: 163): "Marxists nearly always concentrate on letting economic cats out of ideological bags," Orwell thought, with the result that "most of their propaganda misses its mark" (V: 174). Second, and relatedly, he insisted that appeals to ethically laden sentiments were effective, more effective than the concerns identified by Marxists, and that "international Socialism [is] as weak as straw in comparison" (XII: 392), an unsurprising result of his sentimentalism discussed in Chapter 4. Third, he rejected the determinism that the Marxist critique depended on. I noted in Chapter 3 that Orwell doesn't clearly accept determinism, but even insofar as he allows that situational factors can circumscribe the sort of person we will be and what we will do, he still thought that the view that "If you hold such-and-such opinions it is because you have such-and-such amount of money in your pocket" was "blatantly untrue in detail" (XI: 105). Fourth, he rejected Marxist conceptions of class in favor of a sociological conception. "Economically, no doubt, there are only two classes, the rich and the poor," he thought, but he also insisted that "socially there is a whole hierarchy of classes" (V: 208) and that "the issue of class, *as distinct from mere economic status*, has got to be faced more realistically than it is being faced at present" (V: 208, emphasis added). It was essential to understand that "English class-system . . . is *not* entirely explicable in terms of money" (V: 114), he explained, and that "the old classification of society into capitalists, proletarians, and petit-bourgeois" was "almost obsolete" since "the same kind of life . . . is being lived at different levels" (XII: 407–408). In sum, Orwell thought it was Marxists who were politically impotent and theoretically misguided, that their attempts to organize the middle and working classes were unlikely to be effective since they misunderstand the people they are trying to organize along with their interests.

Orwell did not only critique Marxism, and the most obvious evidence of his ethical socialism is discernable in his critique of capitalism, a critique that advanced on multiple fronts but was most plausible when his attacks were manifestly ethical ones.

Orwell's Case against Capitalism

British socialism expressed its opposition to capitalism in the language of moralism, but also in the language of rationalism (capitalism is inefficient) and inevitability (capitalism is doomed) and still more.[22] Orwell too expressed his opposition to capitalism using the language of rationalism insofar as he contended in *The Lion and the Unicorn: Socialism and the English Genius* that capitalism is "inefficient and out-of-date" (XII: 403) and that "The inefficiency of private capitalism has been proved all over Europe" (XII: 421). He expressed his opposition using the language of inevitability and contended that capitalism's demise was imminent when he recorded his thought that "What is quite obviously happening . . . is the break-up of *laissez-faire* capitalism" (XII: 110). He also contended throughout the early 1940s that England could defeat Germany only if it rejected capitalism, that "We cannot beat Hitler without passing through revolution, nor consolidate our revolution without beating Hitler" (XII: 346) and "We cannot win the war without introducing Socialism, nor establish Socialism without winning the war" (XII: 421). Clearly, some of these arguments have not aged well. Others were and are more plausible, especially those framed in the language of moralism.

For example, while he never explained what he means by 'exploitation'—perhaps he understood it in the familiar sense of taking unfair advantage of someone,[23] perhaps in the Marxist sense of extracting surplus value from the worker—Orwell thought capitalism was unjust because of its tendency to exploit. He identified "the right to private property" with "the right to exploit and torture millions of one's fellow-creatures" (XI: 323) and "economic liberty" with "the right to exploit others for profit" (XII: 394).

---

[22] Wright, "Introduction," in *British Socialism*, pp. 5–6.
[23] Gerald A. Cohen, "On the Currency of Egalitarian Justice," *Ethics*, Vol. 99, No. 4 (1989), p. 906.

Animal Farm had its origins in his thoughts that "if only . . . animals became aware of their strength we should have no power over them, and that men exploit animals in much the same way as the rich exploit the proletariat" (VIII: 113). Orwell also affirmed that "The real enemies of the working class are not those who talk to them in a too highbrow manner; they are those who try to trick them into identifying their interests with those of their exploiters" (XI: 154). It is also worth noting that in *The Road to Wigan Pier*, he called on socialists to "hammer two facts home into the public consciousness": "One, that the interests of all exploited people are the same; the other, that Socialism is compatible with common decency" (V: 214). In this vein, he criticized the British Empire for its exploitive tendencies: he chastised "these kind-hearted English [who] have exploited their fellow-creatures with a kind of callous selfishness unparalleled in history (XI: 354), insisted that "To continue exploiting them [that is, colored peoples] is incompatible with the spirit of Socialism" (XVII: 247), and explained that socialism "means better material conditions for the white proletariat" but also "liberation for the exploited colored peoples" (XIX: 439).

Orwell had reservations about making exploitation central to his case against capitalism, mostly because he worried that the goals of securing better material conditions for the white proletariat and liberating colored peoples were, at least "temporarily," going to be "incompatible" (XIX: 439). If exploitation abroad was "incompatible with the spirit of Socialism," ending it "would entail a difficult reconstruction period during which our own standard of living might fall catastrophically" (XVII: 247).[24] The tension is especially evident in passages like this one from his "Toward European Unity":

The European peoples, and especially the British, have long owed their high standard of life to direct or indirect exploitation of

---

[24] Cf. Colls, *George Orwell: English Rebel*, p. 25.

the coloured peoples. . . . To the masses everywhere "Socialism" means, or at least is associated with, higher wages, shorter hours, better houses, all-round social insurance, etc. etc. But it is by no means certain that we can afford these things if we throw away the advantages we derive from colonial exploitation. (XIX: 165)

Orwell insisted that "European nations *must* stop being exploiters abroad if they are to build true Socialism at home" (XIX: 165), but he despaired at explaining that to potential socialists: he recorded a hard truth in "Writers and Leviathan" when he noted that "the workers were won over to Socialism by being told that they were exploited, whereas the brute truth was that, in world terms, they were exploiters" (XIX: 290).

Still, if Orwell was reluctant to appeal to the wrongful exploitation of colonized peoples in making his case against capitalism, his egalitarianism demanded that he condemn it: exploitive relationships are clearly not the relations of social equals. If the working class at home had the surplus value of their labor wrongly extracted or were otherwise taken advantage of, so were subjects of empire abroad who were not equal participants in the planning that utilized their labor and were dominated in a way hostile to social equality and treated merely as a means. All of them, as the argument goes, were treated as inferiors, not as social equals.

Orwell also critiqued capitalism on the ground that it alienates. Alienation was part of Marx's early critique of capitalism contained in his Paris Manuscripts of 1844, where he suggested at least four ways in which workers are alienated under capitalism.[25] First, they are alienated from what they produce, such that the product of their labor becomes controlled by someone else, capitalists, who dispose of it as they see fit. Second, they are alienated from the productive

---

[25] In what follows, I follow John Rawls, *Lectures on the History of Political Philosophy* (Cambridge, MA: Harvard University Press, 2007), pp. 362–364 and Jonathan Wolff, *Why Read Marx Today?* (Oxford: Oxford University Press, 2002), pp. 28–37.

activity of labor itself, which becomes external to them, failing to realize their nature or exercise their natural powers. Labor becomes a mere means to an end, a necessary activity to meet other needs. Third, they are alienated from their "species-being," a Marxist term of art. Roughly, the idea is that human labor is typically a social productive activity and human beings collectively produce artifacts, including very socially valuable ones, in cooperation with each other. Only rarely do we make things of great lasting value all by ourselves. Workers are alienated from their species-being when they do not produce in cooperative ways or do not realize that they are producing in cooperative ways. And under capitalism, workers produce in mindless and thoughtless ways, especially when manufacturing mechanisms aim for efficiency and volume that blind us to our cooperative tendencies. Thus, they are alienated in this third way. Fourth, they are alienated from each other as human beings. Under capitalism, we tend to regard each other as antagonists with incompatible interests and differences or at least fail to recognize the ways in which our social and productive lives are entwined.

Orwell couldn't have thought that the working class was alienated under capitalism in all four ways, but his remark in "Writers and Leviathan" that "most people" are "truly alive only in their leisure hours, and there is no emotional connection between their work and their political activities" (XIX: 292) suggests that something has gone wrong. As I noted in Chapter 2, Orwell counted creative work among our needs, and he despaired that the progressive mechanization of life would weaken our consciousness and dull our curiosity (XVIII: 32). So, whether we work or not, there is some sense in which we are alienated from our labor under capitalism and thereby made worse off, since one of our human needs, our need for creative work, is frustrated: the productive activity of labor becomes external to us and fails to exercise our natural powers.

Orwell's interest in alienation gives rise to another moralistic argument against capitalism. In Spain, Orwell observed "Human beings . . . trying to behave as human beings and not as cogs in the capitalist machine (VI: 4). Workers deigned to live with low wages and poor social standing and compelled to engage in dull repetition in isolation from others may well come to regard themselves as disposable units, the cogs in the machine that Orwell noted. In short, capitalism threatened the self-respect of workers, a feature of decency discussed in Chapter 5, and thus threatens decent personhood itself.

If Orwell's case against capitalism was expressed in multiple languages, an especially important case was couched in the language of moralism and implicated many of the ethical commitments noted previously, including his relational egalitarianism, his theory of well-being, and his concern with decency and self-respect. But Orwell did not offer merely a moralistic case *against* capitalism. He also offered a moralistic case *for* democratic Socialism, one that I try to reconstruct below.

An Argument for Democratic Socialism

Orwell was not proud of *The Lion and The Unicorn* and hoped it would go out of print (XII: 391), but it usefully illustrates how Orwell understood socialism. Sometimes, Orwell seemed to regard socialism and democratic Socialism as the same thing, or at least that 'socialism' and 'democratic Socialism' are synonymous.[26] For example, in a response to a letter from the editor of *The Left News*, he defined socialism as "centralised ownership of the means of production, plus political democracy" (XII: 459). But in *The Lion and the Unicorn*, he noted that "common ownership of the means of production" was "is not in itself a sufficient definition of Socialism." What would suffice? He explained here:

[26] For a contemporary example, see Bhaskar Sunkara, *The Socialist Manifesto: The Case for Radical Politics in an Era of Extreme Inequality* (New York: Basic Books, 2019), p. 30.

One must also add the following: approximate equality of incomes (it need be no more than approximate), political democracy, and abolition of all hereditary privilege, especially in education. These are simply the necessary safeguards against the reappearance of a class-system. Centralized ownership has very little meaning unless the mass of the people are living roughly upon an equal level, and have some kind of control over the government. "The State" may come to mean no more than a self-elected political party, and oligarchy and privilege can return, based on power rather than on money. (XII: 410)

Elsewhere, he explained that "Socialism, if it only means centralized ownership and planned production, is not of its nature either democratic or equalitarian" (XV: 271), so Orwell's official view seems to be the obvious one: there are both democratic and nondemocratic versions of socialism.

I have no plans to spend much time laying out Orwell's case against undemocratic alternatives; he probably didn't think he needed one, having observed the Soviet Union "with plain horror" for some years (XIX: 90). But if one needs an argument, note the tight connection between the demands of relational egalitarianism and democracy, a particularly important constituent of a society in which people relate to one another as social equals rather than as inferiors and superiors.[27] If Orwell's egalitarianism led him to oppose capitalism, it should also lead him to oppose nondemocratic variants of socialism.

Orwell clearly thought that we should be democratic Socialists if we are going to be socialists at all. But what is his case for socialism? His logic is on display in an unpublished draft of a manifesto that Orwell wrote in cooperation with Bertrand Russell and Arthur Koestler on behalf of the League for the Freedom and Dignity of

---

[27] Niko Koldony, "Rule over None II: Social Equality and the Justification of Democracy," *Philosophy and Public Affairs*, Vol. 42, No. 4 (2014), pp. 287–336.

Man. The finished product is "a fine two-page manifesto of aims and objectives,"[28] but in an earlier, four-page draft version housed in the George Orwell Archive at University College–London he explained that "Four basically different social systems operated during the last two centuries of which three still survive." They combined, in his words, "two polarities": "the political polarity of dictatorship versus parliamentarianism, and the economic polarity of national planning versus laisser faire." He then lists four combinations which I reproduce here, slightly edited:

i.   Autocracy plus laisser faire. This combination has become practically obsolete since the French Revolution.
ii. Autocracy plus national planning. The combination is realized in Russia and was probably the potential target of Hitlerite Germany.
iii. Democracy plus laisser faire (U.S.A. and pre-Labour Britain).
iv. Democracy plus national planning. Nowhere.

He concluded this section of the draft with no further comment, but it seems clear enough how the argument is supposed to go: Orwell's case against capitalism should eliminate the two options that combine "laisser faire" economics, and his egalitarianism should lead him to oppose autocracy. That leaves democratic Socialism—democracy plus national planning—an option he thinks is practiced nowhere but could be.

If Orwell's experiences in Spain led to his conversion, his case for democratic Socialism proceeds from his antecedent ethical commitments. But it is an *incomplete* case: there is at least one alternative to democratic Socialism justified by the same reasons that Orwell appealed to in his case against capitalism and for democratic Socialism. I explain below.

---

[28] Crick, *Orwell: A Life*, p. 344.

The Rawlsian Challenge

If it is too much to say that we are all Rawlsians now, it is not too much to say that John Rawls is the most influential moral and political philosopher of the twentieth century. Even his critics allow that "Political philosophers now must either work within Rawls's theory or explain why not."[29] His 1971 masterpiece, *A Theory of Justice*,[30] was widely if not exclusively read as a philosophical justification of a capitalist state augmented with a robust welfare system,[31] and at least one reader called it "a philosophical apologia for an egalitarian brand of welfare-state capitalism."[32] It was not. If there were hints many of us missed,[33] Rawls was transparent in his 1999 *Justice as Fairness: A Restatement*[34] that he regarded capitalism as an unjust regime—his word—and democratic Socialism as a just one. But, and this is the crucial point, he did not think that democratic Socialism was the only just regime: the so-called property-owning democracy was too.

The Rawlsian Challenge makes much of Rawls's arguments that democratic Socialism and the property-owning democracy are consistent with justice as he understood it. If the property-owning democracy is just and just *for the reasons that Orwell*

---

[29] Robert Nozick, *Anarchy, State, and Utopia* (New York: Basic Books, 1974), p. 183.

[30] John Rawls, *A Theory of Justice*, Revised Edition (Cambridge, MA: Harvard University Press, 1999).

[31] For lists of commentators who understood Rawls this way, see Richard Krouse and Michael McPherson, "Capitalism, 'Property-Owning Democracy,' and the Welfare State," in *Democracy and the Welfare State*, edited by Amy Gutmann (Princeton: Princeton University Press, 1988), p. 79 and William Edmundson, *John Rawls: Reticent Socialist* (Cambridge: Cambridge University Press, 2018), p. 3.

[32] Robert Paul Wolff, *Understanding Rawls: A Reconstruction and Critique of "A Theory of Justice"* (Princeton: Princeton University Press, 1977), p. 195.

[33] For example, in a 1977 paper, Rawls affirmed that "the principles of justice do not exclude certain forms of socialism and would in fact require them if the stability of a well-ordered society could be achieved in no other way," adding that the principles of justice "may be realized either by associational socialism or property-owning democracy." See Rawls, "Fairness to Goodness," in his *Collected Papers*, p. 277.

[34] John Rawls, *Justice as Fairness: A Restatement*, edited by Erin Kelly (Cambridge, MA: Harvard University Press, 2001).

thought justified democratic Socialism then his case for democratic Socialism is incomplete. The Rawlsian Challenge does not purport to show that democratic Socialism is unjust, only that Orwellians have work to do to show that justice requires it.

In the remainder of this chapter, I introduce the property-democracy. I then explain why Rawls thought welfare-state capitalism was not consistent with the principles of justice as he understood them and why the property-owning democracy was. I then explain why the Orwellian too should suppose that property-owning democracy is just if democratic Socialism is: they correct for the same flaws that doomed capitalism and promote values of egalitarian relations and self-respect. Briefly: Orwellians should suppose that the property-owning democracy is just if democratic Socialism is. If so, then Orwell's case for democratic Socialism is incomplete.

Two Principles of Justice, Two Just Regimes

Rawls does many things in *A Theory of Justice*, but his overarching aim is to articulate a theory of justice for a liberal society, *justice as fairness*. Justice as fairness gets content from Rawls's two principles of justice which apply to the basic structure of society, governing the assignment of rights and duties and regulating the distribution of social and economic advantages. Famously, Rawls affirms that:

First: each person is to have an equal right to the most extensive scheme of equal basic liberties compatible with a similar scheme of liberties for others.

Second: social and economic inequalities are to be arranged so that they are both (a) reasonably expected to be to everyone's advantage, and (b) attached to positions and offices open to all.[35]

---

[35] Rawls, *A Theory of Justice*, p. 53.

The two principles are part of a more general conception of justice expressed by the thought that "All social values—liberty and opportunity, income and wealth, and the social bases of self-respect—are to be distributed equally unless an unequal distribution of any, or all, of these values is to everyone's advantage," such that injustice "is simply inequalities that are not to the benefit of all."[36] The two principles also highlight the fact that Rawls conceives of a society as a fair system of cooperation between citizens as free and equal persons who regard themselves as such.[37]

In *Justice as Fairness*, Rawls identified the main features of a well-ordered democratic regime that realizes his two principles. To this end, he proceeds as follows:

> Let us distinguish five kinds of regime viewed as social systems, complete with their political, economic, and social institutions: (a) laissez-faire capitalism; (b) welfare-state capitalism; (c) state socialism with a command economy; (d) property-owning democracy; and finally, (e) liberal (democratic) socialism.[38]

In a remarkably short span, Rawls argues that each of "the first three kinds of regimes, (a) to (c) . . . violates the principles of justice in at least one way." His argument against (a), laissez-faire capitalism, is exhausted by his claims that it "secures only formal equality and rejects both the fair value of the equal political liberties and fair equality of opportunity" and that "It aims for economic efficiency and growth constrained only by a rather low social minimum."[39] The first real surprise is that (b), welfare-state capitalism, is also inconsistent with the principles of justice, for reasons I discuss below. As for (c), a socialist state with a command economy, it too is inconsistent with the two principles since it "violates the equal basic

[36] Ibid., p. 54.
[37] Ibid. pp. 131–132.
[38] Ibid., p. 136.
[39] Ibid., p. 137.

rights and liberties, not to mention the fair value of these liberties" and "makes relatively little use of democratic procedures or of markets (except as rationing devices)."[40] That leaves (d) and (e), property-owning democracy, and democratic Socialism. But first things first.

Spending some time articulating Rawls's case against welfare-state capitalism will help later. Welfare-state capitalism too "rejects the fair value of the political liberties" because "It permits very large inequalities in the ownership of real property (productive assets and natural resources) so that the control of the economy and much of political life rests in a few hands."[41] The fair value of the political liberties is ensured, he thinks, only if similarly gifted and motivated citizens have roughly an equal chance of influencing the government's policy and of attaining positions of authority irrespective of their economic and social class.[42] But, he warns, if considerable wealth and property accumulate in a few hands, then "these concentrations are likely to undermine fair equality of opportunity, the fair value of the political liberties, and so on."[43] Thus, Rawls appears to think that "the fact of domination" is a fact, that is, that those in possession of greater political influence tend to entrench and extend their influence, and that they will exert their influence to gain, secure, and extend other advantages, economic and social, to promote comprehensive conceptions of the good that others might reasonably reject,[44] a position that echoes Orwell's contention that "Inevitably, because of their position and upbringing, the ruling class are fighting for their own privileges, which cannot possibly be reconciled with the public interest" (XII: 414).

[40] Ibid., p. 138.

[41] Ibid., pp. 137–138.

[42] Ibid., p. 46.

[43] Ibid., p. 53. Elsewhere, he suggests that one reason "for controlling political and economic inequalities is to prevent a part of society from dominating the rest," adding that "When those two inequalities are large, they tend to go hand in hand." See John Rawls, *Lectures on the History of Political Philosophy*, edited by Samuel Freeman (Cambridge, MA: Harvard University Press, 2007), p. 245.

[44] Edmundson, *John Rawls: Reticent Socialist*, p. 60.

Another Rawlsian objection to welfare-state capitalism is worth recording. It is crucial, he thinks, that "the least advantaged feel that they are a part of political society, and view the public culture with its ideals and principles as of significance to themselves."[45] But in a welfare-state that redistributes resources to persons who fall below a minimum standard, "there may develop a discouraged and depressed underclass many of whose members are chronically dependent on welfare" who feel "left out" and do "not participate in the public culture."[46] To reframe things slightly, welfare-state capitalism is unjust if it fails to secure what Rawls called the social bases of self-respect for all. Note that Rawls thought that "Among the basic rights" recognized by justice as fairness "is the right to hold and to have the exclusive use of personal property" and that "One ground of this right is to allow a sufficient material basis for personal independence and a sense of self-respect."[47] We do not need access to the means of production to secure self-respect, apparently, but securing the material basis for self-respect does require a right to private property.

Rawls has still more objections to welfare-state capitalism: it also does not recognize a principle of reciprocity to regulate economic and social inequalities."[48] But it should be clear enough *that* he rejected it and for reasons that Orwell would acknowledge as legitimate since some of them—namely, equality and self-respect— were also part of Orwell's case against capitalism and case for democratic Socialism. Having rejected (a)–(c), we are left with (d) and (e), the property-owning democracy and democratic Socialism. Rawls explains that "their ideal descriptions include arrangements designed to satisfy the two principles of justice" and "guarantee the basic liberties with the fair value of the political liberties and

---

45 Rawls, *Justice as Fairness*, p. 129.
46 Ibid., p. 139–140.
47 Ibid., p. 114.
48 Ibid., pp. 137–138.

fair equality of opportunity," among other considerations.[49] Democratic Socialism has a rival.

There is much still to explain. What is a property-owning democracy? Aren't welfare-state capitalist regimes property-owning democracies? Rawls allows that "they both allow private property in productive assets" and he lamented that the distinction between the two was "not sufficiently noted,"[50] a "serious fault" of *A Theory of Justice*.[51] He has since made the distinction rather clearer.

The Property-Owning Democracy: A Primer

The terminology "property-owning democracy" was used by Conservative British politicians during the 1940s to distinguish their redistributive objectives from those of socialists, making clear that they favored expanded private property ownership and not nationalization of the means of production.[52] Rawls used it to distinguish the property-owning democracy from a welfare-state capitalist regime that used redistributive mechanisms, especially taxation, to bring about more egalitarian distributions. Much of what Rawls says about a property-owning democracy is in relief of welfare-state capitalism. For example, while welfare-state capitalism permits a small class of society to have a near monopoly of the means of production, "the background institutions of property-owning democracy work to disperse the ownership of wealth and capital, and thus to prevent a small part of society from controlling the economy, and indirectly, political life itself."[53] It also avoids the

---

[49] Ibid., p. 138.

[50] Ibid., p. 135, ffn. 2. In the 1987 Preface to the French Edition of *A Theory of Justice*, he suggested that "Another thing I would now do differently is to distinguish more sharply the idea of a property-owning democracy ... from the idea of a welfare state." See John Rawls, *Collected Papers* (Cambridge, MA: Harvard University Press, 1999), p. 419.

[51] Ibid., p. 139, ffn. 5.

[52] Jackson, *Equality and the British Left*, pp. 209–210.

[53] Rawls, *Justice as Fairness*, p. 139.

concentration of wealth and capital, "not by redistributing income to those with less . . . but rather by ensuring the widespread owner- ship of productive assets and human capital."[54] The institutions of a property-owning democracy "must, from the outset, put in the hands of citizens generally, and not only a few, sufficient productive means for them to be fully cooperating members of a society on a footing of equality" including means of human capital, "that is, knowledge and an understanding of institutions, educated abilities, and trained skills."[55]

The passages I have quoted so far highlight some but not all of what property-owning democrats have called for. Their aims in- clude at least the following[56]:

1. *Wide dispersal of capital*: The *sine qua non* of a property-owning democracy is that it would entail the wide dispersal of the owner- ship of means of production, with individual citizens controlling substantial (and broadly equal) amounts of productive capital (including both human and nonhuman capital).

Instead of using redistributive mechanisms, advocates of property- owning democracy utilize *predistributive* mechanisms which aim for fairer initial distributions of capital endowments, including endowments of human capital, while allowing citizens to engage in mutually advantageous free market economic activity.[57] Opening access to educational resources is key, and the idea that fair equality of opportunity demands substantially opening opportunities to invest in human capital and substantially reducing inequalities in initial endowments of skills and talents is "integral to the ideal of

---

[54] Ibid., p. 140.

[55] Ibid., pp. 139, 140.

[56] Martin O'Neill, "Free (and Fair) Markets without Capitalism," in *Property-Owning Democracy: Rawls and Beyond*, edited by Martin O'Neill and Thad Williamson (Malden, MA: Wiley-Blackwell, 2012), pp. 80–81.

[57] Gavin Kerr, *The Property-Owning Democracy: Freedom and Capitalism in the Twenty-First Century* (New York: Routledge, 2017), p. 4.

a property-owning democracy."[58] There are no shortage of other mechanisms that a property-owning democracy might employ: it will likely invest in high quality job training and skill development; it may promote strong unions to encourage fair wages and job protection and adopt living wage requirements; it might utilize universal basic income or make "baby bonds" available to citizens to ensure that they have financial capital upon reaching adulthood; it may adopt policies attractive to left-libertarians, noted in Chapter 7, that give all citizens access to important natural resources. But whatever the property-owning democracy does, it will aim at empowering its citizens with early access to capital making continual redistribution later largely unnecessary.

2. *Blocking the intergenerational transmission of advantage*: A property-owning democracy would also involve the enactment of significant estate, inheritance, and gift taxes, acting to limit the largest inequalities of wealth, especially from one generation to the next.

Intergenerational policies to neutralize the brute good luck of being born into wealth are needed to preserve the fair value of the political liberties. To minimize such excessive concentrations of wealth, the property-owning democracy will tend to utilize estate taxes or other restrictions on bequests and inheritance.[59] Some contend that estate taxes impose "an especially cruel injury" as they deprive the dead of one of their last chances to secure the goods that they want when "all they can do is pass on worldly goods to intended beneficiaries."[60] But even ignoring the various ways that typical

---

[58] Krouse and McPherson, "Capitalism, 'Property-Owning Democracy,' and the Welfare State," p. 89.

[59] Alan Thomas, *Republic of Equals: Predistribution and Property-Owning Democracy* (Oxford: Oxford University Press, 2017), p. 119.

[60] Loren Lomasky, *Persons, Rights and the Moral Community* (New York: Oxford University Press, 1987), p. 270.

bequests are unlike the genuine "one last chance" afforded by the deathbed promise—well-planned bequests prepared well prior to the deathbed in consultation with expensive estate planners are more than a little unlike deathbed promises—it is unclear why an injury is imposed if honoring a bequest would have done serious harm to third parties. Short of prohibiting inheritance or functionally eliminating it by imposing exceptionally high estate taxes, the property-owning democrat might favor Rigano schemes, which permit inheritance to be taxed at a greater rate when it rolls over— that is, when it gets passed down more than once—and hasn't been utilized to promote any public good.[61] The idle rich—whom Orwell called "an entirely functionless class, living on money that was invested they hardly knew where" and "parasites, less useful to society than his fleas are to a dog (XII: 402)—will see their unbroken transfers of wealth terminate upon realization of the property-owning democracy.

3. *Safeguards against the "corruption" of democratic politics*: A property-owning democracy would seek to limit the effects of private and corporate wealth on politics, through campaign finance reform, public funding of political parties, public provision of forums for political debate, and other measures to block the influence of wealth on politics (perhaps including publicly funded elections).

Rawls repeatedly noted the unfairness of elections influenced by the dominance of a wealthy few,[62] and while he was rarely cynical, he sometimes seethed when describing the role of money in American political campaigns.[63] Property-owning democrats

[61] Daniel Halliday, *The Inheritance of Wealth: Justice, Equality, and the Right to Bequeath* (Oxford: Oxford University Press, 2018), pp. 59, 61, 152.

[62] Rawls, *Justice as Fairness*, p. 131; *Lectures on the History of Political Philosophy*, pp. 11–12.

[63] "When politicians are beholden to their constituents for essential campaign funds, and a very unequal distribution of wealth obtains in the background culture, with the

will follow Rawls and favor public funding of elections, but also restrictions on campaign contributions, the assurance of access to public media, and still more mechanisms to safeguard the corruption of politics.

Note that the property-owning democracy does not suffer from the flaws that Rawls thought doomed welfare-state capitalism. Consider the concerns of James Meade, the Nobel Prize–winning British economist whom Rawls credits (wrongly) for introducing the term "property-owning democracy,"[64] expressed here:

> A man with much property has great bargaining strength and a great sense of security, independency, and freedom; and he enjoys these things not only vis-à-vis his propertyless fellow citizens but also vis-à-vis the public authorities. He can snap his fingers at those on whom he must rely for an income; for he can always live for a time on his capital. The propertyless man must continuously and without interruption acquire his income by working for an employer or by qualifying to receive it from a public authority. An unequal distribution of property means an unequal distribution of power and status even if it is prevented from causing too unequal a distribution of income.[65]

The fortunate property-owner enjoys bargaining strength, including strength vis-à-vis public authorities, suggesting that he can influence the political order whereas the propertyless man can not. The property-owning democrat aims to disperse capital widely to even out disparities of power and influence that plague the pitiable

great wealth being in the control of corporate economic power, is it any wonder that congressional legislation is, in effect, written by lobbyists, and Congress becomes a bargaining chamber in which laws are bought and sold?": John Rawls, *The Law of the Peoples* (Cambridge, MA: Harvard University Press, 1999), p. 24, ffn. 19.

[64] Rawls, *Justice as Fairness*, p. 135, ffn. 1.

[65] James Meade, *Efficiency, Equality and Ownership of Property* (London: George Allen and Unwin, 1964), p. 39.

condition of the propertyless man, but she will also want improve the self-esteem of the propertyless man and make it more likely that he will be able to pass the eyeball test, unafraid to look his fellow citizens in the eye without feeling dominated. Again, Rawls objected that welfare-state capitalism cannot preserve the fair value of the political liberties and damages the self-respect of the disadvantaged. Those problems are explicitly tended to in a property-owning democracy.

We are operating at an abstract level, but hopefully the property-owning democracy is more clearly distinct from rival regimes like welfare-state capitalism and democratic Socialism. If so, the Rawlsian challenge can be mounted more explicitly.

The Rawlsian Challenge, Issued

Again, Orwell objected to capitalism for myriad reasons, but his most plausible objections were ethical ones: capitalism is exploitive and undermines social equality; it alienates and damages the well-being of many of those laboring under it; it is destructive of decency. His case for democratic Socialism is also motivated by ethical concerns, especially his egalitarianism. But Orwell wrongly supposed that all alternatives to democratic Socialism were tried and failed by those standards. I submit that, even if Orwell's critique of capitalism is sound, *he has not ruled out a rival that is justified by the very ethical concerns that he thought justified democratic Socialism*. Since that rival is the property-owning democracy articulated by Rawls, I dub this the Rawlsian challenge and, if sound, it renders Orwell's case for democratic Socialism incomplete.

I hope to have said enough to make the case that the property-owning democracy advances those ethical concerns implicated in Orwell's case for democratic Socialism. If not, consider the policies he recommended in *The Lion and the Unicorn* intended to turn "England into a Socialist democracy":

1. Nationalization of land, mines, railways, banks and major industries.
2. Limitation of incomes, on such a scale that the highest tax-free income in Britain does not exceed the lowest by more than ten to one.
3. Reform of the educational system along democratic lines.
4. Immediate Dominion status for India, with power to secede when the war is over.
5. Formation of an Imperial General Council, in which the coloured peoples are to be represented.
6. Declaration of formal alliance with China, Abyssinia and all other victims of the Fascist powers. (XII: 422)

These first three policies are at least consistent with the major aims of the property-owning democracy: the third is baked into it and the second is the expected effect of predistributing capital. Admittedly, the property-owning democracy does not call for collective ownership of the means of production and historically was understood as an alternative to it, but if the goal of socialism, as Orwell thought, is to facilitate social relations between equals, then the property-owning democrat and the democratic Socialist merely disagree about the means to secure, say, social equality and the social bases of self-esteem, a fairly uninteresting disagreement if, as some prominent socialists think, collective ownership of the means of production is orthogonal to the real concerns of the democratic Socialist. The influential socialist economist John Roemer contends that "socialists have made a fetish of public ownership," that while "public ownership has been viewed as the *sine qua non* of socialism . . . The link between public ownership and socialism is tenuous."[66] In reality, he thinks, what socialists really want are equal opportunity for self-realization and welfare, political influence, and

[66] John E. Roemer, *A Future for Socialism* (Cambridge, MA: Harvard University Press, 1994), p. 20.

social status[67] and they should be "open-minded about what kind of property rights" will facilitate.[68] So, despite his call for nationalization, I submit that Orwell did not make a fetish of public ownership and, more importantly, that his specific proposals are entirely consistent with the property-owning democracy.

Again, if the Rawlsian challenge is sound, then Orwell's case for democratic Socialism is incomplete. I do not say that it cannot be completed.

The Rawlsian Challenge, Considered

How might the democratic Socialist respond to the Rawlsian challenge? She might, with Rawls, "ask whether a liberal socialist regime does significantly better in realizing the two principles," supposing that, if it does, then "the case for liberal socialism is made from the standpoint of justice as fairness."[69] Why think that democratic Socialism would do significantly better in realizing the two principles? I speculate here,[70] but perhaps the toleration of private ownership of the means of production will, over time, undermine the stability of a property-owning democracy for one of two reasons.

First, while the property-owning democrat pins her hopes on various predistributive mechanisms to ensure that all citizens have sufficient capital, there can be no guarantee that wide gaps in capital will not emerge over time. Given the fact of domination, we should expect that those with more capital will seek to maximize their advantage. And while the property-owning democracy will legislate in ways that safeguard against the corruption of politics, recent experience doesn't suggest much cause for optimism. Perhaps

---

[67] Ibid., p. 11.

[68] Ibid., p. 20.

[69] Rawls, *Justice as Fairness*, p. 178.

[70] For a sustained and complicated argument that the property-owning democracy will fare worse with respect to realizing the two principles, see Edmundson, *John Rawls: Reticent Socialist*, esp. pp. 139–169.

it will take longer for the fair value of the political liberties to be undermined in a property-owning democracy, since it will take longer to marshal an unfair degree of political control, but so long as some persons get to privately possess a larger share of the means of production those liberties could, over time, be undermined.

Second, one gets the sense that the property-owning democrat makes some dubious assumptions about moral psychology. One dubious assumption seems to be that if persons have *enough* then they will be largely unconcerned with those that have *substantially more*: if I have lots of capital, why be envious or spiteful of those who have more? But jealous eyes may well fall on those who privately own large shares of the means of production even when all citizens are afforded substantial capital from the start, and Rawls acknowledged that sentiments like envy and spite can undermine a seemingly just regime and render it unstable.[71] If so, then there has to be some worry that we are simply not the sort of creatures that can sustain a stable property-owning democracy.

There is a danger of being too cynical here—must the wealthy *always* seek to maximize their political power? Are we *invariably* going to be envious of those who have more? Orwell insisted that "Experience shows that human beings can put up with nearly anything so long as they feel that they are being fairly treated" (XII: 535). It is easy to slip into political misanthropy and think that human beings are too flawed, too vicious, to be governed by anything but a modus vivendi, in which case a just state is not to be had. But while Orwell knew that we are sometimes governed by darker sentiments, one of the lessons from Chapter 4 is that we are also moved by more admirable sentiments that can be marshalled to overcome the darker ones. The property-owing democrat should contend that she can do at least as good a job convincing citizens that they are being treated fairly in comparison to the socialist, and seek stability there.

---

[71] Rawls, *Justice as Fairness*, pp. 88–89.

There are also reasons to think that the property-owning democracy would do comparatively better in realizing the two principles. Perhaps the moral agency of persons is compromised when the means of production are publicly owned and controlled.[72] Perhaps the secure holding of capital, including the means of production, is connected to the Western political tradition that regards self-sufficiency, prudence, and immunity from improper influence as virtues.[73] Insofar as Rawls thought that we must "look to society's historical circumstances, to its traditions of political thought and practice, and much else"[74] when assessing whether property-owning democracies or democratic Socialist regimes will better realize the two principles, it is not obvious that socialist regimes are to be preferred. Joe Sutton's play, *Orwell in America*, includes the following exchange between the fictional Orwell and his handler:

ORWELL: Whatever else you may think you have *heard* . . . whatever else you may *know* . . . know that first and foremost. I am a man of the Left. I believe in Socialism.

CARLOTTA: You can't say that.

ORWELL: Why not?

CARLOTTA: You . . . Mister Orwell, be serious?

ORWELL: I *am* being serious! It's the whole point!

CARLOTTA: It is not the whole point.

ORWELL: It is!

CARLOTTA: You can't tell an American audience you're a *socialist!*[75]

Carlotta is not wrong to anticipate American hostility toward socialism: a 2020 Gallup poll suggests that less than half of Americans,

[72] Kerr, *The Property-Owning Democracy*, p. 173.
[73] Thomas, *Republic of Equals: Predistribution and Property-Owning Democracy*, p. 114.
[74] Rawls, *Justice as Fairness*, p. 139.
[75] Joe Sutton, *Orwell in America* (New York: Broadway Play Publishing, Inc., 2017), p. 5, stage directions omitted.

45 percent, would vote for a self-identified socialist candidate for president while 53 percent would not, a decrease from a 2015 poll that suggested 47 percent would vote for a socialist candidate. Only socialists did not receive majority support in either poll.[76] Such historical circumstances have got to matter when trying to anticipate how Rawls's principles of justice ought to be implemented in the home country of free yanks from Milwaukee, Wisconsin, like me, and probably speak against attempts to implement democratic Socialism. But in any case, a complete case for democratic Socialism must exclude a rival that Orwell did not, the property-owning democracy.

Conclusion

The twin theses of *George Orwell: The Ethics of Equality* are that, first, there are ethical principles and concepts that pervade Orwell's work consistently and ground some of his better-known positions and pronouncements, and second, insofar as philosophy can help to identify and articulate those ethical principles and concepts it can help us better understand him and his work. I regard this chapter as a demonstration of both theses: Orwell's democratic Socialism was grounded in his ethical sympathies, especially his egalitarianism and theory of well-being and concern for decency, and the weakness in his case for it is evident given some reflection on social and political philosophy. What he was—a democratic Socialist—has been clear enough for some time, but why we should regard him as one and whether we should continue to regard him as one are philosophical questions that we are now, hopefully, better positioned to answer. I do not pretend to have written the last word on Orwell's ethics; to the contrary, my hope is that more philosophers and philosophical outsiders will be interested in his

[76] See https://news.gallup.com/poll/285563/socialism-atheism-political-liabilities.aspx.

ethics and his philosophical sympathies and commitments generally, some of which have previously only been hinted at if they have been remarked upon at all. But I do hope to have done some justice to the nuanced and impressive ethical thought that a philosophical outsider like Orwell was capable of. I am inclined to think that philosophy is useful at helping to understand authors whose work becomes more timeless when tied to my favored discipline, but of course a philosopher would.

How timeless is an author who, like Orwell, was self-consciously influenced by the time and place that he wrote? I close by noting that Orwell posed a similar question. He closed one of his early AIP columns with an anecdote about picking up a copy of Lemprière's *Classical Dictionary*, a "*Who's Who* of the ancients." Apparently at random, he opened to a biography of Laïs, daughter of the mistress of Alcibiades and famous courtesan. Orwell recorded her biography in the passages in quotation marks below and then wondered aloud:

> "She first began to sell her favours at Corinth for 10,000 drachmas, and the immense number of princes, noblemen, philosophers, orators and plebeians who courted her, bear witness to her personal charms. . . . She ridiculed the austerity of philosophers, and the weakness of those who pretend to have gained a superiority over the passions, by observing that sages and philosophers were not above the rest of mankind, for she found them at her door as often as the rest of the Athenians." There is more in the same vain [sic]. However, it ends on a good moral [!], for "the other women, jealous of her charms, assassinated her in the temple of Venus about 340 B.C." That was 2,283 years ago. I wonder how many of the present denizens of *Who's Who* will seem worth reading about in A.D. 4226? (XVI: 27–28)

How many indeed!

A Note on Citations

I quote Orwell a great deal in *George Orwell: The Ethics of Equality*, and to spare readers from an absurd number of footnotes, I use parenthetical citations to reference the twenty-volume *The Complete Works of George Orwell*, edited by the late Peter Davison, which has become the industry standard for Orwell scholarship: Roman numerals correspond to the volume, Arabic numbers correspond to the page number of that volume. All twenty volumes are referenced at some point and I list them here:

I: *The Complete Works of George Orwell*, Vol. 1: *Down and Out in Paris and London*, edited by Peter Davison (London: Secker & Warburg, 1997).

II: *The Complete Works of George Orwell*, Vol. 2: *Burmese Days*, edited by Peter Davison (London: Secker & Warburg, 1997).

III: *The Complete Works of George Orwell*, Vol. 3: *A Clergyman's Daughter*, edited by Peter Davison (London: Secker & Warburg, 1997).

IV: *The Complete Works of George Orwell*, Vol. 4: *Keep the Aspidistra Flying*, edited by Peter Davison (London: Secker & Warburg, 1997).

V: *The Complete Works of George Orwell*, Vol. 5: *The Road to Wigan Pier*, edited by Peter Davison (London: Secker & Warburg, 1997).

VI: *The Complete Works of George Orwell*, Vol. 6: *Homage to Catalonia*, edited by Peter Davison (London: Secker & Warburg, 1997).

VII: *The Complete Works of George Orwell*, Vol. 7: *Coming Up for Air*, edited by Peter Davison (London: Secker & Warburg, 1997).

VIII: *The Complete Works of George Orwell*, Vol. 8: *Animal Farm: A Fairy Story*, edited by Peter Davison (London: Secker & Warburg, 1997).

IX: *The Complete Works of George Orwell*, Vol. 9: *Nineteen Eighty-Four*, edited by Peter Davison (London: Secker & Warburg, 1997).

X: *The Complete Works of George Orwell*, Vol. 10: *A Kind of Compulsion, 1903–1936*, edited by Peter Davison with Ian Angus and Shelia Davison (London: Secker & Warburg, 2000).

XI: *The Complete Works of George Orwell*, Vol. 11: *Facing Unpleasant Facts, 1937–1939*, edited by Peter Davison with Ian Angus and Shelia Davison (London: Secker & Warburg, 2000).

XII: *The Complete Works of George Orwell*, Vol. 12: *A Patriot After All, 1940–1941*, edited by Peter Davison with Ian Angus and Shelia Davison (London: Secker & Warburg, 2002).

XIII: *The Complete Works of George Orwell*, Vol. 13: *All Propaganda is Lies, 1941–1942*, edited by Peter Davison with Ian Angus and Shelia Davison (London: Secker & Warburg, 2001aqz).

XIV: *The Complete Works of George Orwell*, Vol. 14: *Keeping Our Little Corner Clean, 1942–1943*, edited by Peter Davison with Ian Angus and Shelia Davison (London: Secker & Warburg, 2001).

XV: *The Complete Works of George Orwell*, Vol. 15: *Two Wasted Years, 1943*, edited by Peter Davison with Ian Angus and Shelia Davison (London: Secker & Warburg, 2001).

XVI: *The Complete Works of George Orwell*, Vol. 16: *I Have Tried to Tell the Truth, 1943–1944*, edited by Peter Davison with Ian Angus and Shelia Davison (London: Secker & Warburg, 2001).

XVII: *The Complete Works of George Orwell*, Vol. 17: *I Belong to the Left, 1945*, edited by Peter Davison with Ian Angus and Shelia Davison (London: Secker & Warburg, 2001).

XVIII: *The Complete Works of George Orwell*, Vol. 18: *Smothered under Journalism, 1946*, edited by Peter Davison with Ian Angus and Shelia Davison (London: Secker & Warburg, 2001).

XIX: *The Complete Works of George Orwell*, Vol. 19: *It Is What I Think, 1947–1948*, edited by Peter Davison with Ian Angus and Shelia Davison (London: Secker & Warburg, 2002.

XX: *The Complete Works of George Orwell*, Vol. 20: *Our Job Is To Make Life Worth Living, 1949–1950*, edited by Peter Davison with Ian Angus and Shelia Davison (London: Secker & Warburg, 2002).

I have tried to preserve Orwell's original spelling and to use British English when quoting him, but some inconsistencies are bound to arise.

Index

For the benefit of digital users, indexed terms that span two pages (e.g., 52–53) may, on occasion, appear on only one of those pages.

Humean moral psychology, 103–9
  ethical sentimentalism, 109–12
  the Humean Theory of
    Motivation, 103–5

idealism, 13, 14–15
incompatibilism. *See* free will
the inerudite interpretation, 7–
  18, 27–28
  and A. J. Ayer, 15–16
  and Bernard Crick, 8–9, 11–
    12, 15
  strong version of, 8, 9–10
  weak version of, 8–9

Johnson, Samuel, 4–6, 81–82
Julia (from *Nineteen Eighty-
  Four*), 45–46
justice, 6–8, 62, 92, 111–12, 124–25,
  126–28, 130, 132–33, 136,
  139–40, 148–49, 153–54,
  158, 159–60, 161, 162, 165,
  167n.36, 168–69, 172–73,
  174, 176–77, 176n.56,
  185–86, 197, 200–1, 213–14,
  221–22, 223–24, 232–33,
  234–35, 236
  the concept of justice, 130
  connection to self-
    respect, 139–40
  as distributive justice, 159–
    60, 161
  retributive justice, 168–69
  as undefined by Orwell, 6–7
  two principles of (*see* John Rawls)

Kane, Robert, 84
Kant, Immanuel, 6, 34, 85, 103
Kierkegaard, Soren, 64
Koestler, Arthur, 38, 166–67, 230–31

Labour Party, 179–80, 189, 190n.10,
  208, 231

left-libertarianism, 188, 189–
  217, 238–39
  as anarchism, 191–92
  and ownership of natural
    resources, 191, 197, 201–5
  and self-ownership, 191, 197,
    198–201
  theory of, 196–206
  and voluntary slavery, 200–1
Leiter, Brian, 85–86
The Liars' School, 54. *See also* BBC
liberty, 6–8, 23–24, 71n.17, 72, 92,
  93–94, 104–5, 111–12, 185–
  86, 188, 190n.10, 196–99,
  200–1, 204–5, 209, 212n.68,
  216–17, 225–26, 234
  and equality, 188, 196–97, 200–1,
    204–5, 216–17
  as the right to tell people what they
    do not want to hear, 23–24
  as undefined by Orwell, 7–8
Locke, John, 112–16, 201–3
  On personal identity, 113–16
  On the right to natural
    resources, 202
luck. *See* egalitarianism
  bad luck, 164–66
  brute versus option, 160–61

"man is the measure," 31–33, 35, 50,
  101n.13
Marx, Karl, 157–58, 221–22
Marx, the Orwell's dog, 221–22
Marxism, 102, 107–8, 117–18, 124–
  25, 219–20, 221–22, 223–
  24, 227–28
Meade, James, 241
Merleau-Ponty, Maurice, 17–18
Meyers, Jeffrey, 58n.60, 145, 220n.8
Mill, John Stuart, 4n.27, 9, 44–45,
  167n.36, 200
Miller, Henry, 35–36, 44, 134
moral realism, 111–12

        70, 71, 72, 74, 75–76, 80, 90–
        92, 168–69
    could not have done otherwise, 66,
        67n.11, 68, 84, 89, 92
    Frankfurt-style compatibilism, 63,
        64, 70, 73, 75, 90
    and free will, 90–91, 168–69
    and politics, 80
    and the Principle of Alternative
        Possibilities (PAP), 65, 66, 70,
        71–72, 84
    and reactive attitudes, 64, 67n.11,
        91n.61, 92, 135
    Semicompatibilism, 90–91
    wholehearted satisfaction as a
        condition of, 74–80
Mosley, Oswald, 22–23, 56

Newspeak, 79
The Nicomachean Ethics x–xi
Nietzsche, Friedrich, 6, 16–17, 63,
        83, 85–86, 87, 89
    on free will, 84–87
    quoted by Orwell, 16–17

O'Brien (from *Nineteen Eighty-Four*),
        3–4, 13, 14, 32–33, 45–46,
        62–63, 73, 76–77, 79, 106
    as an anti-realist, 3–4
    and free will, 62–63
    and idealism, 13–14
    as the Party philosopher, 13
    on power, 106
offensive speech, 2, 18–21, 23–25,
        133n.46
Orwell, Eileen (neé O'Shaughnessy),
        x–xi, 222–23
Orwell, George
    List of themes
        as an absolutist about political
            morality, 59–60
        as an adversary, 29–30

    on alcohol and
        philosophy, 10–11
    on anarchism, 108, 192–94
    as an anarchist, 191–96
    as an anti-intellectual, 4–6
    on "are not done," 150–51
    on arguments against free
        will, 81
    on attachment, 52–53
    his attack on the Principle of
        Alternative Possibilities
        (PAP), 66–70
    and bed-wetting, 68
    his best argument against
        consequentialism, 49–50
    on birth control, 210–11
    as bourgeois, 120, 121,
        123, 139
    on the British press, 21–22
    and British socialism, 222–
        23, 225
    and cancel culture, 18–27
    on capitalism, 225–29, 242
    his case for democratic
        socialism, 221–47
    on caste, 182–84, 200–1
    and the catapult, x–xi
    on censorship, 24, 25–26,
        207, 209
    on Christianity, 16–17, 98
    on civilian immunity, 56–57
    on class as a social
        concept, 223–24
    on class breaking, 121–23
    on class difference, 118, 120,
        121, 122
    on coercion, 206–7
    his compatibilism about moral
        responsibility, 64–80
    and compatibilist
        propaganda, 92
    his conception of
        decency, 136–54

258   INDEX

Orwell, George (*cont.*)
on consciousness, 13, 42, 43, 68,
80, 113–14, 119–20, 222–23,
226, 228
on conscription, 207, 208
as a conservative, 189
as contradictory, 4–6
his conversion to socialism,
109–10, 218–19, 231
as cruel, 18–19, 100, 184
on democracy, 143, 166–67,
176–77, 178, 211, 229, 230,
231, 242
on democratic Socialism, 6,
184, 218–19, 229
as a democratic socialist, 31,
128, 190n.10, 216–17, 218–
19, 220n.8, 247–48
on determinism, 83, 223–24
and disgust, 27, 95n.9, 109–11
his dislike of philosophy (see
the inerudite interpretation)
his dislike of Sartre, 10
on divine retribution, 101
as an empiricist, 103
on "the ends justify the
means," 45–46
on the English and
philosophy, 9–10
on equality and income, 176–
77, 230, 243
on the ethics of broadcasting, 54
on exploitation, 225–27
on fatalism, 87–90
as a Frankfurt-style
compatibilist, 64, 66–73, 76–
77, 80, 90
on free speech and expression,
26–27, 209
on free-will, 80–90
on the functions of the
state, 166–67
on Gandhi, 50–51

on goodness, 34
on good and evil, 16–17, 48–49,
102, 121, 137, 150, 221–22
on government, 192–93, 206–
7, 230
on happiness, 36, 39–40, 42,
106, 117, 151–52, 219–20
as a harsh reviewer, 71–72
on hedonism, 39–40, 41–44
and Hegel, 71
on hierarchy, 178–80
as homophobic, 18–19, 184
as honest, 59–60
on human brotherhood, 117
on human nature, 35, 126–
28, 147
on human needs, 42,
43, 181–82
on humanism, 31–32, 35,
39n.26, 50–51
as a humanist, 30–33
on humanitarians, 31
his Humean moral
psychology, 103–9
on the idle rich, 239–40
on immortality, 93, 95, 96–98,
102, 112–13
on imperialism, 49, 49n.45, 60
and the Independent Labor
Party (ILP), 219–20
as "John Freeman," 117
as a Kantian, 103
and the League for the Freedom
and Dignity of Man, 230–31
as a left-libertarian, 189–
91, 206–17
as a libertarian socialist, 189–91
on liberty and equality, 196–
97, 216–17
on logic, 9–10
as lower-upper-middle
class, 120
as a luck egalitarian, 164–76